The Jewish Contribution to English Law

Through 1858 to Modern Times

Barrington Black

❈ WATERSIDE PRESS

The Jewish Contribution to English Law: Through 1858 to Modern Times
Barrington Black

ISBN 978-1-914603-03-7 (Paperback)
ISBN 978-1-914603-04-4 (EPUB ebook)
ISBN 978-1-914603-05-1 (PDF ebook)

Copyright © 2021 This work is the copyright of Barrington Black. All intellectual property and associated rights are hereby asserted and reserved by the author in full compliance with UK, European and international law. No part of this book may be copied, reproduced, stored in any retrieval system or transmitted in any form or by any means without the prior written permission of the publishers to whom all such rights have been assigned worldwide.

Cover design © 2021 Waterside Press.

Main UK distributor Gardners Books, 1 Whittle Drive, Eastbourne, BN23 6QH. Tel: (+44) 01323 521777; sales@gardners.com; www.gardners.com

North American distribution Ingram Book Company, One Ingram Blvd, La Vergne, TN 37086, USA. Tel: (+1) 615 793 5000; inquiry@ingramcontent.com

Cataloguing In-Publication Data A catalogue record for this book can be obtained from the British Library.

Printed by Severn, Gloucester, UK.

Published 2021 by
Waterside Press Ltd
Sherfield Gables
Sherfield on Loddon, Hook
Hampshire RG27 0JG.

Telephone +44(0)1256 882250
Online catalogue WatersidePress.co.uk
Email enquiries@watersidepress.co.uk

Table of Contents

Publisher's note *iv*
Acknowledgements *v*
About the author *viii*
Dedication *ix*

1 Introduction 11
2 The Attraction of the Law 19
3 Oaths and Vows 23
4 Early Days in England 29
5 The Laws of England Concerning Jews 43
6 Conversion and Return 59
7 'We May Give You the Laws, But … ' 65
8 The First Jewish Lawyers 69
9 Bar and Bench 77
10 Into the Twentieth Century 101
11 Judicial Appointments High and Low 137
12 Jewish Lawyers in Politics 161
13 The Doors Were Open to All 171
14 Some Notable Jewish Solicitors 177

Epilogue *219*

Selected Bibliography *222*

Index *224*

Publisher's note

The views and opinions in this book are those of the author and not necessarily shared by the publisher. Whilst every effort has been made to ensure the accuracy of the information contained in this work readers should draw their own conclusions concerning the possibility of alternative views, accounts, descriptions or explanations.

The author has asked to make clear concerning explanations, assumptions and apologies that so far as historical events and people are concerned the passage of time decides what and who is important and worthy of memory and praise.

The more recent and present holder of office, or practitioner is more difficult to judge. For in his or her case the jury is still out. In fact the evidence has not all been heard.

'I place myself in the position of juror for I can only write on the basis of those whom I have heard of, or know, through reputation or what I have read in reports and journals.

For this reason I emphasise that the lists of those whom I have described as notable is by no means comprehensive, and there will be those whom I may have unintentionally omitted, do not know about or have progressed and to whom I unreservedly apologise, for I do not derogate from their skills.

Equally, I have broken that important piece of advice "never assume." There may be some instances where, because of name, either self or parental, place of birth and education I have made an assumption as to their Jewish connection. If I have done so incorrectly, then similarly I apologise.'

Acknowledgements

The Pandemic has been a serious and often tragic period for many, to whom my sympathy is extended. On the other hand, lockdown was an opportunity for comfortable solitude which should be cherished, and determined positively.

As part of my own 'lockdown therapy' I set about doing what many did, 'clearing out.' In my case this included the difficult task of deciding which of my many old books merited removal from my not inconsiderable library. Precisely none. In fact it was a case of being pleasantly nudged into reading some works for a second time. What is more, at a leisurely pace, picking-up on matters I'd skimmed over at first reading. Those authors with whom I renewed acquaintance and to whom I am particularly grateful include Cecil Roth, Elizabeth Pearl, Henry Henriques, John Luxon, Simon Schama, Chaim Bermant, Lord David Young, Lord Arnold Goodman, Sir Martin Gilbert and Frederick Morton.

I also came across various editions of the magazine of *The Jewish Historical Society of England* as well as the many notes I had made over probably 50 years of giving talks to groups and organizations. What resulted is this volume.

From the moment that I indicated my thoughts on a book arising from the 1858 Act I received nothing but encouragement from Bryan Gibson of my publishers Waterside Press. It went further, his own ideas for developing the theme by including a brief history of the oath, together with my own curiosity about Parliamentary Acts specific to religious minorities provided avenues to be explored.

Once my manuscript was complete and I'd submitted it to Bryan and his eagle eye went over it, I was grateful for the numerous matters he raised, which necessitated further examination and re-writing to satisfy editorial requirements.

My thanks are also due to Alex Gibson of Dived Up for his research and sourcing of the images.

I must also thank author Brian P Block JP BPharm PhD BA MA LLM MSc MPhil CBiol MIBiol who kindly read the book before it went to press and made a number of valuable last minute suggestions that I was able to incorporate into the text.

And a special thank you to Matthew Black for the photograph on page vii.

I hope that I have accomplished what I set out to do, though it would not have been possible without the co-operation of my wife Diana, who nudged me towards the necessities of life, such as daily exercise and sustenance and for this I am grateful. I should also, on her behalf, and mine, thank those who invented the iPad and Zoom, which together contributed to our peaceful domain.

Will life ever get back to normal?

Barrington Black
August 2021

The author.

The central theme of this book concerns judges and the judicial oath that they were barred from taking until ten years after the landmark Jewish Relief Act 1858.

Photo Matthew Black.

About the author

Barrington Black became one of the UK's best-known criminal solicitors. The founder of a Leeds practice known as Barrington Black & Co, now amalgamated with various other practices and known as Black's, he went on to serve as a Metropolitan Stipendiary Magistrate (district judge) then Circuit Judge, rounding-off his judicial career as a Supreme Court Justice in Gibraltar.

As a lawyer, the author appeared in many high-profile cases, including when he represented Donald Nielsen ('The Black Panther') on a charge of murder and kidnapping. A regular correspondent in the letter columns of *The Times, Telegraph* and *Jewish Chronicle* he contributed as legal expert to Yorkshire TV's *Calendar* and BBC TV's *Look North*.

A long-time resident of Harrogate, where he was a local councillor and Parliamentary candidate, he lives in North London with his wife Diana and they have four children and ten grandchildren. His autobiography *Both Sides of the Bench* was published in 2015.

To the pioneers and those who continue to open doors
to the law, the legal profession and the judiciary.

'Justice, and only justice, you shall pursue'

Deuteronomy 16.20

The word 'justice' is repeated as an exhortation both to the judge and the litigant who should always speak the truth, and the repetition denotes whether it should be to their advantage or disadvantage. Even more important that they should seek a reliable tribunal to decide their case. This was the interpretation of Rashi (1040–1105).

CHAPTER 1

Introduction

It would be easy if Jews could simply be divided into *Ashkenazim* or *Sephardim*, or even Orthodox and Secular, but it is not so easy. There are as many kinds of Jews as leaves on a tree. There are those who do everything that their fellow citizens do except eat pork or shellfish. There are those who do not eat pork or shellfish at home but might be tempted when 'out,' that is in a restaurant, to nibble on a schnitzel or pick out a prawn. There are those who would not eat even food permitted at home when out for fear of becoming desecrated by plates or cutlery that might, on some previous occasion, have hosted forbidden *fruits de mer*.

There are those who would eat at a friend's house because they have implicit trust in their host not to harbour indiscretions. There are those who would not eat at a friend's house despite promises of propriety. There are those who observe the laws on food but only visit the synagogue three days a year. There are those who only go there every Saturday, and those who go on Saturday plus three times a day for the rest of the week.

There are Jews who wear a hat only when they go to the synagogue, and those who wear a hat all the time, from awakening to sleeping. There are even those who wear *two* hats all the time and keep *an extra* hat by the side of the bed in case the other two have fallen off and they dream they are in a synagogue. There are those who love Israel and go there to visit the Hilton and the opera, and those who hate the State but love The Wall and post a note there. Each one of these, if asked, would say, 'Yes, I am a Jew.'

The question for the purposes of this book is, 'Although they may say they are Jews, what is their status in the eyes of others?' In the eyes of the Nazi party in Germany from the 1930s onwards it was not just a simple question of what people ate or didn't eat, nor of whether they had ever taken a footstep inside a synagogue. It was down to their blood. Did they have any Jewish blood coursing through their veins? In fact, such a question arose well before the Nazis came to power. Before 1875 there was no civil marriage in Germany, so where two people, one Jewish and the other Christian wished to marry, one spouse had to convert to the faith of the other and it was almost inevitable that the Jew would do the converting.

Under the Nazis, a decree was introduced in April 1933 known as the First Racial Definition, to determine whether a person was a Jew, or of mixed-blood, in German a *Mischling*. Under this law there were degrees of Jewishness, the utmost being that a person would be regarded as a Jew if they had one Jewish parent, or even grandparent.

There are other laws which need to be examined, including the Jewish law itself. At its simplest this would deem a person Jewish if either their mother is Jewish or they have properly converted to Judaism (see *Chapter 6*) according to Jewish laws called *Halachah* (or *Halakha*) that guide religious practice and everyday behaviour. This is the Orthodox way, meaning 'religiously compliant.' By contrast the Reform Judaism movement[1] will accept a patrilineal relationship, i.e. where the mother may not be Jewish but the father is, and it should be noted that the Reform conversion procedures are not as strict as the Orthodox ones and therefore much more popular.

Israel's Law of Return (*Chapter 10*) holds that a person can be admitted to citizenship of the State of Israel conditional on having a Jewish mother or a valid conversion, and for an Orthodox marriage documents need to be shown to the rabbinate relating to both would be spouses' parents. Failure to do this can create problems for any children which may issue from the marriage, so this is usually done by showing a certificate issued in the country where the parental marriage took place.

Maternal succession in the Jewish religion in some ways follows Roman Law. This line of reasoning may seem strange in view of several biblical family situations whereby the child followed the status of the father as in the case of both Joseph and Moses, each of whom married non-Israelite women. Happily,

---

1. See www.reformJudaism.org.uk

the answer to this given by the Orthodox authorities is that both their wives converted before marriage, although the evidence for this is scant.

This examination of who is a Jew becomes relevant in considering those who became candidates for the bench or other positions which this book deals with.

Jewishness: Acknowledged and Unacknowledged

Apart from Duarte Brandon who is mentioned at the start of *Chapter 6* and examined more as an oddity than a serious contender for inclusion in my book, the status of those mentioned hereafter shows that they are (or were in the case if those departed), in the majority, Jewish *without doubt*, in that they have proclaimed their Jewishness by their extra-curricular activities, and by examination, in most cases, of their parentage and ancestral connections. It may well be that there are those included in the book who either do not wish to be thought of as Jewish or no longer have any active Jewish connections, and I hope this has been made clear.

Some years ago, at the annual Remembrance Day parade held in Whitehall attended by the Association of Jewish Ex-Servicemen, the inspecting officer was Major General Richard Nugee CBE, who surprised, and delighted everybody at the reception following the parade by indicating his Jewish blood arising from one of his ancestors, and thereafter he became a patron of that association. By this indication, it would mean his brother, Lord Justice Christopher George Nugee, the husband of Emily Thornbury MP, was similarly a descendant. Not so far as I can tell that either claims now to practise Judaism in any form and I have included neither.

There are indeed those at one end of the scale who make no mention of their affiliations whereas others do, e.g. our current Lord Chancellor (and Deputy Prime Minister/ex-Foreign Secretary), Dominic Raab, who before politics was a solicitor with Linklaters, was brought-up by his mother as a Christian. He has spoken of his Jewish father (who in 1938 escaped the Nazis in Czechoslovakia), the murder of his grandparents and the systematic elimination of other of his ancestors in the Holocaust. He is very open-minded and has lived in Israel and worked with one of the principal Palestinian negotiators in seeking to resolve the long-running Israel-Palestine conflict. Raab issued pictures of his grandparents that were published in the *Daily Mail* when he ran for the leadership of his party. He also spoke of the need for tolerance and to stamp out anti-Semitism.

The above individuals are not the only ones so placed. In his excellent book *The Cousinhood* (1971), Chaim Bermant refers to,

> 'Loyal sons of their community for a generation or two, and then vanished into Christendom to restock the thinning ranks of the English Aristocracy.'

Amongst the aristocratic Jewish descendants Bermant names are the Marquess of Crewe, Lord Ludlow, Viscount Bledisloe, the Duke of St Albans, Lord Thurlow, Lord Donington, the Countess of Loudoun, Viscountess St Davids, Lord Grey of Ruthin, and a former Duchess of Norfolk.

The extremities shown, however, in the degree of religious observation by Jews are reflected across a wide spectrum by those who in the fullness of time were appointed to the judicial bench, practised law or were appointed to help Governments as described in later chapters. As to the judiciary, at one end is the resident judge at a large London Courts Centre who would bring not only his own strictly *kosher* lunch into the judges dining-room, but also his own crockery and cutlery. Similarly, the resident judge at Harrow Crown Court, where I sat, Her Honour Myrella Cohen QC (*Chapter 11*) presided over her court with the gentle force of 'a Jewish grandmother.' She was never more annoyed than with a Jewish defendant who came into court wearing his *phylacteries*[2] together with a prayer shawl. Myrella Cohen admonished him, saying,

> 'This is no time for demonstrative prayer. That should have been said before you contemplated sin, or in your case probably also afterwards.'

Judges and the Oath

The central theme of early chapters of this book concerns judges and the oath. I explain in *Chapter 3* that it was necessary for judges to swear an oath in order

---

2. A small box containing parchment with religious verses, worn strapped to the head and on the arm, near the heart.

to take their place on the bench. This was not possible until ten years after Parliament passed the Jewish Relief Act in 1858 that opened the outer door. Before that the focus was on Parliamentary candidates who, having been elected and wishing to take their seat in the House of Commons, found they couldn't do so because their conscience would not allow them to swear the oath then required, i.e. 'upon the true belief of a Christian.' The 1858 Act provided for the omission of those words but was restricted to Parliament. Judicial office was in fact specifically excepted, and it was not until 1868 that this exception was deleted, and the full 1858 provisions also applied to the judicial oath (see *Chapter 5*).

Prior to 1858 other Acts were passed which excluded the problematic words 'on the true belief of a Christian' from oaths pertaining to the grant of degrees by the universities of Oxford and Cambridge, making it easier to graduate and hence gain admittance to both branches of the law (as also described in *Chapter 5*). Consequently, this book looks not just at judges but also members of the Bar and solicitors who, though they did not achieve the bench, seem to me to be of equal importance whether for their work as individual practitioners or, e.g. because they were summoned to assist Government—not for their political aspirations, but more their intellectual capacity and legal training.

I have also included a number of Jewish lawyers whose primary reputation is based on them being pioneers, legal reformers or campaigners, but I had to draw a line, e.g. at listing those Jewish legal experts who did not also practise as lawyers. However, I have been able to mention within the portraits of some practising lawyers and judges in later chapters that they also taught or wrote about the law and even in some cases became law professors (university vice-chancellors in some instances) in retirement.[3]

In the course of the progress of Jewish lawyers there were, and still are, those who were appointed to the circuit bench and also at district judge level (i.e. in the magistrates' courts or county court) to whom the necessity of taking the oath applied. Although no oath was required to practise as a solicitor, and restrictions might be circumvented by avoiding Oxford or Cambridge to obtain a degree and instead getting one from the 'Godless Tower of Gower Street,'

---

3. Neither does my book extend to Jewish lay magistrates, who are not lawyers or part of the professional judiciary. A 2016 freedom of information (FOI) request elicited that although the Ministry of Justice publishes diversity information in its *Judicial Statistics* these do not appear to classify Jewishness specifically. Certainly there must today be many hundreds of Jewish JPs, historically barred by the same oath-taking hurdle discussed here.

as University College London became known, it is right also to reflect that by their admission to that profession, the laws of this country were advanced.

A Reflection

It is the 15 July 1997 at St Paul's Cathedral, the Memorial Service for Lord Chief Justice Peter Taylor (Baron Taylor of Gosforth: *Chapter 11*), one of only two Jews then to have held such office. He was born to Jewish parents, his wife also Jewish. At that service Lord Harry Woolf (also *Chapter 11*), then the Master of the Rolls, also destined to become Lord Chief Justice, begins his address:

> 'Some Jews were surprised at this Memorial Service being held in St Paul's Cathedral. However Peter Taylor thought of himself as a Lord Chief Justice who happened to be Jewish, and would, on many occasions attend such services himself, as part of his duties.'

The cathedral is packed. Over 800 people are present, and although a Jewish minister, Reform of course, is involved, the service is largely conducted by the resident Christian clergy. Towards the end of it, Peter Taylor's son stands up, and places on his head a small cap, once known as a *yarmulke* but now, more often, as a *kippah* and starts to recite, in Hebrew, the *Kaddish* or Memorial Prayer. As he does so, the hands of many present (including my own) reach into their pockets, and out come similar small head coverings as we all join in the appropriate Hebrew responses, with a final 'Amen.'

Introduction

Peter Taylor was always conscious of his Jewish background. He rose to become Lord Chief Justice but might easily have been a concert pianist. Taylor prosecuted in many high-profile cases and conducted the Hillsborough Inquiry that led to all-seater stadiums for elite sport. Modest, refreshing, down to earth he is one of several Jewish lawyers in this book from the North of England. I had the pleasure of instructing him several times (*Chapter 11*).

The Jewish Contribution to English Law

CHAPTER 2

The Attraction of the Law

The professions of medicine and law have long attracted Jewish people. Medicine, because the practical benefits combined with a love of learning were conducive to the aims of rabbinical scholars to provide healing of both the body and the mind, and furthermore it was a skill which was transportable and for which there would always be a demand.

Some of the most famous and highly respected rabbis, such as Maimonides (1138–1204), who was one of the great, prolific and influential *Torah*[1] scholars of the Middle-Ages, were medics, so he is a fine illustration, combining this by serving as the personal physician to Saladin the first Sultan of Egypt and Syria. There were Jewish doctors who tended to successive royal families, a notable example being Roderigo Lopez in-house physician to Queen Elizabeth I despite this being during the long period of the expulsion of Jews from England (*Chapter 5*). Exceptions to regulation are therefore not the prerogative of modern-day Governments.

The other favoured profession, the one covered in this book, is the law, an orderly discipline which was a necessity for a 'stiff-necked' people, as Jews are described on no less than 18 occasions in the Testaments, a description reflecting their reputed stubbornness, argumentative disposition, and reluctance to be led; and they were to find the mysteries and vagaries of the various interpretations of the laws which they had been given provided considerable justification for being so described.

---

1. The *Torah* is the scroll of Jewish law. Usually meaning the first five books of the Hebrew Bible; Genesis, Exodus, Leviticus, Numbers and Deuteronomy.

Eve, it was said by someone unfamiliar with the biblical background, was the first Jewish mother who wanted one son to be a doctor and the other a lawyer. The problem was that she, of course, was not Jewish. Judaism hadn't been invented at that time, and as Adam asked, looking around his beautiful garden, 'Where will they find any patients or clients?' In any event, sibling rivalry in its most extreme form put paid to Eve's aspirations for her offspring.

And so it was that when I flew into Gibraltar in 2012, to take up a position post-UK retirement as a member of their Supreme Court that I was met by an official of their Ministry of Justice who, on our way to the Governor's residence for me to be sworn in, casually asked if I had any special preference as to the holy book on which to take the judicial oath. Although I carried with me a small travelling prayer book, a gift from a recent wedding we had attended in Israel, I found when I arrived that they did have at least some idea of my religion. Lying on the table was a miniature *Torah* which had been presented by the local Jewish community who'd been there since 1703.

The ice was broken at that first meeting when I commented to the Governor, Vice-Admiral Sir Adrian Johns, that this would be the sixth oath I had taken, the earlier ones being as stipendiary magistrate (now called district judge (magistrates' courts)), Crown Court recorder (part-time judge of that court), circuit judge, on joining the Army, and when commissioned as an officer. We spent the rest of the morning talking about my military rather than legal background.

The Bishop of Gibraltar exchanged words with me after the service for the commencement of the legal year. This is an occasion when the entire legal profession of this British territory chants a Catholic version of the prayer *Kol Nidre*, regretting any mistakes (which in any event might result in a trip to the Court of Appeal, or very rarely the Privy Council in London). The recitation also sought divine inspiration for the coming year in a fascinating combination of English law and Gibraltarian precedents.

It was intriguing to see, despite the Mediterranean temperature, black-robed and curly wigged lawyers walking through the main street to that most English-looking of buildings, the Gibraltar Supreme Court. Although everything is small there, Gibraltarians don't do things in a small way. For this ceremony, the red-robed full-length bewigged judge is transported in a highly polished car accompanied by two motorcycle outriders from the courthouse to the cathedral.

These buildings are only about 200 yards apart, but the journey takes some 15 minutes as the procession goes the long way round a one-way system.

The words the bishop and I exchanged referred to the fact that although the Jewish community (900 citizens out of a total population of 33,000) had been there for very many years, I was the first Jewish judge and he also noted the fact that the oath-taking ceremony had been offered to me with the miniature *Torah*. After all, Gibraltar was ahead of the game. It had cleared-up any misgivings about how the oath should be worded for witnesses in order to accommodate their various religions by a law passed in 1934, but it was not until 1978 that equivalent laws were finally clarified in England.

The Jewish Contribution to English Law

CHAPTER 3

Oaths and Vows

In order to sit as a judge two separate oaths need to be sworn: first an oath of allegiance to the sovereign, and second the judicial oath dealing with the performance of the duties of judge 'without fear or favour.' Having mentioned that the door to the judiciary was opened by a series of Acts of Parliament affecting oath-taking by Jews—let us establish what exactly is meant by an oath. But first whether there is a distinction between an *oath*[1] and a *vow*.

Concerning matters affecting the administration of the legal system, there is first of all the vow which one is expected to make in order to qualify for or hold a position or office; then quite differently in the course of legal proceedings there is the oath of a party or a witness that what they will tell the court will be the truth. In simple terms a vow, relates to the requirement to abide by the rules of a profession, or an appointment, and to follow its requirements with honesty, devotion, fairness and so on. The person making the vow gives an undertaking to that effect by promising to do something in a certain manner. It is a public undertaking, a promise to those who have entrusted him or her with the responsibility, and also to all members of society, not only those who are present at the time, who might be affected by the use of their powers.

With an oath, you are, again put simply, vouching for the truth of something. Both the vow and the oath each contain a promise, and that promise is made to someone else. In the case of an oath, it is made to your God and, to reinforce this aspect, you hold in your hand the appropriate holy book and 'swear' accordingly.

---

1. Ignoring for now the modern-day affirmation which I deal with later in this chapter.

The word 'appropriate' is important because, in England, prior to 1858 the only bible mentioned by statute was that of the Christian faith. But the time arrived when those who were not members of that church or faith but were suitable candidates for office faced a personal problem because they were precluded by that very requirement.

One need only look back at the *Bible* itself, and this applies to those who hold dear to either the *Old Testament* (Jewish People as well as many Christians) or *New Testament* (Christians only but not Jews who part company on matters such as that Jesus Christ is the son of God). The prohibition on stating a falsehood is included in the Ten Commandments of the *Old Testament*, in Exodus 20, verse 14, i.e. 'Thou shalt not bear false witness against thy neighbour.' This is reinforced in Numbers 30, verse 3:

> 'If a man makes a vow to the Lord or takes an oath imposing an obligation upon himself, he shall not break his pledge, he must carry out all that has crossed his lips.'

There are certain elements of small print relating to what happens when a woman makes a vow, as to the responsibility of either her father or husband for her vows, and the requirements upon them to ensure she complies, but with the observation that she is only responsible for a vow if she is over the age of twelve-and-a-half. How this fits with modern ideas of parental responsibility, women's emancipation and gender equality I'm not sure!

Vows, however, were usually discouraged by Jews, because of the risk, and therefore seriousness, of a breach, and the rabbis spoke against the making of vows. Putting it in the extreme it was said that if one broke a vow, one's children would perish. There still is a custom in some places to use, for emphasis, the phrase 'On my child's life' which is, I think, one that really should never be uttered.

Rather than risk having a loose comment interpreted as a vow, the phrase, in Hebrew, *b'li neder* (literally meaning 'not on my vow') would be added to show that, much as they believed their statement, they did not wish to chance it being interpreted as an absolute undertaking. We see therefore, that *neder* means vow. A promise made to God to perform an act. It can also include a promise *not to do* something. By comparison, an oath is a promise to God *to do* something.

Deuteronomy 13 makes it clear that if one does make a vow to God, then it should be observed. So, if you have any doubt, do not make a vow — and thus avoid the risk and consequences of not complying with it.

Many an inquisition, purge or expulsion has followed Jews through time, only averted, in part, by forms of religious conversion. In order to convert to other faiths, many religions had, as part of this process, a requirement for a vow to be made, and if the person converting was able to escape the area or those governing the current political climate, and later wished to revert to Judaism, then the rabbinical authorities devised a route.

One of the holiest days in the Jewish Calendar is *Yom Kippur*, the Day of Atonement, a fast day, one of prayer and self-examination, a day when the Almighty, having commenced his annual stock-taking exercise and reviewed the behaviour of each of his subjects on Earth, will during the period starting ten days before the Jewish New Year (*Rosh Hashanah* from September rather than January), give a final touch to his 'Book of Life,' and reflect during those ten days who shall live and who shall die. In fact, there is a graphic observation as to exactly how death will occur.

Just before, however, on the eve of *Yom Kippur*, most Jews will foregather for the prayer *Kol Nidre* ('All My Vows') and at this stage the plea will be to cancel any vows made and allow the individual a fresh start. There is one important caveat. That cancellation refers to the vows between that individual and the Almighty. It does not refer to vows *inter alia* with fellow Jews, or for that matter other fellow human beings.

Vows don't feature often these days, but one popular exception is seen each sabbath in synagogue when someone is 'called-up' to read the weekly portion of the *Torah*. That individual will make a donation and the cantor (who leads the congregation) will say, *'Ba-avur she-nadar'* which means, 'In as much as he (or she) has vowed.' For this reason, let us concentrate, as we started, upon oaths rather than vows.

The Early Jewish Courts

In early Jewish courts, an oath would only be taken in *civil* cases, never in matters involving *criminal* acts; and strangely would only be taken where no evidence was produced, or if insufficient evidence was available. This may seem perverse to modern eyes, and one must ask, 'If there was no evidence then who would take the oath?' The answer is simply that a party to the proceedings would do so, but that party would be the defendant, and it would be taken when he or she gave evidence to refute a claim. This would mean that where there had been either documentary or oral evidence, presumably unsworn, then the oath was imposed only on the defendant, as a purgative measure. In other words, by taking oaths, God was being called as a witness. However, if the witness was popularly considered a person not disposed to telling the truth, the oath would not be offered. The dictum was 'possession is nine tenth of the law' and 'whosoever would oust a possessor must bring evidence to establish his claim, his positive assertion alone is not sufficient.'

Over the centuries there were various requirements relating to oaths which varied with the biblical, Mishnaic and Rabbinic periods.[2] But it remained that throughout these times oaths were not taken in criminal cases and for the reason that, 'According to principles of Jewish jurisprudence no-one charged with a criminal act could be believed even upon oath.' They had much in common therefore it seems with events in the Halifax Magistrates' Court of the 1960s!

There were other exceptions: no oaths for rulers, no priestly oaths, no oaths for officials of any kind, for they were supposed to do their duty without them. Someone said, 'The multiplication of oaths tends rather to the corruption of morals.' The *Bible*, however, tells of many extra-judicial oaths, used widely as props to a weak will: oaths of agreement and promises to abjure the realm (leave the country), concerning international security, oaths by one's father and mother, and for a while even the judicial oath in the name of God, which was later abolished.

In the tenth century, Byzantine Law required Jews to wear 'a girdle of thorns,' and stand in water when they took an oath; in Europe until the 15th century

---

2. Mishnaic refers to the early-first to the early-third centuries in recognition of the centrality of the *Mishnah*, a Hebrew compilation of traditions. Rabbinic signifies the mainstream form of Judaism from the sixth century onwards.

similar debilitating practices were followed. The *Sanhedrin* (a local tribunal in ancient Israel) was more civilised; a witness would be reminded of the result of lying, that it was a dreadful sin, and warned that, if they lied, they would face the same punishment as the defendant.

In present-day Israeli courts, the official indication on giving evidence states:

> 'The witness is notified of his or her duty to testify truthfully and is informed that there are penalties under law for giving a false testimony. The witness must then confirm that he or she understands this and must undertake to testify truthfully in addition the court may require an oath or affirmation if there are grounds to believe that doing so would uncover the truth.'

The Oaths Act 1978

In modern times in England, we are governed by the Oaths Act 1978, which, for the first time, properly clarified the taking of oaths; and it allows the witness a choice of swearing an oath (on a holy book) or making an affirmation (a solemn promise). Either has the same force and effect in today's multicultural society, so that everyone irrespective of religion or belief is treated with respect when asked to give evidence. The 1978 Act specifies the wording of both the witness oath and affirmation. For the oath:

> 'I swear by (almighty God/name of the God, e.g. Allah/name of the holy book) that the evidence I shall give shall be the truth, the whole truth, and nothing but the truth.'

And for an affirmation:

> 'I do solemnly, sincerely, and truly declare and affirm that the evidence I shall give shall be the truth, the whole truth and nothing but the truth.'

What is important is that the person swearing an oath or making an affirmation is aware that it binds his or her conscience. Those administering oaths, etc., judges or court staff, should remember to ask the individual what their preference is. No-one should assume that merely because the person appears to come from a particular ethnic community, he or she prefers to swear the oath connected with that community. Too often perhaps the *Holy Bible* is automatically placed into the witness' hand with the instruction, 'Raise your arm and read out the words on the card.'

So, two important factors:

- Does it appear to those administering the oath that the deponent considers it binding?

And secondly:

- Is it one which the deponent considers binding on themselves?

The proper practice is to make sure the witness uses the correct book and understands what he or she is promising to do — solemnly tell the truth; and he or she should have the opportunity to carry out all practical customs, such as taking-off their shoes, washing their hands, and with due deference to their preferred holy text.

CHAPTER 4

Early Days in England

Before considering the arrival of Jews in England we should review how they even came to be in the region, going back to the start. It is difficult to be specific about pre-biblical times. One can only surmise that the reason anyone was in the 'Fertile Crescent' around 2000 BCE was entirely due to the word 'fertile.' They had gathered there because the land was well-watered and could be cultivated. It ran from the River Nile delta in the West, rose North-East to Hebron (where Abraham died), then further North-East to Syria, where it turned South-East to Mesopotamia, then towards Babylon — and thus it formed a crescent.

Abraham (or Abram) is the common 'father' of various religions including Judaism, Islam and Christianity. In Judaism, he is regarded as the one who created the special relationship between the Hebrews and God. He came from a place called Ur on a bend in the River Euphrates, South-West of Baghdad in a country called Canaan (roughly speaking the present-day West Bank) where he died in 1275 BCE. Until his time, although the sun and moon were subjects of devotion, there were also other, closer targets: idols, statues, items made of stone or wood, which could be destroyed, and when this happened the followers of those gods did not know where to turn. Abraham had a brainwave. He recognised the need for an alternative, invisible, God who could not be destroyed by man.

Most of those later referred to as Hebrews, or Israelites, lived in an area between the Mediterranean and the Dead Sea. It was from there that they were forcibly moved by the Egyptians to build stone cities (not, as is sometimes suggested, pyramids) just to the North of the 'left finger' of the Red Sea close to where the Suez Canal is now. It was from there that they were guided by a lengthy, protracted and somewhat circuitous route around what is now The Negev, and North 'to the left' of the Dead Sea, in effect, right back where they started from. Some even moved across the River Jordan.

There were 12 tribes, or families, making-up the Jews as a community or 'people,' and their total number varies in different accounts between a few hundred and many thousands. There are sceptics who point out the lack of any physical evidence of their journey, let alone the detritus that would have been left by a large number of travellers. It can, however, be accepted that the tribes separated: several went to the centre of what is now Israel, some to the North, though there appears to be movement towards Damascus in the North-East by many, and a settlement in the 'elbow' of the River Euphrates, sounding not dissimilar to 'Ibris' or 'Ivrim' or 'Ebra,' meaning those who came from the other side, which became 'Hebrews.' Also, in that location were the Jebusites, a Canaanite tribe inhabiting Jerusalem, and there is a belief that the Israelites developed as a sub-culture from the Canaanites. This is supported by the biblical indications in the 'Book of Samuel' that King David took control from the Jebusites, and his Jerusalem became the capital of Judea. Even before David and his son Solomon, a woman was in charge, Deborah. Although described as a prophet, she was really a judge, for in those days judges were considered worldly wise.

During the period of King David (c1000 BCE), followed by his son, King Solomon, there was an inclusion of what is now Syria, Jordan and Lebanon into the Kingdom of Judea, but this was reversed by the invasion of the Assyrians in 732 BCE, and next the Babylonians in 597 BCE, who forced Jews into detention ('Babylonian' still being a word used to describe a cruel, totalitarian form of administration or policing). Upon their release, many of those detained in Babylon made their way to India and formed a Jewish community in that area which remained for many centuries. There then came the Persians in 450 BCE, after that the Greeks under Alexander in 323 BCE, and then Ptolemy, a man who though born in Egypt was in effect a Roman Pharaoh.

The effect of the death of King Solomon was that the nation was divided into Israel, the larger area to the North, and Judah, the smaller area to the South, which despite its size retained Jerusalem firmly as its capital. We are now well and truly in biblical times and the 12 tribes had become divided even more, particularly by the Assyrian invasion. The prophet Isiah (also a judge), who was more into ploughshares and pruning hooks than swords and spears, reflected their despair in a song which became popular and is sung to this day. Their sadness turned to mortification when Nebuchadnezzar, a Babylonian king, destroyed the temple in 586 BCE—despite another, albeit erroneous song which begins, 'Nebuchadnezzar, King of the Jews, bought his wife a pair of shoes…'

The Romans and the Jews

The Romans arrived in 63 BCE and remained until 300 AD. There was considerable military activity against the Jews, including a brave episode at Masada by the Zealots. There was guerrilla warfare masterminded by Judah the Maccabean (sometimes spelled Maccabias: see *Chapter 10,* 'Sir John Balcombe'), also known as 'The Hammer,' but despite this the Romans treated the Jews in other parts of the Roman Empire to which they travelled and settled in a positive manner, despite the destruction of the second Temple in 70 AD and other restrictions placed on them. They were, at least, not conscripted into the Roman Army, and an allegiance grew between the Roman Emperor Antonius and the editor of the *Mishnah* (above). Most importantly, they were allowed the freedom to practise Judaism.

King Herod (37 BCE), despite being Jewish was crowned by the Romans, really as a puppet monarch. Not the ideal example of a family man, he exhibited this by killing his wife, three sons—and mother-in-law as an encore. By this time, the Jews had moved along the North-African coast, and it is estimated that, in all, at least five million of them lived in areas that the Romans conquered. Conveniently this path became a stepping-stone to North-Africa, Spain, Sicily, Italy, France, and to the Balkans and Turkey.

Although welcomed by the Romans there were problems with other sections of indigenous populations. An example of the severity they faced was their treatment at certain times in Spain and Portugal. Arising from this there was a continued movement North-Eastwards towards France and Germany, and then from Germany through Poland and further East to Russia. The Jews took with them a language, a mix of *Hochdeutch* ('high' German) and Hebrew, and thus *Yiddish* came about.

The Black Death, Russia and The Pale

Quite apart from prejudice and basic hatred of Jews one of the important motivating factors for population movement was plague. In 1349, the Black Death spread throughout Europe, and a large proportion of the population was wiped-out, and of course the Jews were blamed for poisoning the wells amongst other things. However, King Boleslav of Poland had been an exception, and prior to the plague extended a welcome to the Jews based on the benefits from their commercial experience and aptitude. The Black Death put an end to this.

It was not for another 100 years that the welcoming attitude was restored, and Jews were allowed to live and work where they chose, and to enjoy religious freedom. This was the foundation of the large Jewish populations that settled in Poland and other parts of Central Europe and Russia. By 1795, Russia became home to two million Jews but a far from happy Czar Alexander I decided to confine them to an area around 200 miles wide called The Pale of Settlement (from the Baltic Sea to the Crimea). The word 'pale' means 'enclosure' (as also used to refer to the containment of populations in other places such as Ireland) and this remained for nearly 100 years. From the beginning, poverty existed in The Pale, but rarely violence. Families lived in extremely poor conditions but made the best of things. Many, but not all, were farmers. The perception of everybody living in a *shtetl* (or large village, as depicted in the hit stage musical 'Fiddler on the Roof') though common, was not inevitable, for many Jews lived in towns, and from time-to-time were compelled to do so. It depended upon the whim of the current Czar as to where Jews should live, in towns or the countryside, and he dictated the type of work open to them.

When Czar Alexander III of Russia (1845–1894) came to power in 1883 things changed considerably and anti-Semitism became rampant. The Jewish population of the whole of Russia had by then grown remarkably and was now seven million. In that year pogroms, of which there had already been a few, became the order of the day. There was murder, rape, and homes were burned to the ground, which resulted in heavy emigration.

Early Days in England

The West and Other Places

Jews aimed in the main to head towards America, the New World, a welcoming, opportunity-laden country, with great reports feeding back from those who had ventured there. Many Jews had paid for tickets which they thought would get them to New York but on closer examination found their destination was Hull on the North-East coast of England. A third of the Eastern European Jewish population set out for other countries through fear of the pogroms, and arrived there in their millions, but many landed in England and stayed here. A considerable number, mainly from Lithuania, made the far longer journey to South Africa.

It should be noted that those Jews who had originally moved more East to such countries as Persia and Iraq also suffered reversals of fortune, including expulsions, and found it necessary to leave areas where in some cases they had lived for centuries. As they gradually moved back, following a similar route to the earlier Jews, along the African Coast, towards Morocco and then Spain, and having retained many of their own peculiarities in terms of food, forms of ritual, language, and prayer, they joined those who had previously arrived in Spain, but needed to back-track to North-Africa or even move towards Holland. Because of the Spanish majority in their numbers, they were known as *Sephardim*[1] the Hebrew word for Spain. Although things were peaceful for a time, they again faced problems.

Early Jewish Arrivals in England

By 1882, the Jewish population of the United Kingdom was 46,000. By 1900, it was 225,00. These were the two periods of largest admission, so clearly the Jewish population grew to a far greater extent during these times than by the influx following the 400-year period of expulsion from 1290 to 1690 described in what follows. And far more came in the 1800s than during the escape from Nazi Germany in the 1930s and 1940s when the number was around 100,000.

---

1. Of which much more later in this chapter. *Sephardim* is sometimes spelled *Sefardim*.

Elizabeth Pearl's translation of D'Blossiers Tovey's *Anglia Judaica: The History of the Jews in England* (1990) suggests that Jews were known in England prior to William the Conqueror who arrived here in 1066, and despite the popular belief that he is the person who introduced them. Tovey and Pearl point out that the *Canonical Exceptions*, published in AD 740, contain a paragraph in which Egbert, Archbishop of York, forbids Christians to attend Jewish feasts. Prior to Egbert, the Archbishop of Canterbury from 668 to 690 AD was called Theodore, and during the office of each archbishop there were a not inconsiderable number of canons and regulations relating to the Jews. It was, e.g. provided that:

'A Christian woman committing fornication with a Jew should undergo severer penalties than if guilty of the same offence with a Christian.'

Enlarging on the earlier edict above concerning 'feasts' it was explained:

'If any [person] celebrated the feast of Passover with the Jews he should be expelled from every church...If any Christian received unleavened bread or any food or drink from the Jews he should do penance on bread and water for forty days...[nor might] mass be celebrated where the bodies of Jews or infidels were buried [...and no Christian was to] turn Jew or take part in Jewish feasts.'

Tovey and Pearl also draw attention to the thoughts of Sir Henry Spelman (1564–1641) an ecclesiastical and legal historian who, referring to the laws of Edward the Confessor, notes, *'Judei et amnia sun, Regis sun'* (the Jews and all that belongs to them are the property of the King). This appears to be the only law we know of which vests Jewish property in the Crown, and surely shows that Jewish people did live here at that time. However, it goes further than that in that as they were banished from England at the start of the eleventh century, so they must have been here 200 years before Edward. This can be seen in the Charter of Witglass (AD 833). The King of Mercia endowed on the Monks of Croyland, 'All the property they had been given by any Christian *or* Jew.' It follows that if they had property which could be taken from them, they must have been here and owned it in the first place.

Competing Theories

Going back even further in time it has been said that the first Jews in England came as part of the Roman legions in AD 43. In fact, at the time of Jesus Christ there were more Jews spread around the Roman Empire than within the actual province of Judea, so no wonder it is suggested they came with the legions. However, there is no tangible evidence to support this, other than the discovery in the City of London about 100 years ago of a strange brick believed to depict Samson driving foxes into a field of corn. There were also traces of burnt corn on the site. The belief was that the Romans had a granary there and the brick was attributed to their own 'God of the Granaries,' Hercules in place of Samson. The problem was the Romans themselves could not have known about the story of Samson; it is more probable that some Jews came here shortly after the destruction of the temple. London was a port, traders might have settled there, and on the brick in the granary is shown the story of their deliverance from the Philistines.

When the second temple was destroyed in AD 72 the Jews moved around, some to the East and Babylon in particular was a popular destination. Others took an easier, quicker route to Egypt, even the sea route, although more challenging, which took them as far as France and Spain, the latter being particularly attractive because with the passage of time, by the seventh century, the Muslim influence was more amenable than that of Christianity.

The Christians, however, made up for lost time, and before long there were massacres and torture, long before the dreaded Spanish Inquisition began in 1478. The direction the Jews took in escaping Spain was either South to North-Africa, or East to Italy, Greece and then Turkey. Others travelled West to Portugal, though that country offered no better so far as an inquisition was concerned.

Similarly, those who made for Italy and particularly France had good reason to doubt the wisdom of their choice, for they found themselves right in the middle of the route taken by the crusaders, who although primarily targeting the Muslim infidel were not beyond rape, pillage and robbery of other 'infidels' such as the Jews whom they encountered *en route*. For these reasons it seems that the Jews who had either come with the Romans, or more probably later with William the Conqueror from the Rouen, Normandy region of France had made a better choice. That the Jews actually came to England with the legions is based on the supposition that, as the invasion took place after they had invaded the Middle-East and Jerusalem in particular, it would have been normal for them to enlist men from amongst those they had defeated, and who formed part of their support group—'The Pioneer and Logistics Corps'!

Rather than military contributions, it is more likely that a more realistic and reliable source of information is to be found in the Norman Conquest when William, whose origins, as indicated, were in Rouen, was aware of the Jews' commercial abilities and knowledge of coinage and finance. It was with this in mind that he invited a group of merchants to come over three or four years *after* his arrival. It is not known exactly how many were brought over, but they were extremely fortunate. They had moved over the Alps and spread into Northern France and Germany, in the ninth century. Charlemagne found favour with the Jews and eased some restrictions on their travel and admission, which in turn was followed by other sovereigns and 'influencers' over a period of time in the Rhineland. The Jews who lived there were called 'Ashkenazi' as *Ashkenaz* was a Hebrew word meaning Germany; as opposed to those who had come to Europe via the Middle-East, North Africa, Spain and Portugal, the *Saphardim,* for that was Hebrew for Spain or Spaniard. The *Ashkenazi* group produced many famous rabbis and had centres of learning in Mainz and Troyes.

Good and Bad Fortune

I have described those Jews who were introduced to England by William the Conqueror as 'fortunate.' I have done so because some 30 years after their arrival the first Crusade was decreed by Pope Urban II in 1095 which resulted in the deaths of thousands of Jews in Europe.

An appeal had been made by the Byzantine leader to Rome for help in removing the Turks (who were Muslims and had taken over a large region from Constantinople to Jerusalem). The purpose of the Crusade therefore was to redeem the Holy Land and in particular the Church of the Holy Sepulchre in Jerusalem. In reality, the crusaders were not the disciplined armies that are often portrayed and they numbered over 50,000. They were dressed as one might imagine knights to be, bearing a red cross on the chests of their white tunics.

Early Days in England

But they yielded to temptation on their journey. If that temptation involved ransacking villages through which they passed, or which may even have been a little off the beaten track, they would indulge, and if the village had a Jewish community all the better. The takings would be greater, and the odd gold or silver ornaments to add to their luggage were always welcome.

If a charitable view is taken it might be explained that—as the Muslim infidels in the Holy Land were the prime target—then any infidels discovered on the journey might just as well be dealt with. Nor is this a trifling aside. It is said about a quarter of the *Ashkenazi* Jews were destroyed. It is true that protection was offered by some, such as the Bishop of Worms, but 800 were killed there for no reason other than that they refused to convert to Christianity.

Similar disasters occurred in Prague, Metz and parts of Bohemia. There were eight crusades in the 12th and 13th centuries, and throughout Europe there were persecutions, ghettos, and other restrictions abounded. Forcible conversions were commonplace, and word of such activities was brought home to England and followed by Richard the Lionheart, for it was at this time that 'blood libels' and ritual murder charges evolved.[2]

These hard times came about despite a dependency which had evolved upon the trading acumen of the Jews. Their skill and consequent means of livelihood was therefor of money lending and a knowledge of medicine. Only Jews were permitted to lend money at interest, including because the Catholic church considered this sinful. Despite bestowing privileges not available to others, like free movement about the country without paying tolls, of buying and selling goods, but not land (though this restriction was soon removed), selling pledges after the due period of a year and a day, rather like pawnbroking, and being tried by their peers, and of particular interest as a precursor of the 1858 Act described in the next chapter there was a special Jew's oath. But all was not plain sailing, William was more friendly than some who followed him. There were attacks on Jews in Oxford and Norwich, but both King Stephen and Henry II shielded Jews and did not limit their financial activity.

---

2. These manufactured tropes accused Jews of murdering Christians (or other gentiles) especially children. They featured alongside other false, anti-Semitic accounts such as that the wells were being poisoned by Jews, sacrilege (including allegation of participating in the so-called Black Mass) and witchcraft. Fabrications, sometimes called 'anti-Semitic canards,' can be traced back thousands of years, and forwards via Nazi, Communist and similar propaganda, but particularly during the Holocaust and Soviet purges.

Settlement and Sponsorship

What is surprising is the number of areas where Jews settled. A map in Sir Martin Gilbert's extremely useful *Atlas of Jewish History* (1990) shows settlements between 1070 and 1290 in 70 different towns in England and Wales, which apart from London, Cambridge, Norwich, Canterbury, Windsor and Reading contains more remote and widespread centres of Jewish population. Despite all this, Jews were only permitted to bury their dead in London prior to 1177. As they were so spread out the King was able to require financial contributions, secured by demand notes on the sheriffs in the counties.

During this period, the Jews financed the conquest of Ireland, a crusade against Saladin, and at one time a windfall tax amounting to a quarter of the wealth of every Jew. The Jew Aaron of York (Aaron fil Josce), a financier and Chief Rabbi of England, was one of the richest men in the country (if not the richest) and the King's wealth increased enormously on Aaron's death in 1253. This was a peaceful period, one of good relationships with non-Jews, and the clergy, to whom Jews gave help building monasteries and abbeys. It was however the Crusades which had precipitated a feeling of ill-will, and as usual where a community waxes great financially there is envy. In this case from an impecunious upper-class.

Richard I Onwards

King Richard I was a different kind of monarch, spending much time at the Crusades. It was during his absence that physical attacks on the Jews took place in Stamford, Colchester, Bury St Edmunds and other places. Perhaps even worse these were the precursor and reason for the self-destruction of 150 Jews who had sought refuge in Clifford's Tower at York Castle on 17 March 1190, on the Jewish sabbath, before Passover. Following this tragedy, it was several hundred years before any semblance of a Jewish community returned to York. There is a plaque commemorating the event at the entrance to the tower which stands next to the city's criminal court.

There is an element of irony in the fact that when Assizes were converted into Crown Courts in 1972, amongst the early recorders who sat in judgment there were Judge Arthur Myerson QC and Judge Paul Hoffman (both Jewish lawyers: see *Chapter 13*). My wife, Diana sat on the magistrates' bench in Harrogate, and as York was the nearest Assize centre would also sit alongside the York judge sometimes. She described how from Court No 2 she experienced the strange sensation of looking directly out of the window onto the mound of Clifford's Tower where the mass suicide took place but yards away. She wondered how many of the descendants of those who clamoured for the blood of the Jews now appeared in the dock of that very court where she played her part in their judicial disposals.

The personal success of the Jewish community in commerce was accepted by various sovereigns who followed, including King John and Henry III, all of whom were eager to extract financial payments from the Jews as they were deemed chattels of the king. Nor did Church laws provide discouragement, though at the same time there was recognition of the rabbis and even a chief rabbi known as 'The Presbyter of All the Jews of England'; and at one time the *Beth Din* (rabbinical court). This was as near to a conventional court that the Jews could reach, and any business was conducted by the friars, the lawyers of whom were recognisable from the white quiff worn on their heads, to be replaced in medieval times with a flat black cap, and eventually, in seeking to equate with the gentry, the horsehair wig.

Expulsion

It was King Edward I who grasped the nettle and made the decision to expel the Jews from England in 1290, and as far as expulsions go it was comparatively civilised. Specific departure ports were designated, a window of time was given (by All Saints Day 1290) and there were firm instructions that the Jews were not to be hindered in the course of their departure. Although the expulsion which is further explained in *Chapter 5* (that looks at statutory provisions against Jews) affected the vast majority of them, there is ample evidence of a Jewish presence over the following three centuries, when several hundred 'Marranos' who came to England from Spain and Portugal converted to Christianity, or at least pretended to convert because many of them still met in secret to celebrate Passover and *Yom Kippur*.

James Shapiro in his *Shakespeare and the Jews* (1997) considers the Elizabethan prejudices and paranoia about Jews, which enables one to understand his introduction of the frequently considered question, 'Had Shakespeare ever met a Jew?' There *were* Elizabethan prejudices, and certain beliefs about the Jews, which help explain his creation of Shylock, the stereotype grasping moneylender, whose conversion to Christianity forms the climax to *The Merchant of Venice* written around 1600. It is known that before Shakespeare, Henry VIII, apart from rescuing Diogo Mendes (the head of a Dutch Jewish family who conducted business with England and who was arrested for 'overstepping the mark') had him released. Mendes had been accused of not just doing business but at the same time practising Judaism whilst visiting this country. It was also Henry VIII who, loving music at court, in around 1540 hosted the return of Jewish musicians, composers and instrument makers to this country, entirely it seems because of their talents in that regard. Less happy is the tragic story Roderigo Lupez (below). Friar Roger Bacon observed in the 13th century that, 'Christian physicians were not up to the Jewish ones as they did not understand Hebrew or Arabic, which was the language used in those medical works which existed.'

In modern times, Jews have been leaders in the world of medicine and medical science. This is brought home by reading obituaries in *The Times* newspaper, and in particular of the great loss to Germany as well-educated Jews fled the Nazis. The hypocritical attitude of both national and religious leaders can be seen by anti-Jewish rules, regulations, and religious constraints which existed at the same time as the demand for the service of Jewish physicians grew.

Historically, there is the recorded case of Dr Elias Sabot, an eminent physician from Bologna, a centre of medical learning, who was summoned to attend Henry IV in 1410. His full name was Elia de Sabbato, upon whom Roman citizenship was conferred five years previously because of his knowledge of medicine.

Dr Roderigo Lopez is another such an example. A tragic one. Born in Portugal in 1525, his father was Jewish and his family converted, and he qualified at Coimbra, but was suspected of secretly practising Judaism. He had to leave Portugal and chose London, where he changed his name to Lopez. At that time, to practise medicine in England, a degree from Oxbridge was essential, and as this was well before 1856–1858 (see later), that was not possible. If you did not have such a degree you had to go before a board for individual assessment. It is presumed he achieved this, for he practised at St Bartholomew's Hospital in the City of London, and later became a Fellow of the Royal College of Physicians.

Lopez quickly gained a reputation amongst the higher echelons, and his patients were of similar status. He acted as a surgeon, and specialised in stomach ailments, for which he had created prescriptions with ingredients which would have kept even our current Prince Charles content. They were said to have beneficial effects and were confirmed as antioxidant. He was granted a monopoly by Queen Elizabeth I to import prescribed plants and seeds. She approved to the extent that she appointed him her physician-in-chief. She was not his only patient, one of his aristocratic clients was the Earl of Essex.

Whether it happened intentionally or otherwise, Lopez either deliberately or accidentally revealed to another person that he was treating the Earl, and alas that was his undoing. Bad enough to talk about a patient, but to disclose their illness, when that illness is venereal disease, one is just asking for trouble. That there is any connection between the disclosure and Lopez' arrest and being charged with poisoning is but a matter for conjecture, but things moved fast.

Lopez was charged and convicted within a short space of time, and the sentence to be hung, drawn, and quartered swiftly exacted. It was the appellate procedures which, as ever, caused delay in his execution. The queen who had put an enormous amount of trust in Lopez was reluctant to believe his treasonable activities, but public opinion felt otherwise. There were cries of 'Hang the Jew' from the multitudes, and that is what they did, in public.

Despite the precarious nature of the role, Lopez remains so far as I can tell the only royal physician executed in English history. His lawyers were apparently not entirely dissatisfied with the outcome, as Elizabeth insisted that his property should pass to his relatives rather than be forfeited to the Crown (as was the norm in treason cases).

Despite Lopez' fall from grace, royal families continued to indicate a preference for, and were tolerant of Jewish doctors coming to this country. The Merranos (Spanish and Portuguese Jews who had often been forced to convert to Christianity) continued with their medical administrations, but it was mainly their fiscal skills which helped them along, and this expertise in commerce influenced the sovereign and the country so as to overcome any prejudice. Moreover, they were foremost in the trading world, particularly in the overseas territories.

International Trade and Religious Teaching

One of the important places of trading was in Holland, where a large section of the population was comprised of Jews who had moved West from Poland, via Germany. Trade such as that in diamonds was much in their hands, still being one of the commodities easily portable should the necessity arise. We are told that converted Jews were engaged teaching Hebrew at Oxbridge. Many English clergymen engaged them either temporarily or permanently as members of their households because a knowledge of Hebrew was deemed essential to advance in any religious post in either academia, the church or otherwise. Traders and explorers were quick to realise the talents of the Jews as linguists on expeditions to the Middle-East and Far East. They clearly helped adventurers and explorers when 'getting to understand the natives.'

CHAPTER 5

The Laws of England Concerning Jews

English laws with specific reference to the Jews are few but in early times they could be draconian. As noted in earlier chapters, anti-Semitism is nothing new. It existed in England as long ago as medieval times, if not before, so although formal measures and statutory laws against Jews might be a novelty anti-Semitism and prejudice were not.

The Edict of the Badge

Repressive measures begun by Henry II were reinforced under Henry III by the Edict of the Badge of 1218 which contained 13 'provisos' (paraphrased):

- Every Jew should wear a badge conspicuously on the chest.
- Jews could remain in England but only if they 'served the kingdom' in some way.
- No new synagogues could open, only those existing circa King John.
- Jews should 'lower their voices' in synagogues, so as not be heard by Christians.
- Jews should make some payment to their local Christian church.
- Christian wet-nurses and servants should not work for Jews.
- Nor should Christians eat or live in a Jewish household.
- Jews should not buy or eat meat during Lent.
- Jews should not disparage the Christian faith.

- There should be no familiarity' between Jewish men and Christian women; likewise Christian men and Jewish women.
- Jews should not enter Christian churches except 'in transit.'
- No Jew should hinder another Jew's conversion to Christianity.
- Jews needed a licence to live in any town where an established Jewish community did not already exist.

Furthermore, the Edict required that 'justices of the Jews' enforce the above dictats failing which their chattels would be forfeited to the Crown.

The Statute of Jewry 1253

The Statute of Jewry of 1253[1] was the very first Act to be 'aimed at the Jews', and was passed so the King as Head of State could:

> 'Keep [Jews] under control, in a specific place, and make them wear a badge so they can be recognised.'

Made by King Edward I, the 1253 Act sought to inhibit the influence of the Jews especially in financial trading by among other things outlawing the lending of money at interest. In the short time that the Jews had been in England they had achieved what was considered disproportionate influence in money trading, but this had really come about by default in that such trading by Christians had been banned by the church itself. Effectively, the Jews—who were not so restricted by their own laws or beliefs—had stepped in, to everyone's benefit, and some achieved comparatively great wealth.

Apart from the usual portable commodities ('goods') that could be bought and sold, land (known as 'real property') had also become marketable, as it could be used as security for a loan. Not only in England, but this was also common in France, Provence and Gascony, in particular, resulting in expulsions of Jews from those places. However, the English royals hit upon the idea of turning this to their advantage. The Jews were making profits, so the king

---

1. *Statutem de Judaism 1253.*

taxed them on these; their payments were needed not only for building works in this country, particularly the abbeys, but also to finance military excursions abroad and incursions at home.

Statute of Jewry 1275

By 1275 things were clearly getting out of control, so the Statute of Jewry of that year aimed, among other things, to reign in usury. The Act (paraphrased):

- Outlawed usury (lending at unconscionable rates) in every form.
- Released Jew's debtors from certain such obligations.
- Banned Jews from living outside certain cities and towns.
- Stepped-up existing requirements by providing that Jews over the age of seven must wear a yellow felt badge on their outer clothing, in the form of two tablets of a certain size.[2]
- Demanded that all Jews over the age of 12 pay an annual tax of three pence.
- Entrenched the requirement that Christians could not live with Jews.

But the 1275 law did contain some redeeming elements. So, on the positive side:

- It gave Jews time to re-adjust and they were, e.g. allowed to buy farmland for a living, for the next 15 years.
- Jews could also make a living in other so-called 'respectable occupations' as merchants, craftsmen, or soldiers.

The Edict of Expulsion 1290

This was a decree issued by Edward I whereby he ordered the sheriffs of each county in England and Wales to ensure that all the Jews were gone from the

---

2. It is worth noting that the two white bands worn at the collar of modern-day lawyers, 'tabs,' represent the 'Tablets of the Law.'

country by All Saints Day, 1 November 1290, and penalised the sheriffs if they did not do so. The Expulsion lasted throughout the rest of the Middle-Ages, until Oliver Cromwell eased the situation in 1657 as described in *Chapter 6*. One of the reasons put forward for the Edict was that the 1275 Act had not been faithfully followed. Neither this nor the Edict of 1218 were ever repealed.

At the time, the total Jewish population of England was no more than 2,000. Some of those expelled moved to Scotland, others to France, The Netherlands and Poland, where a Jewish community had existed since the 12th century and their rights were at times better protected. Despite the Edict some Jews remained, and complaint was made that the Lombards were Jews.[3] However, with the exception of a few larger transactions, involving the abbeys, Jews were mainly involved at the lower end of the scale of money movement, as shown, e.g. by them running arrangements similar to pawn shops. The higher echelons, however, owed much to the fiscal movements of the Lombards, with their connections to Italy, especially Rome. In London they did business with the Jews: the origins of Lombards Bank.

The Jew Bill of 1753

It might be appropriate, so soon after the lengthy debates of 2018–19 in the UK Parliament on Brexit[4] to suggest that the disagreements, consumption of parliamentary time, numerous votes, and other emotive arguments, have only been equalled by the to-ing and fro-ing of the debates on the Jew Bill of 1753 and associated legislation with a similar theme. That this Jew Bill was introduced in May 1753 and the resulting Act repealed in November of that year indicates the vulnerability of such measures. It can be described as an Act intended to give comfort to a comparatively small number of Jews who had not been born in this country, and whose trading facilities were commercially disadvantaged as compared with those born here.

Jews were, in addition, not permitted to own land in this country. The solution seemed to lie in a private Act of Parliament. The debates on the Bill

---

3. Lombardy was a part of Italy and the *Langobardi* were members of a Germanic people who once ruled those parts, some of whom in due course came to England.
4. The UK's departure from the European Union.

pre-empted a public outcry. Newspapers, leaflets, cruel pictures, and even attacks on Jews were the order of the day.

There *had* been a Bill which constituted an exception to the rigours against which the 1753 Jew Bill was aimed. This led to the Plantation Act of 1740,[5] which allowed those who had previously lived in the American Colonies for seven years, and had then lived in England for three years, to become naturalised without any religious problems concerning taking an oath. There remained however those who were deeply conscious of the risk to their own businesses and were strongly opposed to the Bill so that, although passed, the 1753 Act was an afterthought, and hence its repeal some six months later.

Once the Jew Act was repealed, calm was restored. An attempt was made to also repeal the Plantation Act, but this failed. It may well have been that Parliament did not seek to be a platform for further openly anti-Semitic speeches. Although things quietened down, there were still odd displays of this, but it is said that the success of the Jewish boxer and East End prize-fighter Daniel Mendoza (1764–1836) whose fame elevated the status of Jews and deterred would-be thugs and assailants from attacking them. The 1753 Act did however leave a bitter taste in the mouths of many people, who became more entrenched in their views be they for or against emancipation.

The Debates of 1833

A prime example of the range of opinions concerning Jews progressing to positions of status is shown in a debate on that very subject during 1833. A flavour of the atmosphere in the House of Commons during the many debates which took place during the 30 years prior to the eventual passing of the landmark Jewish Relief Act of 1858 (below) can be gleaned by a closer look at the debates in the Commons and Lords, which were high on eloquence, long in time, and emotive in content as can be seen from *Hansard* for the 17 April 1833. There was a strange atmosphere. The place was full. They came in from every corner of the realm to vote against the possibility of their august institution being diluted by the presence of the Jew.

---

5. Also known as the Naturalisation Act 1740.

The chief supporter of emancipation on this day was Robert Grant (1779–1836) MP, a Liberal. He was born in India his father being chairman of the East India Company. Educated at Magdalene College, Cambridge University, called to the Bar, a King's Serjeant,[6] he was elected MP for four different seats, two in Scotland and Finsbury and Norwich in England (at different times!). He became Judge Advocate General and Governor of Bombay and wrote many works including a book of hymns. His support of the Jewish cause, no doubt motivated by the purest of intentions, might well have been influenced by his religious disposition, and perhaps, just perhaps, by his father's position with the East India Company, an organization with which the Rothschild dynasty were known to be connected. Grant's argument in the House of Commons included these amongst many other words:

> 'In every civilised community no man ought to be excluded from any civil right on account of his religious sentiments being different from those of the community at large... An Hon gentleman once said that he could not contemplate being on dining terms with the Jews, and seemed to think that his own repugnance in this respect constituted a satisfactory reason for excluding such individuals from Parliament. This is a lamentable state of ignorance on this subject as many Hon Members present, who could testify from personal experience that the cookery of the Jews is not the worst thing about them... Throughout the whole of history they have distinguished themselves as an orderly, industrious, obedient, religious people. In political principles and moral and loyal conduct the Jews evinced that they had common interests with ourselves, so was it just that they should be excluded from common honours?... The Jew was interested in defending the country which contained his family and property, so open up to him the Army and the Navy.'

It may be recalled in connection with the last sentence of the above quote that when Napoleon opened-up the European ghettos, and young Jewish men were enabled to work outside of them, to travel and to take up new occupations,

---

6. The name given to members of a group of elite lawyers who wore a distinctive white skull cap, as previously worn by the friars.

they often joined the Army, and within a short period made up a fair proportion of the officer class in several countries in Central and Eastern Europe.

Grant continued:

'The Jew is so deeply interested in the Laws of the country, place him on the bench if qualified. He is interested in upholding the King and Constitution, let him serve the King as his other subjects do.'

His main opponent in the debate that day was Sir Robert Inglis, second baronet, the Conservative member for Dundalk, Ripon and Oxford University. A man with staunch high church views and perhaps an obvious person to challenge Grant. He made it clear that he believed the Jews were 'alien,' and that they had no allegiance to this country and were damaging to Christianity. He likened Buddhism to idolatry and opposed a grant to a Catholic seminary.

Although Benjamin Disraeli (whose Jewish parents had converted to Christianity) was not necessarily one to openly speak for Jewry, he and Inglis did not see eye-to-eye, and Disraeli was particularly scathing, perhaps unfairly, taking-up Inglis on the lack of power in his advocacy, the cause of suffering in Ireland, and saying he deplored absentee landlords. Inglis' criticism of the potential emancipation of Jews can be seen from his speech where he asks:

'Would the Parsee, the Brahmin, the Mussulman [Muslim], the Jew, be fit to be entrusted with the ecclesiastical as well as civil interests of this country?'

Though it is necessary to search carefully for the proposition actually being canvassed in the debate he maintained:

'The nationality of the Jews was a strong argument against their admission place them in Poland, Prussia, France or Algiers or in China, they still regard themselves as a separate Nation...the promotion of Joseph in Egypt and Daniel in Babylon as a proof of their promotion in High Stations was a miraculous promotion carrying into effect the will of the Almighty, and not an argument to show Christian people should admit Jews to power...'

'That Jews in Poland, though the subjects of Russia, aided the escape of Buonaparte...'

'They came back after the expulsion for their own purposes and speculation...'

'Strangers and sojourners the Jews must be till they find their own home, in Jerusalem...'

'Would you place a Jew on the judicial bench, where perhaps his first task would be to try a person on an act of blasphemy?'

The resemblance between some of the arguments put forward on this occasion and those heard in recent times is perhaps not surprising, for anti-Semitism has existed throughout the ages. However, one speaker in favour of the Bill argued that if you deny the Jew parliamentary influence it seemed to follow that you might deny him his landed property, and if you take his landed property then why not take his funded property? If you take his property, then why not his liberty? And if his liberty then why not his life? How is it possible to leave a man in possession of vast property he asked and yet deprive him of political power.

Can there be kinder words than these uttered in April 1833 by Thomas Babington Macaulay, later Lord Macaulay. He was a noted historian, educated at Cambridge University, a poet, essayist, and Whig politician, Secretary of War and Paymaster General. In this debate he made his maiden speech on the emancipation of the Jews. He was a noted orator, who composed the famous poem *Horatius*:

'How can man die better, than facing fearful odds,
For the Ashes of his fathers, and the temples of his Gods.'

But it was his words about emancipation that influenced and gave much strength to the cause he supported:

'Let them open the doors of that House—let them open to the Jews every career of honourable competition. Until they did that let no man presume to say, that there was no genius in the countrymen of Isiah, and no valour in the descendants of the Maccabees. In supporting such a proposition, I consider myself supporting the true interests of Christianity.'

In the final days of the debate in 1833, comparisons were made to the position of Catholics. Specific pieces of legislation existed, such as the Roman Catholic Relief Act 1791[7] which admitted them to the practice of the law, permitted the exercise of their religion, and the existence of their schools. It allowed members of the Catholic church to sit in Parliament. In the ensuing debates it was urged that similar relief be afforded to the Jews concerning Westminster, including that the House Lords also be open to them.

The Sheriff's Declaration Act 1835

The adventures of David Salomons built something of a foundation for the cause, as he had clearly found favour in the City of London. Amongst his various accomplishments, he helped establish the National Westminster Bank. His main occupation was that of a banker, but he had also been called to the Bar, though he never practised. He had some determined supporters but having been made Sheriff of London he met oath-taking problems.

Salomans persevered and the law was changed to accommodate him. The Sheriff's Declaration Act of 1835 let him take up office without taking the oath; and when made an alderman of the City, the Jewish Municipal Relief Act of 1847 was passed that allowed him to take the oath without Christian references. He later became Lord Mayor of London.

Salomans was elected to Parliament in 1851. He took the oath but omitted the Christian requirements, then went and sat down on the Liberal benches. He was asked to withdraw. At first, he didn't, then he did, but he came back three days later, voted in a division and was forcibly removed by the sergeant-at-arms and fined £500. He won a seat again in 1859, a year after the 1858 Act (below), and held it until his death 14 years later.

---

7. Also known as the Catholic Emancipation Act.

The Landmark Act of 1858

The most important date in this book is undoubtedly 1858, and the real purpose of this work concerns the gradual and increasing relief afforded by the cumulative effect of the Jewish Relief Act of 1858 and other statutes which together opened-up Parliament, the professions, the universities and the judiciary to Jews (as well as to those of other minority faiths in the United Kingdom).

The 1858 Act was indeed a relief to many in more ways than one, and in fact a compromise, because the question see-sawed between the House of Commons and House of Lords. The Bill achieved acceptance by the Commons then rejection by the Lords, a pause, then renewal, and only in 1858, when it was passed by the Commons sitting as a committee, and separately by the Lords, did it seem that a conclusion had been achieved, though once more, not truly so, because over the following decade it required re-examination.

The Persistence of Baron Rothschild and Earl Russell

Following the 1858 Act and having been elected to Parliament in 1857, on the 26 July 1858, Baron[8] Lionel de Rothschild was allowed to take an oath without needing to add the words 'on the true faith of a Christian.' He was the first Jew to lawfully take his seat, amidst loud cheers.

He had in fact made several attempts to enter Parliament, having first won a seat nine years earlier but after arriving at the House of Commons he said he could not take the Christian oath. On being told to withdraw he did so, in a dignified fashion, and the Prime Minister immediately proposed the removal of civil and religious disabilities by a Bill affecting the Crown's Jewish subjects. This was agreed by 257 to 186 and resulted in the preparation of a Jewish Disabilities Bill which concentrated on the question of allowing Jews to take a seat in Parliament. The Whig proponent, John Russell, the first Earl Russell and Foreign Secretary in a Coalition Government, was a man small in stature but 'big' on reform. Quite apart from his urge to emancipate Catholic and Jew, he had secured social reforms concerning public baths, washhouses, factory hours, working conditions, sewage and clean water. The first improvements in all of these were as result of his stewardship.

---

8. Baron Rothschild was so styled because of his Austrian hereditary title *Freiherr*. It was granted to his father. Being a foreign title it did not exclude him from being 'a commoner.'

The Laws of England Concerning Jews

'Lionel Nathan de Rothschild introduced in the House of Commons on July 26, 1858 by Lord John Russell and Mr Abel Smith.' Painting by Henry Barraud. Rothschild Archive.

Caricature of Baron Lionel de Rothschild from *Men of the Day*. Rothschild was the first unconverted Jew to sit in Parliament. Elected by the voters four times it took eleven years for him to take up his seat because he wouldn't swear the oath 'on the true faith of a Christian.' Picture Alamy.

Russell's Bill on the emancipation of Jews received support not only from his own political party, but several Conservatives. Yet on three occasions the Bill was rejected by the House of Lords, and not finally passed until 1858. This only came about I think because both sides were thoroughly exhausted by the repetitive nature of the arguments. An indication of this was the fact that the Prime Minister, the Earl of Derby, who had strongly opposed the Bill, suddenly seemed to capitulate. He was a Conservative, and the arguments were causing harm within his party, so a simple and basic compromise was reached. It involved creating an oath which would be acceptable to those of the Jewish religion without including any demeaning references to the spiritual traditions of the deponent or anyone else. The final Commons vote on the 1858 Act was 143 to 97 in favour and in the Lords 129 to 55.

After Rothschild's service in Parliament which was, ironically, most inauspicious, for he made *not one single speech*, Queen Victoria was approached to consent to him entering the House of Lords. She refused, not just unamused, but positively irate at the thought. Eventually his son Nathaniel de Rothschild, despite Victoria's misgivings, was granted a peerage in the aftermath of enormous financial assistance and advice on the purchase of the Suez Canal, various railways in England and Europe, personal assistance during her visits to Europe, and the common appreciation of Prime Minister Benjamin Disraeli, turned-on perhaps by his flattery, and despite his Hebraic origins.

Once passed, the Act of 1858 enabled Jews to take an oath which did not include the words 'on the true faith of a Christian,' meaning they could take-up a seat in Parliament. As we have seen the debates were many, they had ranged across the years, and had dealt with general principle, both in the House of Commons and House of Lords. The divisions were numerous, the repetition of arguments tedious, the persistence of those on either side who were for or against Jewish entry to Parliament full to the brim with tenacity.

Following the vote on the 1858 Act there were days of discussion as to whether this had been a 'one-off,' or if it applied to those Jews who, in the future, might gain election for other constituencies. It was accepted that this would now be the case. And although other legislation had already, just a couple of years earlier, opened-up the universities (see next section), progression to the judiciary was expressly excluded by the 1858 Act.

A Growing Jewish Population

By the time of these pieces of legislation the number of Jews in England had increased from 20,000 to at most 30,000 out of a total population of 17 million following anti-Semitic incidents in Eastern Europe, which were the precursor of the later pogroms. Although the wealthier Jewish families were known by name and accomplishment during the comparatively short period since the unofficial 'Return' in the time of Cromwell, the majority were quite poor. They were immigrants from Holland in the case of *Sephardim* Jews[9] who had made a gradual passage from Spain, which is what *Sephard* means, through South-West and Central France, and the *Ashkenazi* or German, who came from Russia, Poland and Germany. The latter were in the main artisans and in minor trades. The principle of charity was strong in the minds of the wealthy, and once other Jews arrived here, through synagogues, various charitable institutions were created. There was a movement from London, and a revival in some of the 60 centres where in medieval times Jewish communities had, if not flourished, existed. The more religiously observant however tended to stay in London, but there was a general movement and quest for improvement in education amongst the middle-classes, their aim being to gain status and respectability.

Those who had been in England for some while, were known as 'the Jewish aristocracy.' Some, indeed, were part of 'The Cousinhood,' so called because of frequent intermarriage with other wealthy families, thus cementing family ties and the total value of wealth amassed: the Cohens, Rothschilds, Montefiores, Montagus, Salomons. They had been successful in commerce and banking, providing facilities not only to kings and princes but also by using their international connections to their advantage. It was therefore natural that parents would have ambitions for their sons. The daughters would benefit in marital advantage arising from the wealth of their parents, both in and out of the faith, but sons would have to be provided with the best education possible, and a legal qualification would be a traditional ambition. There were however two problem areas arising from the same prohibition.

---

9. The largely interchangeable descriptions *Sephardi*, *Sephardic* or *Sephardim* Jews signifies those who came mainly from Spain but it was also applied to those from Portugal—or even parts of the Middle-East—hence also the term 'Hispanic Jew.'

The first of these problems would preclude them from the ultimate educational targets of Oxford and Cambridge, the second from the ambition of many a lawyer, to achieve a seat on the bench and the knighthood that usually goes automatically with appointment to the High Court and above. The prohibition related to the oath, which in the first case had to be sworn prior to graduation, and the second before assuming a judicial post, and for that matter a seat in Parliament, or even basic entry to certain other posts or professions. The oath taken at that time needed to be on the *New Testament* as a Christian. The Jews Relief Act 1858, as later amended, changed all of that.

Opening-up the Universities

Until just before 1858, Jews were not allowed to have a degree from Oxford or Cambridge, thus barring a key qualification route to the Bar (from which the judges then usually came). The Oxbridge barrier was removed by the Oxford University Act 1854 followed by the Cambridge University Act 1856. These Acts abolished religious 'tests' precluding non-Christians from having certain degrees conferred on them. The position was improved further by the Universities Tests Act 1871 which forbade religious tests for any degree. However, before that time, candidates were not entirely prevented from being called to the Bar, as seen by the success of those who went to University College London as described in *Chapter 1*.

Opening-up the Judiciary

The 1858 Act, though advancing the principle of equality, precluded, by a specific exception relating to oaths taken upon appointment to the bench, appointment to the judiciary. That exception was removed by the Promissory Oaths Act which began as a Bill in 1866 and was passed by Parliament two years later in 1868. This repealed the section in the 1858 Relief Act which prevented Jews holding certain offices of State and preserved for these the previous forms of oaths and declarations contained in former statutes. It is interesting to note that although Jews were, by this change, placed on a level footing with Christians, there was still one restriction which—one might think not unreasonably—remained, and that was that they could not exercise ecclesiastical patronage attached to any public office they might hold. Obvious, really.

Opening-up Other Higher Legal Roles

Sir George Jessel (*Chapter 9*) became the first Jew to be appointed Solicitor-General in 1871, and as will be shown in later chapters Jews served as privy councillors, judges, including as Lord Chief Justice, Master of the Rolls, Lords of Appeal, Presidents of the Supreme Court, colonial governors, Cabinet ministers, and although there were arguments to the contrary, no acceptable reason was ever shown as to why a Jew should not hold the position Lord Chancellor. We shall see in *Chapter 9* that Farrer Herschell, 'a Jew by race,' eventually did manage to progress to this ancient office as did Dominic Raab as this book went to press.

It took 50 years for the effect of the changes of the 1850s to reach the top shelf, when in 1913 Sir Rufus Isaacs (*Chapter 9*) became Lord Chief Justice. Then after an interval of 70 years (and 150 years after the Jewish Relief Act), over a period of 16 years between 1992 and 2008, rather like waiting for a bus, three came along almost at the same time: Peter Taylor, Harry Woolf and Nicholas Phillips (*Chapter 11*). To cap it all, as the President of the Supreme Court, Phillips became the first head of that court in 2009 and then another Jew, Lord David Neuberger in 2012.

At the time of writing there have been several recent appointments of Jewish lawyers to the higher echelons of the judiciary and politics; both the present Master of the Rolls (and his immediate predecessor); the new President of the Queen's Bench Division of the High Court (and her predecessor); the Attorney-General; and under-secretaries of State at the Ministry of Justice.

This caused me to reflect upon the initial prohibition barring such appointments, about how some had mysteriously circumvented the requirements of the former oath and of the great men who had become able to hold office as a result of a critical enabling step, the Jewish Relief Act of 1858, the significance of which should never be underestimated, not only for the Act itself but as the springboard for many post-1858 reforms.

CHAPTER 6

Conversion and Return

I mentioned in earlier chapters that some Jews chose—or were forced—to convert to Christianity. This even though they might remain Jews in mind or in private. The following story is about one such person, Sir Edward Brampton described as 'once a Jew, but who afterwards laved in the sacred font by King Edward,' in other words, converted to Christianity, presumably for his own purposes. It also tells of one London institution catering for 'converts,' whilst the later part of this chapter describes 'the return of the Jews' to this country when legal barriers were no longer enforced and later abandoned.[1]

The Doubtful One: Sir Edward Brampton

In the 15th century there came about the legal case of a man with the unusual name of Perkin Warbeck. He claimed to be Richard Duke of York, the second son of King Edward IV, and the younger of the two princes murdered by Richard III in the Tower of London. Had that boy lived then he would have had a claim to the English throne, that is, if his elder brother had died first, so a possibility, no more.

If there had been a word like 'scammer' in medieval times he would have fitted the bill. He swanned around the various courts of Europe for three years from 1492. He made many strange claims, and he ended-up on the scaffold.

---

1. I should mention that there are occasional references in this book to the Law of Return which has quite different connotations to the return of the Jews to England. Rather it is associated with the notion of a Jewish State or homeland and centres on who can be a citizen of the Jewish, ancestral, biblical, call it what you believe, homeland in what is now Israel.

Perhaps his strangest claim was that he was a Jew. This may have been to get better food in prison whilst awaiting his fate, but he was certainly not a Jew, although he might have been brought up by one.

Warbeck may have been *the pretender* to the throne, but as we shall see Sir Edward Brampton (1440–1508) was *a pretender* when it came to conversion. As Warbeck's date with the executioner drew nigh, he wrote down the details of his parents, and of where he had been brought-up, and explained that he had, at the behest of his father, been sent to various parts of Flanders for what was described as an opportunity 'to learn the language.' He thereby claimed that, in effect, he was an *au pair* and some time 'escort.' As part of his duties, he found himself on one occasion accompanying Sir Edward's wife on a voyage by ship. We do not know whether Sir Edward knew that Warbeck was doing so, or in what precise capacity, but let us grant him the benefit of the doubt, and assume it was all quite *kosher* and that Sir Edward had knowledge of and gave his full support to that voyage by his wife and her companion.

Actually, Sir Edward was born in Portugal and reference to his birth appears frequently in the chronicles. It seems he was young when he first came to the notice of the king, and he converted later in life. There was a House of Converts, the *Domus Conversorum*, established in 1232 in a building in Chancery Lane, London for poor Jews who had converted, and which provided a communal home and low wages to those converts who had been compelled, as part of the process, to forfeit their possessions to the Crown. It housed between 40 and 80 'converts' and it still existed into the 16th century. Moreover, the warden was given this appointment as an addition to his main office, none other than Master of the Rolls.

An examination of the house's records shows that in 1468 there appears the name Edward Brandon. There is clearly a similarity between Brampton and Brandon, and there are other possibilities which point to it being the same person, particularly as there had been an influx of Jews from Portugal where they had been treated badly. Brandon is not an uncommon name amongst Jews of Spanish and Portuguese origin, for example Brandon Lewis, Minister of State for Northern Ireland, and a recent chair of the Conservative party is Jewish.

Edward Brandon advanced, he was given a commission in the Army and then made a naval officer, being handed command of one of Her Majesty Queen Elizabeth I's ships. He was eventually created Governor of Guernsey and was

Conversion and Return

greatly loved by the royal family and knighted in 1484 by Richard III. Not bad for a converted Jew from Portugal.

But let us not allow the success of Brandon to cause us to forget the other inmates of the *Domus Conversorum*. Lest it be thought that this was a peaceful refuge for asylum seekers, then think again. Life there was no bed of roses. Writers of the time describe a litany of offences which the miscreants who lodged there had committed. The same writers had some novel ideas about the occupants of that house, including that in 1290, following the expulsion from England, they had been sent to Scotland, and that this explained 'why the Scots were so close-fisted, and did not eat pork.'

Sir Edward Brampton whose wife toured Europe in the company of scaffold-bound pretender to the throne Perkin Warbeck. My 'doubtful tale' of Brampton explains why I think he may have ended-up destitute in a 'House for Converts' in London before becoming Governor of Guernsey (if he's the same person that is).

The Return of the Jews

Contact with Jews was not new. By the end of the 16th century, many English travellers and trade-seekers who ventured abroad, met with Jews whom they would not ordinarily come across in England. They came together through trade in Morocco, Turkey, Holland and Italy where communities of Jews existed and were at the forefront of their various livelihoods, and in dealing with commodities which British travellers sought. It was not until 300 years had passed and Charles I had been beheaded in 1649 that the Jews felt it was safe to return following a petition by Rabbi Menasseh Ben Israel to Oliver Cromwell, who was a devout Puritan. Cromwell also had the common sense to realise the advantage of allowing Jews to return, for after all they had been expelled by Edict of a king, not by any Parliamentary law. Amongst the devout it was believed that the second coming of Christ would not happen until there were Jews throughout the world, and there was the overriding problem of rebuilding the national economy following the lengthy Civil War.

Cromwell gathered for a meeting in Whitehall with merchants, clergymen, and some of the judges. The judges were happy at the idea of the Jews returning, but the merchants and clergymen were less enthusiastic. Cromwell felt frustrated that he could not achieve unanimity. But rather than abandon the idea he adjourned the meeting and used the interim period to take matters into his own hands with a compromise. This was to invite some wealthy Jews to England from Holland, and to encourage them to move their trading base with Spain to London.

This was the reason that about 300 Marranos, that is Jews who when in Spain and Portugal had converted to Christianity *de jure* (legally speaking) but remained Jewish *de facto* (in fact) were able to be more open about their religion, and in 1701 they established the Bevis Marks Synagogue.[2] This is Britain's oldest synagogue, in Aldgate in the City of London and has continued at the same address for the last 300 years.

Those Jews who came from Holland were *Sephardim*, having travelled to that country from Spain and Portugal, and they were followed by the *Ashkenazim* who came from Germany, Poland and Eastern Europe. They travelled

---

2. *Qahal Kadosh Sha'ar ha-Shamayim.*

via Holland because of massacres in the Ukraine and Poland in the 17th century which were distinct from the pogroms in Russia, Lithuania, Latvia and Poland of the late-19th century, and the more modern ones in Germany and Austria of the 20th century. However, in the England of the mid-17th century all did not go smoothly.

Despite the support of Cromwell there were groups of religious activists, and people in commerce, who were concerned about losing out and who made attempts to vanquish the Jews once more. This, despite knowing that the Jews had brought vast amounts of capital into the country. They financed the Duke of Marlborough's wars against the Spanish and during the Jacobite uprising in 1745 were particularly loyal, offering not only finance but also volunteering for the army battalion created to defend London. Their financial activities provided one twelfth of the nation's surplus, and a twentieth of its foreign trade.

To affirm this re-settlement the first practical gesture was the Act of Parliament of 1753 known as 'The Jew Bill' mentioned in *Chapter 5*. This allowed them to become naturalised as British citizens. Although passed by the House of Lords, the Bill did not pass in the House of Commons, because there were those who believed that such a step would be seen as weakening Christianity. It is not surprising therefore that many prominent Jews, such as Benjamin Disraeli allowed their children grow up as Christians, and acceptance was slow.

Thus, the return to England was a gradual process because there had not been any legislation which specified a change in policy and an identifiable entitlement. It was more a case of saying we will not say that we will allow you to enter the country, but we will not do anything to prevent you coming here. There were those in this country, such as politicians, who expressed fierce objections whilst there were others including the Quaker community who showed enthusiasm for the return of the Jews, and the fact that there had been emancipation of the Catholics was looked upon as a good omen.

There were one or two false starts in the journey towards full emancipation, including the attempts at Parliamentary intervention cited in *Chapter 5*. But nothing which could be defined, and those who came to England were, with the notable exception of the medical practitioners who held qualifications in Holland and other European countries, still almost entirely engaged in trade or finance.

Given the period of the Expulsion being 1290–1657, it is extraordinary that it only took a further 43 years for the first knighthood to be awarded to a Jew. Solomon De Medina (approximately 1650–1730) lived in Amsterdam. He travelled to England and gave great assistance to King William III as a supplier of goods and arms. William was a staunch Protestant and De Medina[3] found great favour in his eyes. As did several other Jews who joined his columns. Medina was introduced to Lord Marlborough and financed his battles in Spain. This was precisely what the Rothschilds had done for the Duke of Wellington. In 1700, De Medina was knighted. He was a great supporter of the Bevis Marks Synagogue mentioned earlier.

In 1837, Queen Victoria knighted Moses Montefiore (*Chapter 8*), and four years later Isaac Lyon Goldsmid received the first hereditary award, a baronetcy, for his work for Jewish emancipation concerning the Jewish Disabilities Bill (*Chapter 5*), which eventually led to the granting of basic civil and political rights to Jews. Amongst other achievements by Goldsmid were his part in the building of some of the railways of southern England, the London Docks, and establishing University College Hospital in the vicinity of Euston and Bloomsbury. But, as yet, of Jewish lawyers, not a trace.

---

3. Known as 'The Jew of Medina.'

CHAPTER 7

'We May Give You the Laws, But...'

Most civilised countries owe much to Jewish law, yet in England it was a case of, 'We may give you the laws, but we aren't allowed to provide the lawyers.' For the background to Jewish law-making it is useful to examine a few lines from the Book of Deuteronomy, Chapter 16:

- 'Judges and Officers shalt thou make. Tribe by Tribe, and they shall judge the people with righteous judgment.'
- 'Thou shall not wrest [that is pervert] judgments.'
- 'Thou shalt not respect persons' [which does not only mean you shall not be awed by the rich and ignore the poor, but equally you shall not favour the poor because of their deficiency. Decide on the issues, 'keep your eye on the ball.']
- 'Neither shalt though take a gift, for a gift doth blind the eyes of the wise, and pervert the word of the righteous.'

In this last context I must admit that when first sitting as a judge and about to sentence a defendant I was somewhat thrown when prosecuting counsel and the police detective in the case asked to see me in my private chambers. He and prosecuting counsel came in, as did defence counsel, for one cannot see one side's legal representative without the other being there. The prosecutor opened by saying, 'Your honour, this is a brown envelope case,' and thrust something in my direction. I immediately froze, thinking of the openness of the whole thing, and my bible readings.

The prosecutor then explained that the envelope contained confidential particulars of 'help' the defendant had given to the police, in mitigation of the sentence I was about to impose. I was saved from temptation. But back to my readings of the good book:

- 'Justice, Justice, shalt thou follow, that thou mayest live and inherit the land which the Lord thy God gave thee' [The repetition of the word 'justice' is deemed vital, for repetition means that, whether to your advantage or disadvantage, you shall tell the truth].
- 'A death sentence is only to be imposed if the act is confirmed by at least two witnesses, preferably three.'
- 'If thou, the judge, cannot come to a proper decision then refer the matter to a higher tribunal, where the judge will inquire diligently and decide whether the witness be false.'

I sometimes wondered whether the judges of early times had to take an oath of office (*Chapter 3*), and how it compared to ours.

Nowadays we are entreated to do justice 'without favour, affection, or ill-will.' It used to be 'to do justice indifferently,' and it took quite a long time to appreciate the ambiguity of that phrase. How similar therefore is that line from Deuteronomy 16 to the requirements of English law by way of the Justices of the Peace Act of 1327 which refers to the appointment of 'good and lawful men' in every county to guard the peace.

Moses as Lawgiver

Exodus 18 is about how Moses' father-in-law, Jethro is so worried about how Moses is wearing himself out trying to diminish crime that he shows him that he should install a court where heinous crimes can be tried, and small courts dotted around the country for less serious transgressions. In taking this advice Moses in effect invented the tiers we now have for the Crown Court and the magistracy.

Whenever I visit the Great Hall of Lincoln's Inn and look to the Northern end of that vast room there is an enormous painting, a huge semi-circular

'We May Give You the Laws, But...'

fresco on the wall painted by George Frederick Watts called, 'The School of Lawgivers.' It shows men (always men in those days) who created the laws of some of the world's leading civilisations and religions: Justinian, Confucius, Pythagorus, Alfred, Atila, Minos, Draco, Mano, Charlmagne, Servius. But the central figure is Moses. Despite the dispersion of the Jews it would appear that in the minds of all the others Jewish law was supreme. Despite also the fact that there had been issued various prohibitions, warning Jews against recourse to non-Jewish courts of justice, probably out of fear that the participants would be persuaded to honour idols in whose name those other courts administered their own forms justice.

Perhaps this edict was issued to maintain the internal autonomy of Jewish communities: 'Don't follow the laws of the Egyptians or the Canaanites.' But this prohibition has long fallen into disuse as Jews gradually learnt to look to the courts of the countries in which they lived for relief.

It follows that with this emancipation Jews began to participate themselves in the legal process and with the remarkable results which have evolved, and they have made important contributions to legal thought in most countries of the modern world. In England in particular—first in the 19th century and later as I will indicate—their contribution was not only disproportionate to their numbers in the population but also to the numbers who in fact practised law. In the next chapter I turn to the those who paved the way for this in England.

CHAPTER 8

The First Jewish Lawyers

It is important in evaluating the early contribution of the Jews to English law to record that it occurred in a span of little more than 100 years. This was because, even in so liberal a country as England, Jews were until the mid-1800s excluded from the universities of Oxford and Cambridge (as well as Parliament), and thus mostly from the Bar and solicitor's professions, that is unless they practised forms of Judaism covertly which many refused to do. Perhaps before we deal with those about whom we are more certain, a word or two about the very first Jews to become lawyers, though I must admit doubts arise as to the veracity of some aspects of the first of these accounts as I think will become obvious.

Joshua Montefiore (1762–1843)

It is perhaps inevitable that the name Montefiore should crop up sooner or later in any Jewish historical scenario, so let us get our Montefiores over with right at the beginning. They were first heard of in Moorish Spain, and when expelled from there they had the right idea and moved to Italy. One branch of the family settled in Ancona, and then moved on to Leghorn.[1] In Leghorn the tolerance of the powerful Mediccis gave full scope to Jewish enterprise, and in 1656 Menasseh Ben Israel, a Portuguese rabbi—Portuguese, but born on Madeira—a writer, printer, who in later times would be known as an 'activist,'

---

1. The old English name for Livorno on the West coast of Tuscany.

said that it was because of this tolerance that Leghorn was so prosperous. It was he who influenced the petition to Oliver Cromwell for the re-admission of the Jews to England in 1656 (see *Chapter 6*). One of his less successful projects was to try to show that the South American Andes Indians were the descendants of the lost tribes of Israel. Perhaps the ultimate in losing one's way.

Sir Moses Haim Montefiore was the most famous of that clan. Honoured as the First Baronet Montefiore in 1846, he was a financier and banker, a philanthropist and he became Sheriff of London, but I do not dwell upon his life as he was not a lawyer. He had been born whilst his parents lived in Leghorn, where the family were amongst the leading merchants of the town. His grandfather, Moses Vital (Chaim) Montefiore was married to the daughter of a wealthy Moorish merchant, Masshod Racah, but he himself failed to prosper and in 1758 emigrated to England. He had little capital but nevertheless established himself as an importer of Italian goods. Maybe he didn't have time to prosper as he had 17 children, eight sons and nine daughters.

It is one of those sons, Joshua Montefiore (1762–1843) that we are concerned with. Born in London, he claimed to be the first Jewish undergraduate at Oxford University, the first to be called to the Bar (in 1794) and the first to hold a commission in the British Army (he became a captain in the Yorkshire Light Infantry and served in Martinique and Guadeloupe). It is not surprising that he was described as a 'Baron Von Munchausen character' and these details of his career are based entirely upon his own chronicles.

Joshua Montefiore claimed to be one of the leaders of an ill-fated expedition to West Africa, and that on his return he had been offered a knighthood by George III which he declined. Other sources do confirm that he did go on an expedition but was described as 'a most troublesome fellow.'

What *can* be confirmed is that Joshua Montefiore wrote *A Synopsis of Mercantile Law and Notarial Precedents* (or at least his name is on the book), now published by Forgotten Books (sic). He eventually went to the USA, got married for the second time to a Catholic lady and produced eight children when he was between the age of 73 and 81. He is buried in Vermont. My research does confirm some of the claims he made, but does not answer the question, 'How did he do it?' By which I mean get into Oxford and become a barrister prior to the changes discussed in this book, not produce all those children at that great age. Let us therefore turn to a man of whom there is more acceptable evidence, to whom we can perhaps more safely grant the accolade 'first in line.'

Sir Francis Henry Goldsmid (1808–1878)

Francis Goldsmid (whose image adorns the front cover of this book) was the son of Sir Isaac Lyon Goldsmid (1778–1859) who was knighted in 1841. There had been that previous baronetcy awarded to Sir Moses Montefiore (above), but I do not include Sir Moses as a principal in this section as he did not either have ambition or achievements as a lawyer. Nor indeed did Sir Isaac Goldsmid and neither did Sir David Salomons, who was awarded a knighthood in 1855 as Lord Mayor of London.

Francis was born in Spitalfields in 1808 and read for the Bar at Lincoln's Inn, but when he was actually called to the Bar in 1833 he refused to take the oath on 'the true faith of a Christian.' It was by sufferance rather than right that the benchers[2] agreed to allow him to take an oath of allegiance in a form 'acceptable to his conscience,' as he had explained that it would cause him hardship if this procedure could not be followed. At the meeting which decided this, one learned bencher was heard to dissent, muttering, 'Hardship? Hardship? then let him become a Christian.'

An observant Jew, as were members of his family, who were wealthy, for they were part of the Goldsmid banking dynasty, he could thus afford to be choosy. Moreover, he married his cousin, another Goldsmid. He decided upon the Chancery Bar so as not to have to attend court on the Jewish sabbath or Jewish festivals. Once he had been called to the Bar and as a junior barrister he was described as no more than 'competent' in practice. Nonetheless, he took silk, that is, became a Queen's Counsel, in 1858, the first Jew to attain that rank, but retired the year afterwards on succeeding to his father's title as second baronet. He then entered Parliament as Liberal MP, for Reading, Berkshire in 1860, and sat in the House of Commons for 18 years until his life came to an abrupt end when he fell between the platform and a railway carriage at Waterloo Station.

---

2. The ruling body of his inn of court made up of judges and senior barristers who sit at the top table ('bench') in hall during meals.

Although Sir Francis Goldsmid's parliamentary speeches 'lacked lustre' they were nevertheless concerned with humanitarian issues, working-class housing, rural amenities, popular education, and religious liberty. 'Descended from a race and belonging to a religious community which for centuries were the object of persecution,' he told the electorate of Reading, 'I am attached alike, by a feeling of conviction to the great values of religious freedom.' He practised what he preached, and acquired a large estate, Rendcomb Park near Cirencester[3] and he gave all his tenants improved sanitation and other housing amenities which he sought for the working-class at large. He was a model landlord and Rendcomb became a model village. He was a model of faith in action, the very antithesis of the NIMBY. He was a devout Jew, and although riding was his favourite relaxation, he would never mount a horse on the sabbath. He was the most English of English gentlemen and one of the founders of progressive synagogues. When he died his obituary announced,

> 'It was his desire that the Hebrew should make it evident to the world at large that a rigid observer of Mosaism, a loyal patriotic citizen, capable of serving his country in every office...does meet and combine in the same individual.'

It is interesting that the reference is not to 'the Jew' but to 'the Hebrew,' not to 'Judaism' but to 'Mosaism' (the religious system, laws, and ceremonies prescribed by Moses). Jews and Judaism were alien 'Hebrew' to him and 'Mosaism,' established at home, somehow English. His Jewishness was therefore of a very English type. He and his progressives wanted a place of worship that would not remove them from England. In Upper Berkley Street, the West London Synagogue is such a place: Bevis Marks, 'The Great' and other Orthodox synagogues were part of Judea in exile.

---

3. An Italianate Villa that now houses Rendcomb College.

The First Jewish Lawyers

Caricature of Sir Francis Henry Goldsmid by James Tissot from *Vanity Fair*. Goldsmid was called to the Bar by Lincoln's Inn in 1833 after its ruling body made a 'special accommodation' concerning the oath, making him - by the author's estimation — the first unconverted Jewish lawyer in England.

Sir John Simon (1818–1897)

John Simon became a barrister, a serjeant-at-law, and commissioner of Assize. The status of Queen's Counsel requires little elaboration, it is simply a senior barrister who has attained experience, distinction, and respect amongst his or her fellows, who is said to possess the gravitas and talent which places him or her above the common or garden barrister, of no matter what age, who is referred to as a 'junior.'[4] That status is reflected in the level of case in which the barrister is instructed, and consequently the fees he or she is entitled to charge.[5] There was a time when barristers needed at least ten years in practice before being deemed worthy of applying for such appointment. And, at that time, it was on the 'wink and a nod' principle that barristers applied to become QCs, the same way judges were chosen until modern times.[6]

For Simon, being a QC was also a stepping-stone to the judiciary. A commissioner of Assize was given the power of a High Court judge, but not quite the same status. The role of serjeant-at-law originated in the 12th century at the time of Henry II. Serjeants were an elite group who carried out much of the work in the central common law courts. This preceded the status of Queen's Council/King's Council which was created by Elizabeth I and although the serjeants continued alongside the new breed of leading counsel, their existence ceased with the Judicature Acts of 1875. Another title for a serjeant was 'holder of the order of the coif,' the coif being the white bonnet formerly worn by those friars who in earlier days assumed the duties of a judge in the various abbeys. Sir John Simon was one of the last serjeants when he was appointed in 1864 and as such he also sat as a judge in Manchester and Liverpool, as well as the City of London because the office gave a commissioner of Assize equal powers to the Queen's justices.

Simon was born in Jamaica in 1818, his father being Isaac Simon. At the age of 15 he was sent to Liverpool, where he studied Hebrew. His aim was to

---

4. QCs/KCs are frequently called 'silks' after the material of their gowns (as opposed to the stuff/cotton gowns of juniors).
5. Also, e.g. a KC/QC will often be accompanied in court by a junior who 'does the groundwork,' so that adds to a client's costs. For an unusual case of a junior taking the lead in a murder trial see Dame Rose Heilbron in *Chapter 10*.
6. Since 2006, judicial appointments are the responsibility of an independent Judicial Appointments Commission, by advertisement, open-competition and on merit without reference to ethnicity, race, gender, etc. Before that it was an opaque responsibility of the Lord Chancellor.

become a rabbi. Although his family were Orthodox, he was keen early on to support the Reform movement, but this met with opposition from his father and at the last minute he changed his mind for the law. His interest in the Reform movement lasted throughout his life.

He obtained a degree at the University of London and was called to the Bar in 1842 and was the first Jew to practise at the Common Law Bar.[7] He went back to Jamaica, where he briefly practised law, but returned to England and achieved a good practice on the Northern Circuit, becoming its leader. He also practised in the London courts and acted in some formidable cases, as for example when he secured an acquittal for Dr Simon Francois Bernard at his 1858 trial concerning a plot with Felice Orsini to assassinate Napoleon III in Paris. His first judicial appointment was as a deputy judge in the county court, and thus he became the first Jew to sit as a judge.

Simon was elected to Parliament in 1868 as Liberal member for Dewsbury, Yorkshire where he sat for some 20 years. He was a keen spokesman for reforms to the law, and he also campaigned on behalf of Soviet Jewry, who at that time were suffering the pogroms and rampages of the Czar of Russia. He organized meetings throughout the country, in some 42 towns and cities, and at universities, in protest, and his platforms contained more non-Jews than Jews.

The town of Dewsbury did not have a single Jew on its electoral roll but that did not prevent Simon being described as the 'member for Jewry,' particularly after the death of Sir Francis Goldsmid in 1878. He looked like a typical member of the English nobility, slim upright, well-spoken, with mutton chop whiskers surrounding his chin. It is not surprising that he was one of the founders of the Anglo-Jewish Association. His mantle was carried following his death by his son Oswald John Simon.

---

7. Because Sir Francis Goldsmid (above) had been at the Chancery Bar.

CHAPTER 9

Bar and Bench

Before dealing with four 'great judges' and the progress of Jewish barristers let us first tell the story of one of the more colourful members of the legal profession, not himself a judge, but worthy of a place at the head of any list, though few of those I write about could be considered bland.

Judah Philip Benjamin (1811–1884)

It is 1811, and Judah Benjamin's *Sephardi* parents have married in London. Judah had not quite arrived when they left and were *en route* for the New World with the intention of settling in New Orleans. They had been shopkeepers and having a large family of seven children wished to seek better opportunities. But due to the River Mississippi being blockaded by the USA Government fleet their ship put in at the Island of St Croix in the West Indies. It was there that Judah Benjamin was born and instantly became a British subject, because that island was then held by the British. Its history is somewhat volatile, it had in turn been occupied by the Spaniards, the French, the Danes, and for short periods the British. Currently it is part of the USA Virgin Islands, but when Judah was born, although titled part of the Danish West Indies, probably due to the Napoleonic Wars, it was British.

And so began the life of a man whose strange and romantic career made him a leader of both the American and English Bars, and secretary-of-state of some of the Confederate States of America. If the American Civil War had turned out differently, as it might easily have done, his name would have been remembered as one of the great ones of history, instead of just by lawyers.

When he was two, in 1813, the family found life difficult in the West Indies as the trade routes had been blocked by the British occupation, so they set sail again and settled in North Carolina where maternal uncles were established merchants. They then moved to Charleston, the large Jewish community of which attracted Judah's father who was observant in his religious practices, though he did wander into a Reform synagogue which had become established, attracted possibly by its shorter services and that they were conducted in English rather than Hebrew.

It was Judah's mother who dealt with the practical issue of making a living by operating a fruit stall. The family must have found a degree of success in that and with the aid of a generous benefactor they were able to send Judah to a private school, which proved a good choice as the boy was quite intelligent. At the age of 14 he was admitted to Yale University, Connecticut, but left rather abruptly without taking a degree at the age of 16. It is not clear as to the cause of this, though seemingly it was due to an infringement of the rules, gambling being one of the reasons that have been suggested.

He did not waste time. After going home to Charleston, he rapidly moved again, to New Orleans, with just $5 in his pocket. There he made the most of his 'wit, charm, brain, and energy' for New Orleans was a rapidly growing cosmopolitan port and he found a job in a mercantile office, which though in the lower business echelons was enough to give him an appetite and assistance when he later became the leader of the Commercial Bar, for he was determined to become a lawyer, and succeeded in learning enough Latin in his spare time to make it possible for him to be admitted to the State bar at the age of 21.

From the start, his career as a lawyer was an outstanding success, and within three months of being admitted he was arguing a case in the Louisiana Supreme Court. He had one specific advantage compared to his competitors in that he had language skills in Spanish and French as well as English, and the law of Louisiana was an odd amalgam of Roman, Spanish, English, and French Law. It was this 'side knowledge' of legal systems which enabled him to write *The Law of Sales*, and later in England *Benjamin's Sale of Goods* (now in its 11th edition priced by Sweet & Maxwell at £535!), which he was able to use to his advantage when arguing cases later in England before the Judicial Committee of the Privy Council. Within ten years he had become the leading commercial lawyer in New Orleans.

In 1842, Benjamin decided to enter politics and was elected to the State legislature; and ten years later he entered national politics and was elected to the US Senate. However, just before he was due to take-up his seat in March 1853, he was nominated by the President as a justice of the Supreme Court: the first time such an appointment had been offered to a Jew. But Judah Benjamin declined the offer as he preferred a more active political career. Sadly, that was also curtailed for the simple reason that the American Civil War started, and he was, alas, not on the winning side.

When the Southern Confederacy was founded, Benjamin was appointed its Attorney-General. He firmly-believed in the partition of States in the North and South. It is interesting to speculate that if his advice had been taken by the Confederate Cabinet before hostilities began, then the South may have won the Civil War, having foreseen the coming conflict he urged the Government to ship 100,000 bales of cotton immediately to England in order to buy arms and ammunition with the proceeds—and it was lack of arms which was the main cause of the defeat of the South. His advice was rejected on the basis that his colleagues were convinced that the North would be beaten in a few months. As the war dragged on until April 1865, by when the Southern cause was lost, Benjamin, disguised as a Frenchman obtained a horse and waggon, crossed Georgia, and entered Florida where he hoped to find some means of escaping by sea to the West Indies. He managed to hire a small fishing boat, which was stopped and searched by a Northern gunboat crew at which point he escaped disguised as a cook. We can possibly learn something his appearance, because one of the searchers remarked that he had never seen a Jewish cook working on a boat. It was only after a shipwreck, a fire on the boat, and various other adventures that he finally arrived in England on 20 April 1865, aged 54, still buoyant and hopeful.

It was not easy for a man of that age, having just passed through four years of war to begin a new career in strange surroundings and conditions. He did this by becoming a student at Lincoln's Inn and supporting himself by writing leaders for the *Daily Telegraph*, being paid the princely sum, and it was in those days, of £5 per article. When a student in America he had supplemented his income by teaching languages, and one of the lesser tongues with which he was familiar was Creolel; and he taught a young catholic girl called Natalie Bauche St Martin on the understanding that she would help him to improve his French. This working relationship blossomed, and they married. Her family were wealthy and, in addition to a sum of money, she brought to the marriage as part of her dowry two young slaves. The irony is that slavery, which was rife in the area where Benjamin had lived, New Orleans, played an important part in his court practice, which included a vibrant slave trade component, necessitating his florid speeches on the subject. These did not always reflect his inner-feelings and there was some criticism. His marriage was not a success, and there were those who said he entered into it partly to advance his professional practice. Within a short time his wife went to live in Paris. They had one child, Ninette, and she was raised as a Catholic. They continued to visit each other.

Benjamin had not only grown wealthy from his practice in America, but also from the part-ownership of a sugar plantation, so it was natural once he started work in London that he would have ambitions to return to the high standard of living which he'd enjoyed in America. He was called to the English Bar on 6 June 1866, only six months after enrolling at Lincoln's Inn.[1] This, of course, in addition to taking the necessary legal examinations. Clearly an exception was made, albeit unofficially, in view of his American legal background and reputation. He would then need to obtain a 'tenancy' that is membership of — and a room in — chambers (a set of offices) where a group of barristers share a clerk, expenses, overheads and receive legal briefs and instructions from solicitors.

It was not, however the elegant salons of London which Benjamin enjoyed, because the English legal system involves a geographical division, and parts of the country were known (as they still are) as 'circuits,' a relic of the time when the king (later his royal judges) travelled periodically, round seven separate areas of the country, setting-up places to sit in judgment which became known as Assizes (nowadays part of the Crown Court). Members of the Bar would congregate in those places and often provincial chambers were established. Benjamin chose the Northern Circuit and based himself in Liverpool, his reason being that cotton markets in that area would provide some connection with America and in particular the South.

---

1. A remarkably short time, because the normal rules required keeping 12 terms, that is four in each of three years, without earning at the Bar, and eating a prescribed number of dinners in the collegiate atmosphere of the hall of the would-be barrister's inn of court.

At first his practice was slow to develop, which could have been due to his American accent and manners which may have proved a hindrance, because he did not show judges the deference which is customary in the English courts. In 1867 his fees totalled £493.12 6d (a little under £60,000 today) and to supplement this income he became a writer of legal textbooks, in particular *Benjamin* (already mentioned above), which became the leading authority on the subject, and to this very day has maintained its reputation as a classic of English law. It was his emphasis on clarity which was particularly striking.

From then onwards his career was meteoric. In 1872 he became a Queen's Counsel, most unusually only six years after being called to the Bar (the usual interval being ten years upwards). He was never a 'jury barrister.' Despite his quickness of mind cross-examination of witnesses did not come easy to him, but that was one thing that was not necessary. His practice was in the Court of Appeal, the House of Lords or the Privy Council addressing senior judges rather than a jury, and in the Privy Council his knowledge of foreign laws meant he was unrivalled. He was a bencher of his inn of court, a singular honour which entitled him to sit at the top table alongside high-ranking judges and senior lawyers when dining in hall.

In 1877 he appeared in 36 of the 65 reported cases in the House of Lords (that encompassed Privy Council work in relation to cases from British territories overseas), where his nearest rival was Arthur Cohen, of whom more next in this chapter. Though one of his rare failures in court was that he could not overturn a sentence of 14 years in the *Tichborne Claimant* case, a *cause célèbre* in which Arthur Orton, a butcher from Wagga Wagga in Australia claimed to be Sir Roger Tichborne, a baronet who had vanished some years earlier. The court found Orton had perjured himself when giving his evidence and thus the heavy sentence.

The last dramatic incident in Benjamin's career was in 1881 when, in the House of Lords, he stated a proposition of law with his usual confidence. The Lord Chancellor was reported to have remarked *sotto voce,* 'Nonsense.' At this Benjamin stopped his argument mid-sentence, slowly tied-up his brief with the customary tape, being white in the House of Lords (rather than pink as used in the lower courts), bowed low, and left the room. The next day the Lord Chancellor, no less, sent a message of apology to him and the incident was closed.

In the autumn of the following year whilst visiting Paris Benjamin was seriously injured when he fell from a tram, and soon after that developed heart problems and decided to retire. On 30 June 1883, as was the tradition when a judge or formidable barrister retired, there was a gathering of his friends and admirers, taking the form of a drinks, or maybe a small dinner, but on this occasion the benches were packed to the rafters. In his speech, the Lord Chancellor said,

> 'No man within my recollection has possessed greater learning, displayed greater shrewdness of ability, or greater zeal for the interest entrusted to him.'

The Attorney-General said,

> 'Who is the man, save this one, of whom it can be said he held conspicuous leadership in the Bar of two countries?... Rivalry with him seemed to create, rather than disturb, friendship.'

Benjamin was short and stout, but his striking characteristics were lively amused eyes and a silvery voice, a man of attractive lucidity, a man with confidence that it was the business of the judges to do what was fair and reasonable in the matter before them. His view was that if prior decisions ('precedents') or technicalities (legal rules) stood in the way of this, then they should be modified or recast. He clearly played a part in the development of English Commercial Law, and he prevented it becoming rigid or sterile.

Judah Benjamin died on 6 May 1884. His wife, Natalie, from whom he had lived apart for so long, but from whom he never untied himself, was a Catholic. Benjamin, although born to Jewish parents, married a non-Jew, never joined a synagogue as a member, nor did he actively participate in Jewish affairs. But although he rarely spoke of his Jewish background, he was never ashamed of it — though, unsupported by evidence, it is said that he once spoke in a synagogue in San Francisco on *Yom Kippur*. However, there is reported an exchange (which has also been attributed to Benjamin Disraeli) and it relates to a retort given in answer to an anti-Semitic comment. In the case of Benjamin in the Senate, and of Disraeli in the House of Commons, it arose during a debate on slavery. It is said that an opponent, following mention of Moses being a freer of slaves, described Benjamin as 'An Israelite in Egyptian clothing.' To which Benjamin replied,

> 'It is true that I am a Jew, and when my ancestors were receiving the Ten Commandments from the immediate hand of the Deity, amidst the thundering and lightening of Mount Sinai, the ancestors of my opponent were herding swine in the forests of Great Britain.'

Perhaps the former and more recent USA Supreme Court justice Ruth Bader Ginsburg (1933–2020) summarised his life in the most appropriate way:

> 'He rose to the top of the legal profession twice in one lifetime, on two continents, beginning his first ascent as a raw youth and his second as a fugitive minister of a vanquished power.'

The Times said this:

> 'In his life, which was as various as an Easter Tale, he carved out by his own unaided exertions, three histories of distinction. In America, in England, and it was also inherited, in that resistance to evil fortune which preserved Benjamin's ancestors, together with the same refined apprehension of logical problems, which informed the subtleties of the Torah.'

Judah Benjamin died having been administered the last rites of the Catholic church at the behest of Natalie his wife. There was a church service, and he was interred in her family's crypt, although the grave did not bear his name until 1938 when a plaque was placed there at the behest of an American organization.

Judah Phillip Benjamin who enjoyed success on two continents. Benjamin who was positioned to become US Attorney-General if the Southern States won the American Civil War lost out and narrowly escaped to England disguised as a ship's cook. In the UK he became a leading lawyer and international authority after writing *Benjamin's Sale of Goods*.

Sir Arthur Cohen (1830–1914)

I mentioned that Judah Benjamin's nearest rival was Arthur Cohen. Cohen's life spanned an epoch of Anglo-Jewish history. He was born in 1830 which was a time of considerable Jewish emancipation in England. His uncle was the most famous Jew in England at the time, Nathan Mayer Rothschild (1777–1836) the German born banker, financier and businessman, despite having one great disadvantage, namely his foreign birth. Cohen died a couple of years before Arthur Balfour made his famous declaration for a Jewish homeland in Palestine in a letter to Rothschild's great, great grandson, who bore the same name, and became the second Lord Rothschild.

The character of Cohen was best suited to that era I think because it was one of patriotism and people believed in England's place in the world as a great and responsible nation. But he combined this feeling with a desire to promulgate the good name of the Jew, and his conduct was performed in every way with this aim in mind. He was autocratic and humane, which may be Jewish traits, on the other hand he was aloof and self-conscious and a combination of these qualities may well be attributed to his upbringing and education. His grandfather was a Dutch immigrant who came to England in 1770, Levi Barent Cohen and his father, Benjamin Cohen, was a wealthy broker of bills who became a member of Lloyds. His mother was a sister of Sir Moses Montefiore (*Chapter 8*).

Arthur Cohen was a clever child, a prodigy in fact, a mathematical genius. He was born in Bryanston Square, London W2. It was realised that at that time he would not be able, as a Jew, to obtain a degree from Oxbridge, so in preparation for an alternative *alma mater* he was sent to commence his serious studies at a gymnasium (or high school) in Frankfurt, Germany and from there enrolled as a student at University College London. He did well at both establishments and was fortunate that at this time the family had become known to the Prince Consort, Prince Albert, who had a circle of wealthy Jewish friends. This group of Jewish aristocrats had the advantage of being fluent in several languages, including German, the mother tongue of Prince Albert who was Chancellor of Cambridge University. It has been suggested that it was by Albert's influence that Cohen secured his admission to Magdalene College there in 1849. But there were drawbacks in that although Cohen qualified for a degree, he could not accept it until the Cambridge University Act was passed in 1856 (*Chapter 5*), and thus he was the first Jew to take a degree openly, and indeed in 1853 became President of the Cambridge Union.

Cohen was called to the Bar in 1857 and quickly amassed a large commercial and international legal practice. He was a member of the South-Eastern Circuit and represented the Government in Geneva. He rapidly took silk, and eventually became a bencher and Treasurer[2] of the Inner Temple. He acted for many government departments, including, at that time the all-important India Office.

Cohen also became chair of the Bar Council and chaired several Law Commission matters, and with some irony Cambridge, the university which made him wait seven years to hold in his hands the degree he earned there, appointed him as their standing counsel. In 1874, he fought as a Liberal candidate the constituency of Lewes in Sussex but was unsuccessful. However, six years later he was returned as the Member of Parliament for Southwark which he held until that constituency was abolished in 1885.

One year after taking his seat in the House of Commons, he was given the choice, of resigning and accepting a place on the bench, but declined. The reason caused much gossip and conjecture. In fact, Southwark was not deemed a safe Liberal seat and Cohen had defeated Sir Edward Clarke a Conservative, who was later to be returned for Plymouth and became Solicitor-General. The choice of a judgeship or staying in Parliament was offered by the Lord Chancellor, Lord Selbourne. Cohen asked for time to 'think about it,' but when Prime Minister William Gladstone heard about this, he was most concerned, because he did not want a by-election with the risk of losing Southwark. It was for this reason that pressure was put upon Cohen to decline the offer of judicial appointment, remain in politics, and he was told the offer was 'bound to come around again.' It was indeed the unanimous view of his colleagues at the Bar that he deserved a place on the bench, and that Gladstone would be as good as his word. This view was also held by the judges who wanted to see Cohen amongst them. Sadly, the offer did not come around again. Lord Selbourne retired earlier than anticipated, having become alarmed at the increased radical tendencies of the Liberal party and he broke with Gladstone over Irish Home Rule. He went off and joined the Liberal Unionists.

---

2. The Treasurer is the 'top official' at each of the four inns of court.

Cohen's Relationship With Farrer Herschell (1837–1899)

When Lord Selbourne left office, a new Lord Chancellor, Farrer Herschell, was appointed who was said to be a Jew by race. His father, the Reverend Ridley (Haim) Henry Herschell, had converted to Christianity, and took a leading part in founding the Society for the Propagation of the Gospel Amongst the Jews. The fact that he graduated at University College London could have meant that other avenues were closed to him.

Reverend Herschell was certainly born to observant Polish Jews in Warsaw, and although his original ambition was to become a rabbi he moved to Berlin, and there lived 'a decadent life,' described by him as 'like a Christian.' He eventually moved to France and experienced a dramatic religious conversion. He was baptised in the Christian faith, and married a Christian woman older than himself, but who had a deep interest in Judaism and had learned Hebrew, and amongst their five children was Farrer. He is not reported to have indicated any interest in following Judaism. Sadly, there was considerable antagonism between Herschell and Cohen, so much so that Cohen's 'promised' judicial appointment never materialised. It was the talk of the Temple. Some attributed it to Herschell's 'barely visible Jewishness,' the only clue being his name. One ill-chosen but creative *bon mot* (or *beaux mots*) was, 'What can Cohen expect of Herschell except a Passover?'

Cohen was however appointed judge of the Court of the Cinq Ports, an historic position, dealing originally with piracy, but also disputes amongst the townsfolk and other crimes as well as those arising from collisions at sea. The jurisdiction stretched from Shore Beacon in Essex to Seaford in Sussex. A hearing would be in the town where the incident arose, sometimes taking place in the open air on the seashore, or in bad weather inside a local church. The demands upon his time were not great, and the office was more of an honorary one. Nor did he avoid his responsibilities to the Jewish community, for many years he was President of the Board of Deputies of British Jews, the representative body of the Jews of England, where he succeeded his uncle Sir Moses Montefiore (*Chapter 8*). He was also Vice-president of Jews College, an ecumenical establishment for the training of Jewish clergy.

His obituary included the words, 'There was no person of the bench whose opinion left such a deep mark on English Commercial Law.' Sir William Dicey, a leading constitutional lawyer and one of the foremost legal writers of the day, Professor of Law at Oxford and then the London School of Economics, described him as 'coming as near as any man could to the ideal of an English lawyer.' Cohen did, however, by virtue of his appointment to the Cinq Ports become a Privy Counsellor. He died at the age of 85, 'a lawyers' lawyer.'

Sir George Jessel (1824–1883)

George Jessel was clearly a man of good address, and in 1824 there can have been few better than Saville Row, and for his country house he needed to travel no further than Putney. He was the son of a wealthy merchant, Zadok Aaron Jessel (1792–1864). However, despite all other benefits, the chance to go to Oxbridge, for religious reasons, eluded him, and after private education at Mr Neumegens School for Jews in Kew he took a BA degree in unscientific subjects, followed by an MA, and was awarded a fellowship at University College London, the haven for many of his co-religionists.

Called to the Bar in 1847 Jessel began earning a 'respectable' level fees from the start, and within three years was making £800 per annum, which in current terms (allowing for inflation) would amount to £110,000. Not bad for a newly qualified barrister. His work dealt with conveyancing, that is the transfer of 'real' property (land, houses, estates and the like) and he advanced at a reasonable but not strenuous pace. His appointment as Queen's Counsel was not rushed, and it took time for him to find a parliamentary seat. This was the designated route for a professional man, and Parliament was often the ultimate accolade. It was however his specialist knowledge which 'made him.' Though not a powerful orator, he was a steady and reliable persuader who prepared well and showed a sound knowledge of his subject.

His field had initially been the work of the Chancery Court and Prime Minister William Gladstone noted his abilities. That court involved slow, 'stodgy' processes, but Jessel gave an early indication of working his way more rapidly through the dullness of the lists. He had sound legal knowledge, a good memory, and the ability to deliver a judgment immediately[3] without a lengthy adjournment or preparation time clogging-up the court's list of cases. His work made

---

3. Known by lawyers as *ex tempore* or in common parlance 'off-the-cuff.'

him an obvious candidate for the position of Master of the Rolls, and he was duly appointed to that judicial office.

At one stage there was a the rather elaborate incident of an assassination attempt upon him, made by a deranged clergyman. This was on 22 February 1878 when his assailant was Henry John Dodwell, who was a patient of Broadmoor Special Hospital who raised many actions and complaint about people. Hence Berkshire Records Office notes:

> 'As part of his continuing action, ostensibly about [the Governor of Broadmoor], he met Sir George Jessel, the Master of the Rolls, for the first time. Jessel was to become a hate figure for Dodwell. This hatred never left him, and when the judge died in 1886 Dodwell penned a sarcastic epitaph which survives in his Broadmoor file. At this first meeting, Jessel was sympathetic to the mistake Dodwell had made with his representation, and set aside the judgement to give Dodwell another chance to defend the governors' action. Jessel subsequently heard the case itself. It was here that Jessel experienced Dodwell's approach to the law for the first time: the governors presented their case, and Dodwell presented a list of grievances, mostly about Brighton. Jessel agreed with the governors that Dodwell had not presented a successful defence to their action, and on this occasion he decided for the plaintiffs.' (see Henry Dodwell.doc (berkshirerecordoffice.org.uk))

One of the most important tranches of legislation in English legal history were the Judicature Acts of the 1870s which attempted to fuse the split law and court systems which had existed for years.[4] It was a form of revision and modernisation requiring a determined approach which was steered by Jessel. One of his sayings was, 'I may be wrong, and sometimes am, but never have any doubts.' One particular case lasted 23 days in court and over 100 witnesses were called, Statutes going back to the days of King John were cited and documents piled high in the courtroom, but Jessel delivered an oral judgment (16 pages long when reduced to writing) immediately at the end of counsels' arguments.

---

4. Charles Dickens was never more scathing of the workings of the existing courts than with his fictional case of *Jarndyce v Jarndyce* in Bleak House (1852–53) which dragged on for generations (eating up legal fees that outstripped the estate in question). It remains a byword for any long, drawn-out legal proceedings and a warning not to go to law if it can be avoided: hence the line 'Suffer any wrong that can be done you rather than come here.'

In 1881 Jessel stopped sitting as a judge of first instance, which is what the Master of the Rolls often did (*Chapter 11*), and thereafter sat only in the Court of Appeal. This was because there was no-one of sufficient weight in that court. He was described as one of the greatest English judges, and his bust can be seen in the lobby of the Law Courts in The Strand. He was elected Vice-Chancellor of University College London, became a trustee of the British Museum, and Treasurer of Lincoln's Inn.

He had earlier been appointed Solicitor-General, the first Jew to occupy that position, and was the first to be sworn into the Privy Council, and the first to hold judicial office. He married Amelia, the daughter of Joseph Moses. Though not a totally observant Jew, George Jessel remained a member of an orthodox synagogue all his life. His great, great nephew, Toby Jessel (1934–2018) was the Tory MP for Twickenham for 27 years from 1970.

Sir George Jessel Master of the Rolls who steered one of the greatest changes in English legal history, the Judicature Acts of the 1870s, that transformed the notoriously slow processes of the civil and Chancery courts.

Sir Rufus Isaacs (1860–1953)

Sir Rufus Isaacs is 'the one that everyone knows about and remembers' because he accomplished so much. The Isaacs family have I think now become somewhat anglicised, but the name still rings through in matters Jewish. He was born in London in 1860 (so clearly not part of the developments of 1858 which are a main theme of this book) and his father's family, who traded as M Isaacs & Son, were fruit merchants in Aldgate, London. His mother was a Mendoza, a relative of Daniel Mendoza, the Jewish prize-fighter (*Chapter 2*). And here is some encouragement to my younger readers, Isaacs' school reports were awful, he was the despair of his family and his ambition and attitude to scholarly work were described as 'non-existent.' The initials IDB, explaining that not very bright offspring could blossom 'in daddy's business' had not yet emerged, but this was his path. However, getting-up early to deal with determined shopkeepers was not to his taste, and he didn't last long in the business. This exasperated his father who believed it to be profitable if demanding, and so when young Rufus, feeling particularly stroppy one morning, said, 'I'd rather go to sea,' his father took him at his word and bundled him onto the steam train to Cardiff, to sign on as ship's boy on the *Blair Athol*.[5]

Isaacs senior had heard talk about this particular ship when in the market, and learned that it was owned by a Glasgow firm, and that he had done business with them. He discovered it was due to sail to South America and India on a year long voyage. Not quite the gap year this turbulent teenager had mind, but maybe it would get him over a difficult phase and make him yearn for the comforts of home and the rigours of the family business to a greater degree.

The ship had four officers, three apprentice sailors, and the rest of the crew was composed of Brazilians, Swedes, French, Germans, Portuguese and Italians, rather like the cabin crew of a modern-day cruise liner, but they did not all have the broad smiling faces of such a body, in fact quite a few of them looked rather mean and menacing at this well-dressed, pink-cheeked youngster.

Rufus was introduced to the captain and told that in accordance with custom it would be necessary for him to sign an apprenticeship. Perhaps the very first legal thoughts travelled through his mind at this stage. He was but 16 years

---

5. An iron-built fully-rigged sailing ship of 1,777 tons.

old, so was he eligible by age to sign a binding agreement? Of course, his father would sign it too, but would that bind Rufus? Why was it necessary then for him to sign at all if his father had power to sign on his behalf? He paused with the pen which had been thrust upon him, more especially when he saw that although the trip was expected to last a year this agreement would bind him for two years. This for an occupation he might not feel suited to, and so the turbulent teenager in him came out, and he refused.

This must have created a Dickensian, 'You are asking for more?' moment as he put the pen down. The captain told him that the other apprentices had each signed without tremor, and his father joined in by telling Rufus that he had not come all the way from London to Cardiff for nothing, and flatly refused to have Rufus back home.

Rufus then displayed a further and particularly lawyerly disposition: he came up with a compromise. If he had to go to sea, then he was prepared to sign for one year or for one voyage, whichever was the shorter. In other words, he had come with the intention of going on that one voyage and that was all he would agree to. For the next few minutes, the atmosphere was fraught, his father stomped around, the captain sighed wearily, and Rufus folded his arms, giving out a sign that every parent will recognise.

Eventually Rufus signed on his exact 16th birthday, as a ship's boy, for that one trip, at the generous wage of ten shillings a month. Every Jewish mother's dream. And so it was that in 1877 the *Blair Athol* sailed past Calcutta, up the Hugli River in West Bengal, to Hooghly, a major river port which had been reached by Vasco de Gama the Portuguese explorer around 1500 when opening-up the sea route to India; and travelled by many traders after him. Standing on the deck was young Rufus Isaacs digesting his first glimpse of India, a country which he was destined to return to as Viceroy 40 years later.

When the *Blair Athol* returned to England later that year Rufus was happy to take leave of the ship and return to his family business for a while, but once more found it difficult to settle. So, after three years, he decided to try his luck on the Stock Exchange. He had no experience whatsoever in this field, and it is hardly surprising that when he was 24-years-of-age he was 'hammered,' or expelled, for not being able to pay his debts, embarrassed, ruined, unable to face his friends. The only thing open to him was to flee the country, to get away as far as possible.

He had heard that some of his former friends had found riches in South America: minerals, crops, a New World, a new challenge, just what he needed, so from the family he scraped together enough money for a one-way ticket to the Argentine. A quite extraordinary series of events then ensued. After bidding farewell to his family, most of whom, excepting his mother, could barely hide their enthusiasm, and actually sitting in a compartment of the train due to take him to the departure port of Liverpool, his younger brother arrived, puffing and panting to tell him that since leaving home his mother had been taken ill and he must return home at once.

Rufus Isaacs' mother, Sarah Isaacs, had a great talent, not fairly described as 'acting,' but more as 'engineered histrionics.' It was a last resort utilised with effect just prior to his capitulation, designed with the intent of changing the weight of the argument. I have read one report that his father would say, 'If your mother says it is so, then it is so, even if it isn't so.' He promptly returned home, and of course she had by then almost recovered, but alas the ship had sailed and there was not another for some weeks. It was during those weeks that she persuaded her son to read for the Bar, telling him that even if he did not wish to practise law at least it was 'something to fall back on in the future.'

Rufus Isaacs was called to the Bar in 1887 when he was 27. This was a good age to start out in practice as he would look neither too young and inexperienced nor too old and exhausted. He had, however, found his forte and took to law from the start. He soon developed a busy practice as a junior barrister.[6] His practice was in the common law, as opposed to Chancery, which was the choice of many of his friends. Common law however was extremely wide and covered libel and divorce as well as crime, divorce having previously been dealt with in the Probate, Divorce and Admiralty Division, known as 'Wives, Wills and Wrecks.' This success proved that whatever he had tried and failed at in the past, it was not due to an innate aversion to hard work. So much so that it became clear he did not need more than five hours sleep, and he was able to rise between four and five in the morning to read his briefs and prepare for work that day. Many barristers will work after dinner, well into the night, but this was not his *modus operandi*. At that time, he was earning £30,000 per year, the equivalent in today's terms of almost £4 million.

---

6. 'Junior' meaning any barrister, no matter how old or experienced, who was not yet appointed Queen's Counsel.

Isaacs once said, 'The Bar is never a bed of roses, it is either all bed and no roses, or all roses and no bed.' After only ten-and-a-half years, in 1898, he was appointed Queen's Counsel. As with all English barristers he followed the 'cab-rank' principle, which put simply means that barristers are obliged to accept whatever work is offered by the next client in line, provided he or she is available to do so[7] and always provided the remuneration is reasonable. In turn this meant Isaacs could be prosecuting one day and defending the next, though of course not the same person nor if any other conflict of interest arose.

Thus, Isaacs happened to find that he was prosecuting in what came to be probably his most famous case, that of Whittaker Wright, or 'WW' as he was fondly known, an allegedly crooked financier, and this case is said to have cemented his reputation. The trial in question was unusual in several ways. It took place in 1904 at the Royal Courts of Justice (not in a criminal courtroom such as at the Old Bailey) and before a High Court judge, Mr Justice Bigham, a civil expert, and a specially convened jury.

The authorities, having failed to identify a route through Wright's obfuscations and opaque paper trail, this was a private prosecution by investors in the accused's money-making schemes. Isaacs' incisive approach and experience of the stock market, having worked as a broker, meant he was able to trace and patiently explain matters so that the fraud was exposed. Rather than face the seven years' imprisonment that Bigham imposed, Wright committed suicide on the court premises by taking cyanide. The subsequent inquest revealed that he had also been carrying a revolver (presumably for the same purpose) which had evaded security at this unusually relaxed location.

Isaac's Parliamentary career began when he was elected Liberal MP for Reading, Berkshire at a by-election in 1904, and with deserved promotion some years later he was appointed Solicitor-General, an appointment which George Jessel (above) had held some 37 years earlier. This is the lower of the two legal offices of State, discounting that of Lord Chancellor, the other being Attorney-General, and it so happened that Isaacs rapidly leapfrogged to the second of these. The

---

7. The cab rank principle is said to be grounded in the idea that no-one should ever be denied access to justice which the less attractive might be if barristers were allowed to represent only those who are deserving in their eyes, and how else would they get representation at all? Though there was (and is still) the poor person's 'dock brief' whereby a client may engage any barrister 'lounging' in the courtroom, at a modest fee, though largely now superseded by legal aid.

Attorney-General prosecutes in the most serious, complex, or important cases and where appropriate those impacting on Government affairs.

The responsibility also includes murder cases. The case of Frederick Henry Seddon came well within that remit. Although Isaacs only personally prosecuted one murder case it was that of the infamous poisoner and insurance company swindler Seddon who was hanged in 1912 for the murder of Eliza Mary Barrow. Seddon had taken in Miss Barrow as a lodger and soon persuaded her to hand over her possessions in return for a small annuity to be paid to her by Seddon. However, he hated the tedium of regular but trifling payments, so he decided to kill her, and the way he did this was to introduce a solution of water and arsenic into her food and drink. He obtained the arsenic not by the then far too open procedure of purchasing it from a pharmacist, but by soaking it slowly from fly papers.

Seddon, to those who met him, was an ordinary, black-coated, white-collared member of the working-class. Employed for many years as a clerk with insurance company Industrial Life[8] he lived in a large, terraced house near Finsbury Park, North London. As he had an abundance of rooms, he let the entire second floor to his victim. At his workplace they deemed him a 'safe pair of hands,' reliable as to punctuality and efficient as to his duties. However, there was another side to him, a less pleasant one: he towered in his tyranny over a diminutive wife.

Miss Barrow, who was nearing 50-years-of-age was just a little deaf and had some strange ways. She lived with the child of a distant relative whom she had adopted. Her wealth was kept under the bed in a box in which she had gathered £4,000 in bank notes, some gold coins, and a few small items of jewellery—because she did not trust either banks or people who might try to help her with investments. What could have been a valuable portfolio in today's values, almost half a million pounds lay hidden beneath the bed.

It is hardly surprising that within seven days of commencing her flypaper diet she took ill and the doctor who was called not being told about her unusual intake suggested she was suffering from 'epidemic diarrhoea.' When he left the house, she confided in Seddon that she had no will. As no-one had heard of epidemic diarrhoea, she was unsure if it was terminal, so felt she had better summons a solicitor to draw one up. Seddon, being the obliging sort, offered

---

8. Ironically an honest organization formed, amongst other things, to pay small annuities to widows and spinsters not unlike Miss Barrow.

to do it for her. She left her jewellery and few bits of furniture to the orphan, but no mention was made of the secret hoard of cash, which, apparently, she had 'forgotten about.'

Seddon agreed to be the sole trustee, and all just in time, because two days later she died. The same doctor came along and certified his earlier conclusion as to the cause of death: epidemic diarrhoea. All seemed to be in order for the funeral to be held, after all Miss Barrow had been ill, Seddon had called a doctor, she had died, and the doctor had issued the necessary certificate. Seddon continued his duties as executor by purchasing an inexpensive grave and arranging her funeral. And then came a problem.

There is nearly always a distant relative who turns up at a time like this, and one duly did. Seddon was rather cross to be asked questions, after all he had given freely of his time and done his duty, and so before answering any questions he demanded proof of the purported relative's relationship to the victim. This caused suspicion and the relative called in the police.

In due course Miss Barrow's body was exhumed, traces of arsenic found, and some straightforward police work followed: the clues all matched up. It seems Seddon's daughter had recently bought an unusually large stock of flypapers, yes, the ones containing arsenic. Someone had seen Seddon counting gold coins, and he had taken Miss Barrow's ring to be enlarged and an inscription on her watch re-engraved. Within days he and his gentle-looking wife were both charged with murder. Some were surprised that his daughter was not also indicted.

Rufus Isaacs assembled the evidence and witnesses for the murder trial to find that Seddon was to be defended by the 'great' advocate of that era, Sir Edward Marshall Hall.[9] A fight of the giants. But the case also involved the first truly great forensic scientist, Sir Bernard Spilsbury, as the main prosecution witness and the evidence he presented related to the arsenic content which could be detected from Miss Barrow's body and hair.

Isaacs was more practised in civil and commercial cases, where advocates present evidence in a modulated way, and there is hardly ever fierce or domineering cross-examination conducted in the dramatic style of Marshall Hall. He was not one to argue with a witness, not one to raise his voice, nor one to interrupt.

---

9. A KC who won countless cases during his career for accused individuals, often those charged with murder, in an era when rhetoric, theatrics and jury distraction were the order of the day.

His first question to Seddon (who gave evidence) in cross-examination, was, 'Tell me, did you like her?' None the less Seddon was found guilty, but his wife acquitted, and it is reported that as the jury verdicts were announced he kissed her (for probably the first time in many years). He had been a Freemason, and he was aware that the judge was also a member of that order. The story has frequently been told that immediately prior to sentence Seddon addressed the judge, Sir Thomas Townsend Bucknill, in a masonic formulation that began, 'By the Great Architect of the Universe...' It was at this stage that the judge was seen to assume a whitish hue, and as he sentenced Seddon to death it was clearly with hesitation.

In normal circumstances, the tradition until that time was that if the Lord Chancellor resigned died or retired, and the Government of the day was to continue, then the post would first be offered to the Attorney-General. It was not, however, offered to Isaacs, it went to the philosopher-politician Richard Burdon Haldane (1856–1928). Isaacs however, still as Attorney-General, was offered a role in the Cabinet, that appointment not having previously been of sufficient rank. Fate had other things than the Lord Chancellorship in store for Rufus Isaacs however, and indeed the question was even much later posed as to whether a Jew would have been eligible for that office (see *Chapter 5*).

Before long, as in many legal careers, there came the banana skin, and this one was called Marconi. Isaacs had a younger brother called Godfrey Isaacs, and he was appointed managing director of Marconi Wireless and Telegraphy. To celebrate there would be a banquet in New York, and Rufus, quite naturally was invited to send a message of good wishes to his brother, which he did. It read 'I wish my brother and Marconi every success.' Nothing more. However, Marconi was on everybody's lips, and the company entered negotiations with the UK Government for a contract to establish wireless radio stations. It was due to the efforts of Godfrey Isaacs that they succeeded, but there was a problem, if not two problems. First that Rufus Isaacs held shares in Marconi, and that the Postmaster-General at the time, Herbert Samuel, was also a prominent Jew. The headlines ran 'A corrupt contract between 3 Jews.'

Cecil Chesterton, the brother of G K (Gilbert Keith) Chesterton (creator of the fictional amateur sleuth Father Brown, who was a KC: both of whom at times faced serious allegations of anti-Semitism), was the editor of the magazine *Eye Witness*, and wrote of a 'secret arrangement between Isaacs and Herbert

Samuel that the British people should give Marconi large sums of money for the benefit of the Isaacs.'

Other journalists followed-up the story, and rumour ran rife. A Select Parliamentary Committee was set up which ran for months, and in France *Le Matin* wrote of *'Un Scandal Financial en Angleterre.'* This was the last straw, so the time had come for the matter to be aired in the courts. Isaacs and Samuel were represented by leading barristers Edward Carson KC and Frederck Edwin Smith KC,[10] and *Le Matin* did not defend the claim. The plaintiffs wisely did not ask for damages, this would have made them appear particularly avaricious. They only sought an apology, and they received one. *The Times* observed, 'Lack of judgement is very different to the monstrous offences imputed.' Cecil Chesterton also faced a charge of criminal libel and was fined £100 at the Central Criminal Court.

The Select Committee, acting with unusual speed once the case had been heard, also found there was no corruption. In Parliament the Opposition naturally sought to turn events to their advantage but Isaacs was on top form, and he made a remarkable speech which was accepted by the House of Commons. His career was undamaged.

In 1913 he was appointed Lord Chief Justice, and a year later made a baron. His time on the bench was short because World War I broke out within a year. He was called upon in 1918 to be the UK's Ambassador to the USA. Three years later he was appointed Viceroy of India, and it was in that capacity that he set sail once again for that country, 'once again' because the first time was, as described earlier, 40 years ago as a cabin boy on the *Blair Athol*.

It was Sir David Sassoon as President of Bombay Municipal Council who welcomed Isaacs to India saying, 'I do so in the name of one great Oriental Civilisation, as a member of another, and ... the most distinguished Englishman of his day.' The reply from Rufus Isaacs, by then raised to be Viscount Reading, was, 'I note your sympathetic reference to the ancient race to which I belong, it is my only connection with the East, and will, no doubt be of enormous help.'

Rufus Isaacs was an unobservant Jew, but strongly, aggressively Jewish in sentiment; it is perhaps as a great legal fencer, cool, graceful, strong, accurate, using words like a rapier, that he will be best remembered.

---

10. Universally known as 'F E' Smith (1872–1930) who became the First Earl of Birkenhead.

Sir Rufus Issacs the youthful adventurer and City broker whose mastery of commerce allowed him as King's Counsel to secure the conviction of the country's most notorious fraudster. In a remarkable life Issacs tried several careers, entered politics, became Lord Chief Justice and, as the Marquess of Reading, returned to one of his old haunts as Viceroy of India.

Sir Archibald Levin-Smith (1836–1901)

I dealt in *Chapter 1* with some of the criteria I have applied to the question of whether those I write about are to be considered, or consider themselves, Jewish but let us conclude the 19th century with this man. Although the son of a gentile landowner, his mother was the daughter of a Polish Jewish immigrant, Zadik Levin, a name which is incorporated into his hyphenated surname, but as we cannot establish the religion of Zadik's wife we cannot be certain that his mother was Jewish, for the line of succession so far as religion is concerned runs through the mother. Suffice it to say the records show no more than 'that he had some Jewish ancestry.'

He was educated at Eton, and Trinity College, Cambridge University where he participated in a boat race though his boat sank, but being nearly seven feet tall the water but came up to his neck. After practice at the Bar, he became a Queen's Counsel, then a High Court judge and later a Lord Justice of the Court of Appeal, where his most famous case will ring a bell with all students of the law. Whatever he or she may forget they will always remember the first case they were taught, if only for its peculiar name, that trips of the tongue like the title of a Roald Dahl children's book.

Carlill v Carbolic Smoke Ball Company ([1892] EWCA Civ 1) goes to the very heart of the law of contract. The simple tale was of an advertisement in the newspaper for a flu remedy, the carbolic smoke ball, and the manufacturer offered a reward of £100 to any purchaser who found it did not work as promised. It was decided by the court that the manufacturer had made an offer, and by buying it and using it the purchaser, Mrs Louisa Elizabeth Carlill had accepted the offer and a contract existed on which she could sue the makers for damages. Every essential element of a lawful contract was present including an offer (the advertisement), acceptance (by the customer), consideration (payment by the customer in return for the maker supplying the product) and an intention to create legal relations. The following gives a flavour of Levin-Smith's style and approach:

> 'The first point in this case is, whether the defendants' advertisement which appeared in the Pall Mall Gazette was an offer which, when accepted and its conditions performed, constituted a promise to pay, assuming there was good consideration to uphold that promise, or whether it was only a puff from which no promise could be implied, or, as [has been argued] a mere statement by the [makers] of the confidence they entertained in the efficacy of their remedy. Or...whether this advertisement was mere waste paper...'

Clearly the advert wasn't 'waste paper' or simply a 'trader's puff' and Levin-Smith went on to greater things, serving for a short period towards the end of his judicial career as Master of the Rolls in 1900 and 1901, the year he died, shortly after his wife tragically drowned in the River Spey whilst on holiday in Scotland.

CHAPTER 10

Into the Twentieth Century

As events moved into the twentieth century an increasing number of Jewish lawyers worked in England and they began to progress more and more to senior positions, the bench and higher judicial roles. Before looking at the most senior positions of all in the next chapter, the following legal pioneers deserve a place in this book.

Baron Lionel Cohen (1888–1973)

Lionel Leonard Cohen's father, Sir Leonard Lionel Cohen KCVO, had been a Conservative Member of Parliament for the last two years of his life. Prior to that he was a banker, working in his father's firm, Louis Cohen & Sons, foreign bankers and members of the London Stock Exchange.

What was strange about the politics of Sir Leonard (the father) was that the Jews had largely favoured the Liberal party, but he took the view that his co-religionists should be more independent in their approach. He was devoted to helping the poor of his community and helped establish a board of guardians (to administer the Poor Law), and he brought about a uniting of the synagogues in the City of London, and became warden of 'The Great Synagogue' built in 1690 soon after the return of the Jews.[1] It was via his relationship with the Rothschilds through marriage, and his friendship with the Montefiores (*Chapter*

---
1. This, the first *Ashkenazi* synagogue, was in Duke's Place, Aldgate, destroyed in the Blitz in 1941.

The Jewish Contribution to English Law

5 and *8*) that members of his family belonged to what was known as 'The Cousinhood,' one of the strongest connections in the history of Anglo-Jewry.

The Cohen family were clearly well off and it was hardly surprising that Lionel was sent to Eton, then New College, Oxford University, where he took a first and was then called to the Bar. This was followed in due course by appointment as a member of King's Counsel. In World War I he served in the London Regiment and was wounded. Returning to the Bar after the war, his field was Chancery and in particular Company Law. In 1943 he was elevated to the High Court, and subsequently the Court of Appeal, then given a life peerage as Baron Cohen of Walmer. Probably his most important tasks as Lord Cohen were to chair several business-oriented Royal Commissions and as Head of the 1954 Cohen Inquiry into the loss of two Comet airliners.[2] In communal affairs he was Vice-president of the Board of Deputies of British Jews.

Baron Lionel Leonard Cohen whose family belonged to 'The Cousinhood,' one of the strongest connections in the history of Anglo-Jewry. A barrister, judge and ex-banker, as a Privy Counsellor he chaired several finance-related Royal Commissions. Photo National Portrait Gallery.

---

2. As reported in *Hansard*, 16 February 1955.

Judge Neville Laski (1890–1969)

Impressive as the Jewish communal accomplishments of the Cohen family may have been, they are I believe narrowly overtaken by the record of a man who can be properly described as a leader of Anglo-Jewry. He ticked all the boxes, starting with his education at Manchester Grammar School, in the city where he was born, followed by Clifton College, Bristol, which, having a Jewish house, Polack's, made it the target for many of the scions of the Jewish community. As Clifton College currently describes itself:

> 'For over one-hundred-and-fifty years Clifton College has supported a vibrant Jewish community within its school. It is the only public school with its own synagogue, enabling Jewish students to maintain their Jewish identity...The Polack's House Educational Trust is an independent charitable organization that provides means tested scholarships and bursaries for Jewish children...Recent recipients have gone on to fantastic universities including, Oxford, Exeter, Edinburgh and Bath...Candidates must meet the criteria on being Jewish and demonstrate an interest in Judaism. [They] are expected to participate in and contribute to Jewish activities in the school.'[3]

Polack's House was followed taking a degree at Corpus Christi College, Oxford University.

Laski's communal work included being President of the London Committee of the Board of Deputies of British Jews, Presiding Elder of the Spanish and Portugese Congregation and Vice-president of the Anglo-Jewish Association. At the Bar he was appointed King's Counsel in 1930. He became a recorder of Quarter Sessions (later the Crown Court) and Recorder of Liverpool, and during World War I (with the rank of captain) served with the Lancashire Fusiliers in Gallipoli, Sinai and France.

His daughter was the journalist, novelist and scriptwriter, Marghanita Laski (1915–1988). It is fair I think to mention that she was an avowed atheist, and a campaigner for nuclear disarmament. She appeared regularly on BBC panel

---

3. See www.cliftoncollege.com/admissions/polacks-house-education-trust/

shows such as 'The Brains Trust,' 'Whats My Line?' and 'Any Questions?' His brother was Harold Laski (1893–1950) professor of politics at the London School of Economics and chair of the Labour party, a stalwart of the left, though it would again be fair to mention he repudiated his faith in Judaism by claiming that reason prevented him from believing in God. Despite this he was an ardent Zionist.[4]

Judge Ewen Montagu (1901–1985)

Ewen Edward Samuel Montagu CBE, QC, DL, RNR's grandfather, Samuel Montagu (1832–1911), the first Baron Swaythling, founded the bank that bears his name, Samuel Montagu & Co. He was an orthodox Jew who founded the Federation of Synagogues in the East End of London, a collection of the traditionally observant variety, as opposed, e.g. to the middle-of-the-road collection the United Synagogue,[5] and the more extremely revisionist groups, such as Reform, who were inclined to the anglicising of services and customs. The federation was steeped in traditions brought over from Russia and the *shtetl* (*Chapter 1*), however there are those who would describe it as being more in line with 'conservative anglicising.'

Samuel Montagu was also one of the earlier Zionists, using such influence he could gather to appraise the Foreign Office of this prospect. This Zionist ambition was diametrically opposed by Samuel's eldest son, Louis Montagu (1869–1927), co-founder of the anti-Zionist League of British Jews, who succeeded to the title, but the circle is completed by the emergence of his nephew, Herbert Samuel (1870–1963) who became the first Viscount Samuel, the Liberal politician, Home Secretary in the National Government of Ramsay MacDonald and first High Commissioner of Mandated Palestine.

Louis Montagu, who was educated at Clifton College, Bristol, was opposed to Foreign Secretary Arthur Balfour's Declaration announcing British support for the establishment of a national homeland for the Jewish people in Palestine and in this

---

4. I do not deal specifically with Zionism in this book. Put simply it is a nationalist movement whose goal was the creation of a Jewish State in Palestine, the Jews ancient homeland. Zionism originated in the mid-to-late 19th century and takes its name from a hill in Jerusalem called Zion.
5. See www.theus.org.uk

he was supported by Lionel Nathan de Rothschild. The 'Cousinhood' element continued in that his marriage connected him to the Goldsmids and Rothschilds.

Ewen Montagu had just completed his education at Westminster School when World War I broke out, and he went off to train as a machine gun instructor. After the war he studied at Cambridge University, then Harvard University, USA after which he was called to the Bar. His judicial career progressed to the extent that he was for many years chair of Middlesex Quarter Sessions (the professional judge sitting alongside magistrates for the county). This important court, now subsumed within the Crown Court, dealt with criminal matters sent there by local magistrates for trial or sentence and sat at the Middlesex Guildhall opposite the Houses of Parliament, a building now used to accommodate the Supreme Court.

Montagu was known as a judge who did not suffer fools gladly. His career after the war was also largely taken-up with his position as Judge Advocate of the Fleet, that he held until 1973. He retired with the rank of lieutenant commander. He was President of the United Synagogue from 1954–62, also of the Anglo-Jewish Association. But it is Montagu's part in naval intelligence that he is best-known and remembered for.

He had always been a keen yachtsman and before the war had joined the Royal Navy Volunteer Reserve, but it may have been due to his legal experience that he was appointed as a staff officer in intelligence. It was with a senior air force officer that he thought up a major deception operation to be performed upon the axis powers at a crucial point in the war. Germany's General Rommel was being run out of North Africa, and the next step for the allies would be the invasion of Southern Europe, to be commenced in coordination with an invasion in the North. The question was 'Where?'

The front was vast, stretching from Greece in the East to the Spanish border in the West, and the choice of an ideal location was vital, but equally important was that the Germans and their allies should not know where. Part of ensuring this was to fool them into thinking the invasion would start at a place other than the truly intended one. Thus, was born 'Operation Mincemeat' after Montagu hatched a plan to use a corpse, dressed as a British allied officer, which carried some information indicating that the place of invasion would be Greece, when the actual plan was to invade Sicily.

It was intended that the corpse be washed ashore at a location in Spain, for the simple reason that it was known German agents were rampant there, and

Spaniards finding it were most likely to let the Germans know, in the hope of some reward. The details in the pockets of the corpse would not only be indicative of the planned landing, the false one that is, but there would be others to add an air of reality. Apart from military identification, the deceased would carry personal letters from his girlfriend, photos of her, and other documents indicating the real life of an active serviceman.

The idea was a total success, and the aim of having the information passed on to Adolf Hitler's top brass at his headquarters was later found to have been fully achieved. German forces were diverted to Greece, and the invasion of Sicily took place, although with some opposition but that was diminished by the fruitless volume of troops, equipment and aircraft diverted by the Germans to Greece.

The adventure is the subject of a book which Montagu wrote, and a feature film made in 1956 with the same title as that book, 'The Man Who Never Was' (see *Selected Bibliography*). Ewen Montague received the OBE from Queen Elizabeth II.

'The judge who came in from the cold.' Ewen Montagu (left) 'did not suffer fools gladly.' As a British spy he helped mount Operation Mincemeat. Over a weekend, it is said, he wrote the best-seller *The Man Who Never Was* about those events. Here he meets Clifton Webb, who played Montagu in the 1956 film. Photo Alamy.

Into the Twentieth Century

Sir Seymour Karminski (1902–1971)

Coincidentally, following the previous judge above, Seymour Karminski too served as a lieutenant commander in the Royal Navy Voluntary Reserve in World War II. His father had been born in Germany and Seymour went to Rugby School and Oxford University, taking a first in History, and was then called to the Bar. His speciality was Divorce Law becoming a member of King's Counsel immediately following his discharge from the Navy. Six years later he was elevated to the bench being allocated to the then Probate Divorce and Admiralty Division. He was an active member the Jewish community, being chair of the Welfare Board, and of the Reform Synagogue in Upper Berkeley Street (the West London Synagogue).

Sir Cyril Salmon (1903–1991)

Cyril Salmon was a member of the family that collaborated with Joseph Lyons and Isidore and Montague Gluckstein to set up a 'spin off' from the Salmon & Gluckstein tobacco company, the J Lyons & Co tea rooms and restaurants (known as 'corner-houses' from their frequent positioning on street intersections) and associated catering business.

Salmon went to Mill Hill School, North London and then Cambridge University, and was called to the Bar in 1929. During World War II he served with the Royal Artillery, was attached to the 8th Army in Africa as judge advocate and attained the rank of major. Upon demobilisation in 1945 he was appointed King's Counsel. He was made a High Court judge in 1957 after serving as a Crown Court recorder for some years. One of the cases he dealt with arose from a series following the Notting Hill Riots of the 1950s in which racially-motivated damage was perpetrated. Sitting at the Old Bailey, exemplary, particularly heavy sentences, had been imposed by him of four years each on nine white youths who had gone 'hunting' for black people during an August Bank Holiday weekend. In the debates that followed in the House of Lords, Salmon was praised for saying:

'Everyone, irrespective of the colour of his skin, is entitled to walk through our streets in peace, with their heads erect and free from fear. That is a right which these courts will always unfailingly uphold.'

Seven years later he was made a Lord Justice of Appeal, at the same time as Lionel Cohen (above) was appointed to the Court of Appeal, though there had not been a Jew holding that position for two decades. He then chaired the Royal Commission on Tribunals and Inquiries.

Judge Alan King-Hamilton (1904–2010)

Born in West Hampstead, Alan King-Hamilton was the son of a Jewish solicitor. Educated at York House School, Haberdashers' Aske's Boys' School (both in Hertfordshire), Bishop Stortford Grammar School, and from 1927 Cambridge University he was called to the Bar in 1929. Specialising in Transport Law, in 1954 he was made Queen's Counsel, and became Recorder of Hereford, then Gloucester, then Wolverhampton, moving to the Old Bailey in 1964.

King-Hamilton sat as a judge in several high profile cases, including those of Emil Savundra the Sri Lankan businessman and swindler responsible for the collapse of his Fire, Auto & Marine Insurance Company which left almost half a million UK motorists without cover and who received eight years' imprisonment (1960s); the singer Janie Jones (real name Marion Mitchell) renowned for holding 'sex parties,' jailed for involvement in 'controlling prostitutes' (1970s); Peter Hain the Liberal politician (later Baron Hain) acquitted in his youth of a London bank robbery having allegedly been framed by South African security services for his anti-apartheid stance (1975); and *Gay News* in which that newspaper and its editor, Denis Lemon, were found guilty of blasphemous libel (1977).

King-Hamilton had a reputation for being somewhat eccentric, but with wit. And he could be somewhat forceful, though always courteous to counsel telling them the Test Match scores. He served in the Royal Air Force in World War II with the rank of squadron leader. He was President of West London Synagogue, and Vice-president of the World Congress of Faiths.

Judge Bernard Gillis (1905–1996)

On 11 December 1975, the longest trial at the Old Bailey which had lasted 111 days concluded with several heavy sentences being handed down by Judge Bernard Gillis who was a permanent judge for many years at that court. He was at one time the Recorder of Bradford, where he originally had chambers.

Sir Sebag Shaw (1906–1982)

At the time of his appointment to the bench, Sebag Shaw (formerly Sebag Sochaczewski) was one of the few non-public school judges, maybe due to a review of the accepted configuration by reforming Labour Lord Chancellor, Lord Gardiner. He was the son of a photographer who had come to London following the pogroms in Poland and was educated at London's Central Foundation Boys School, a 'middle-class' establishment, for it was believed that there existed facilities for the children of the rich, and also the poor, but the question was the 'in-betweens' whose parents could afford something but not a great deal towards the costs of their children's education. The list of former notable pupils there is impressive: doctors, lawyers and academics abound and it is unsurprising that there are many Jewish students amongst them. Shaw then advanced to University College London prior to being called to the Bar in 1931.

A childhood affliction, polio myelitis left Shaw with a limp, but he nevertheless became a swimmer, rower, and, unusual for the East End of London, a horse rider. It is also the fact that he remained a junior for nearly 30 years before 'climbing' to Queen's Counsel, but his card must have 'been marked' because he went onto the bench the following year. His years as a junior were clearly not insignificant because, during that time, he was 'second chair' to Aubrey Melford Stevenson QC in the defence in 1955 of Ruth Ellis, the last woman to be hanged (for murder) in the United Kingdom. He was appointed a Lord Justice of Appeal in 1975 and with others of that rank became a Privy Councillor.

Sir Alan Mocatta (1907–1990)

Alan Mocotta was another product of Clifton College Bristol's Polak's House, and Oxford University. He was called to the Bar in 1930. When World War II broke out nine years later, he joined the Royal Artillery advancing from second lieutenant to lieutenant colonel on the General Staff.

The history of Mocatta's family in this country goes back many years. Moses Mocatta came here from Amsterdam, though he was originally from Portugal, and in 1671 established a firm dealing in gold, silver and diamonds. One of his ventures was to export silver to India, where it was greatly prized for making jewellery, and it was much cheaper in the West than in the East. Within a few years the company had also set up as brokers to the Bank of England and the East India Company and Moses was joined by Asher Goldsmid and the company renamed Mocatta & Goldsmid. The family controlled the firm for the next 250 years, but alas various problems arose in more recent times, and it wound down its activities. Well before this happened, the family, with the passage of time, spread its wings into other trades and professions, and it was thus that in the early-19th century, David Alfred Mocatta (1906–1882) became a well-respected architect, responsible for designing many railway stations and synagogues. Examples of the former are Brighton, Croydon, and others on that line. The Montefiore Synagogue in Ramsgate was also to his design.

Alan Mocatta was appointed King's Counsel in 1951, and ten years later to be a High Court judge and he served in that position for 20 years. He also became President of the Restrictive Practices Court set up to judge whether restrictive trading agreements were in the public interest.[6] His communal involvements included being chair of Jews College, an establishment for training Jewish clergy, and an elder and the President for 15 years of the Spanish and Portuguese Synagogue in Hollands Park.

---

6. The RPC was abolished in 1998. Its functions were transferred to the Competition Commission.

Sir Jack Jacob (1908–2000)

Isaac Hai ('Jack') Jacob's family originally came from Iraq, where his father worked for E D Sassoon & Co Ltd an international bank founded by the well-known Jewish banking and merchant family of that name; and who was posted to their branch in Shanghai. It was there that Jack was born and went to school. At 18 he left for England and went to London University where he won the Cecil Peace Prize. He was called to the Bar at Gray's Inn in 1930, becoming what the *Guardian* (1 January 2001) described as:

'The outstanding British exponent of civil court procedure during the 20th century. He was the first to fully grasp the relationship between court rules and the social dynamics which lay behind their operation. He had the ability to enter the minds of the special pleaders of centuries ago, to understand their thought processes, and to reconstruct the essential features of the English system into a modern framework. His vast industry was harnessed by a streak of naiveté in his outward-going personality into a quest to bring the civil court system up-to-date. For he knew better than most the function which procedure plays in protecting fundamental liberties, a role enshrined in article six of the European Convention on Human Rights.'

Jack Jacob's legal career was interrupted by World War II in 1939, when he rose staff captain. Returning to the Bar in 1945 and building a practice in Commercial Law, he was at the point of taking silk when family finances and doubts over his own advocacy skills dictated an alternative route as Master of the Queen's Bench with a guaranteed income. To many this would have been a hum drum, safe, not overpaid but secure position, which involved pre-trial administrative work. But he hit upon a blip in the procedures of civil law, which was clearly in need of reform. The way to bring improvements into effect was through a reconsideration of the 'bible' used by all practitioners, *The White Book*, which as its name suggests is a tome between a white hard cover with thousands of flimsy pages dealing with the nitty gritty of getting a case to and through the civil courts. Nor was this the only book in need of revision: pleadings (the written statements of claim, defence statements and counterclaims, etc. used by lawyers) and forms also needed to be made more useful to speed-up the system and the understanding of judges and practitioners, to say nothing of the general public. So, he revised several leading works known to all civil lawyers, principally *Atkin's Court Forms, Bullen & Leake on Pleadings* and *Chitty's Queen's Bench Forms*.

Jacob was welcomed at places of legal learning to lecture on his findings and reforms. He became senior master, and Queen's Remembrancer, an ancient office which involves testing the quality of coinage at the Royal Mint (known as 'the trial of the Pyx'). He was knighted and made an honorary Queen's Counsel. His wife, Rose, died in 1995, and he was most proud of his two sons, one a law lecturer, and the other Robert Jacob (below) a High Court judge.

Judge Godfrey Heilpern (1911–1973)

Godfrey Heilpern was the Recorder of Salford, Greater Manchester, who as a solicitor advocate and member of Queen's Counsel defended Myra Hindley when she was tried alongside Ian Brady in the infamous Moors Murder Trial of 1965.[7] A Godfrey Heilpern Memorial Scholarship is named after him at Middle Temple.

Judge Sir Rudolph Lyons (1912–1991)

Born in Leeds into a Jewish family engaged in the textile trade, Rudolph Lyons was an eminent Leeds lawyer, who I personally knew, and as a solicitor instructed on several occasions, both when he was a junior and later a member of Queen's Counsel. He was an outstanding after-dinner speaker. He was educated at Leeds Grammar School and Leeds University, took silk in 1953, and became leader of the Northern Circuit and Recorder of Sunderland, and thereafter of Manchester, Liverpool, Newcastle and Leeds. He was knighted in 1976. He was active in Jewish communal activities as well as non-Jewish ones

---

7. By a tragic coincidence, Heilpern's sister-in-law, Rachel Heilpern, aged 56 and the manageress of a dress shop in Salford, Greater Manchester, was found murdered on the first day of Brady's and Hindley's trial: see www.chilternlaw.com/chester-assizes-and-two-sadistic-killers-of-the-utmost-depravity/

in Leeds, particularly 'Children of the Covenant.'[8] He was painstaking in all his duties, with a great eye for detail.

Dame Rose Heilbron (1914–2002)

Described as the 'heart throb' of every young law student when, in 1949, she was appointed King's Counsel, Heilbron was elegantly poised with stunning good looks. She was perhaps one of the best-known barristers in the country, certainly in her home city of Liverpool. The public does love 'a good murder trial' and within six years of her call to the Bar in 1940 she had already appeared in several. At the age of 28 she appeared in a murder case as a junior without a leader (no KC). It is most unusual with such a charge for a junior of whatever age or experience to occupy what the Americans would call 'the first chair.' Some people commented that so many men were in the forces that the field was wide open, but that seems grossly unfair given Heilbron's qualifications—which included a masters degree—and this would not be tolerated today.

Rose Heilbron was the daughter of Jewish hotelier Max Heilbron and attended Belvedere School and Liverpool University (both close to her home in that city). Her legal practice involved personal injury cases as well as crime, though crime was her first choice, and at the extraordinarily young age of 34, on achieving silk, she became the second youngest holder of that position, and one of only two women so appointed.[9] According to a Guardian obituary:[10]

> 'When she appeared at the Old Bailey in 1951, defending Liverpool dockers accused of incitement to strike, the newspapers announced that she received £750 and £150 a day, then the highest brief fee paid to a woman. But it was well earned.'

---

8. *B'nei B'rith:* the Jewish organization concerned with the security and continuity of the Jewish people and combating anti-Semitism and bigotry.
9. As explained by Judith Bourne in *Helena Normanton and the Opening of the Bar to Women* (see *Selected Bibliography*) the less well-remembered Bar pioneer, Helena Normanton (1882–1957), not Jewish, paced Rose Heilbron on certain fronts but was never, unlike Heilbron, so popular.
10. 13 December 2005.

Rose Heilbron became the first woman recorder of Burnley, Lancashire, the first female judge to sit at the Old Bailey, and only the second appointed to the High Court, having previously sat as a Commissioner of Assizes, in effect as a deputy High Court judge.

Heilbron acted in many famous cases such as that in 1944 when she was junior counsel for the West Indian cricketer Learie Constantine in his 1944 case against Imperial Hotels after he was turned away due to his colour; and as defence counsel in a number of murder cases of the 1950s, one in particular of headline proportions, and graphically reported in her daughter, Hilary Heilbron's biography of her mother, *Rose QC* (See *Selected Bibliography*). This is the case of distinguished Jewish solicitor Louis Bloom where after Heilbron's address to the jury he was convicted of the lesser offence of manslaughter.[11]

As a KC she also appeared for the defence in a quite famous miscarriage of justice case in Liverpool in 1950, that of George Kelly who was hanged for the 'Cameo Conspiracy' in which the manager of the Cameo Cinema Wavertree just outside the city was shot dead as the perpetrator grabbed the takings for the evening. Kelly was posthumously vindicated by the Court of Appeal many years later a wholly innocent man having been executed.[12]

Another first for this hero of the Bar was to be the first woman presiding judge of a Bar circuit, and it was naturally the one which included Liverpool, namely the Northern Circuit. One of her most important extra-judicial duties was her appointment by the Home Secretary in 1975 to consider reform of the rape laws. This led to important recommendations, including that the identity of a rape complainant should be kept confidential, and that there should be limitations on the right of the defence to cross-examine a complainant in

---

11. I do not deal with Bloom, who was from Hartlepool, in this book as his greatest claim to fame appears to have been his offence. He killed his girlfriend in the office claiming she'd become hysterical on discovering he was having an affair with a former client (her previous lover had been shot dead by his father!). Bloom grabbed her by the throat and pressed her neck until she died. He then telephoned the police saying, 'I did it.' According to a letter to the *Jewish Chronicle* (20 January 2020) a Martin Levinson recalled the Little Schul in West Hartlepool where 'in the late-1950s a distinguished gentleman by the name of Louis Bloom sat quietly in the back row reading up on the runners and riders, making up the minyan but not overtly participating in the service. He was the Town Clerk of Hartlepool Council, and some years later became the Town Clerk of Sunderland…where he was highly regarded… After serving his sentence for manslaughter, he was fully rehabilitated into society and [remarkably] readmitted as a solicitor.'
12. See the book by campaigning author George Skelly in the *Selected Bibliography*. The accused reportedly said initially that he was not 'having a Judy defend [him],' but he later praised Heilbron for her painstaking defence, which led to her being named the *Daily Mirror's* 'Woman of the Year.'

the witness box on their sexual history. Rose Heilbron was a member of Soroptimists International; and her husband Dr Nathaniel Burstein was a medical consultant (on whose advice she is said to have sometimes relied as an advocate).

Dame Rose Heilbron KC who was one of the first women barristers. Forever associated with her Liverpool home and practice on the Northern Circuit she appeared in several famous trials including defending Jewish solicitor John Bloom on a murder charge. Her daughter Hilary (*Chapter 11*) has followed in her footsteps. Photo Alamy.

Sir Morris Finer (1917–1974)

A proud pupil of Kilburn Grammar School and the London School Economics, Morris Finer was politically allied to Anthony Lester, later Lord Lester of Herne Hill (*Chapter 12*), Sir Geoffrey Bindman (*Chapter 14*), and Michael Zander (*Chapter 14*). Finer supplemented his early Bar earning by writing leaders for the *London Evening Standard*. He was called in 1943, made Queen's Counsel in 1963, and appointed to the High Court bench in 1972, alas only two years before he died. His legal interests were mainly in Commercial Law and probably his most notable case as a lawyer, in 1971, involved three of the Beatles, for whom he acted concerning their management, Apple Corporation. He chaired the committee that in the 1970s produced the 'Finer Report on One Parent Families' but his report as chair of the Royal Commission on the Press was not completed due to his demise.

Judge Aaron Owen (1919–2009)

Born Aaron Leslie Cohen into a Jewish family in the Welsh mining town of Tredegar, a family friend was the Welsh Labour politician and pioneer of the welfare state Aneurin ('Nye') Bevan. After local grammar school, Owen went to University College Cardiff where he took a degree in Hebrew, then completed a doctorate. At the outbreak of World War II he was declined for the Royal Air Force due to poor eyesight; he always wore thick spectacles. Owen was appointed as a minister at the Beth Hamidrash Hagadol Synagogue, Leeds and was called 'The Reverend' rather than 'Rabbi' (I recall this, because he officiated at my bar mitzvah there in 1945!). He left to study law and was called to the Bar as Aaron Owen, describing it as 'Giving up on the Law of the Prophets for the Profits of the Law.' He specialised in Town and Country Planning and was appointed a circuit judge in 1980, becoming in 1986 the resident judge at Clerkenwell county court, then a deputy High Court judge in the Family Division. Extremely sympathetic in matrimonial cases and to what *The Times* in his obituary referred to as 'chained women,' those caught up in the complexities of Jewish marital law, he was a popular individual, with a wealth of stories, and a prolific writer in Jewish journals.

Into the Twentieth Century

Judge Israel Finestein (1921–2009)

Born in Hull, Isreal Finestein got a double first at Cambridge University, was called to the Bar, made Queen's Counsel, and became a circuit judge, deputy High Court judge and President of the Mental Health Tribunal. He was President of the Board of Deputies of British Jews (1991–1994) and a member of the Jewish Historical Society.

Sir Michael Kerr (1921–2002)

Born in the old 'palace area' of Berlin, Germany called Charlottenburg, and therefore believed to have been Britain's first foreign born judge since the 12th century, Michael Robert Emmanuel Kerr's mother was a composer and his father a drama critic. The rise of the Nazis caused their departure from Germany as with many other lawyers, doctors and prominent representatives of virtually every profession.[13] The Kerrs journeyed through Switzerland and France before arriving in England where Michael Kerr attended the 400-years-old Aldenham School, Elstree, Hertfordshire, followed by studying at Cambridge University.

Despite this, at the outbreak of World War II, he was identified as an enemy alien and sent to the Isle of Man, a move dramatically reversed, in that within a short space of time he was being trained a pilot in the RAF, where he became a Flight Lieutenant. Upon demobilisation he returned to Cambridge, graduated, was called to the Bar, and a seat in the High Court was followed by promotion to the Court of Appeal. In 2015, Kerr's son Timothy, who followed his father to the Bar was promoted to the High Court bench.

Sir Sydney Kentridge (1922–)

Sydney Kentridge is a South African born former lawyer and judge, who was also called to English Bar. The son of a Lithuanian-born lawyer and politician, he attended King Edward VII School in Johannesburg, then the University of

---

13. The obituary columns of *The Times* and other newspapers bring this home with frequency.

Witwatersrand, graduating in 1942. He was a World War II intelligence officer in East Africa and Italy.

Kentridge took his Oxford University BA in Jurisprudence obtaining a first-class degree. He was admitted as an advocate of the Supreme Court in South Africa, and appointed senior counsel in 1965. His notable cases include treason trials, defending future South African leader Nelson Mandela, and the Prisons Trial. He represented Steve Biko one of the country's leading black anti-apartheid activists as well as other leading figures of the apartheid era.

Serving at the English Bar from 1977–2013, he was appointed Queen's Counsel in 1984. He represented P & O Ferries after the disaster in which the *Herald of Free Enterprise* roll-on-roll-off car ferry capsized moments after leaving the Belgian port of Zebrugge on the evening of 6 March 1987, killing 193 passengers and crew on board. He was appointed a Judge of Appeal in Botswana, and to the Court of Appeal in both Jersey and Guernsey; also to the South African Constitutional Court. He was knighted (KCMG) in 1999; and given the Helen Suzman Lifetime Achievement award in recognition his career in South Africa and UK.

Sir John Balcombe (1925–2000)

John Balcombe was the son of Alfred Balcombe the founding owner of Alba Radios in 1918, which became a leading wireless and record player manufacturing company and retailer in the 1950s (now part of the Sainsbury group). John Balcombe went to Winchester College and then Oxford University, completing his National Service in the Royal Corps of Signals. He was called to the Bar in 1950 and built a busy, general common law practice, taking silk in 1969 and eight years later in 1977 he was appointed to the High Court, where he sat in the old Probate Divorce and Admiralty division until promoted to the Court of Appeal in 1985.

Balcombe held many extra-curricular appointments including at the Reform Synagogue (West London Synagogue), Nightingale House, a care Home in Norwood and an orphanage. He was President of the Maccabeans, an interesting, somewhat elitist, Jewish cultural group which originated in Victorian times, named after Judas Maccabias, one of the leaders of a revolt of the Judeans.

Originally restricted to professionals and only in recent years admitting others, their main event is a Chanukah Dinner when a toast is drunk to the memory of Judas Maccabias. The Maccabeans administer certain scholarships and lectures on historical matters.

Sir Louis Blom-Cooper (1926–2020)

Born of Jewish parents in London, Louis Blom-Cooper attended Port Regis School, Shaftesbury, Seaford College, West Sussex, the University of British Colombia, King's College London, and studied at the universities of Amsterdam and (Fitzwilliam College) Cambridge. He taught law at the London School of Economics as part of an academic career that continued part-time alongside legal practice. He was called to the Bar in 1952, progressing to Queen's Counsel. He was chair of the Mental Health Commission (1987–1994), and a deputy judge of the Court of Appeal in Jersey (1988–96). Blom-Cooper was a correspondent of *The Observer, Guardian* and other newspapers and one of the founders of Amnesty International. An anti-death penalty advocate and often controversial, he undertook a variety of quasi-official roles and was chair at various times of Amnesty, the Howard League for Penal Reform, and 'think tank' the Homicide Review Advisory Group (HOMRAG) (later Modernising Justice). Well-connected across the legal establishment (senior judges would give him the time of day) one of his book launches was attended by the President and most of the Supreme Court. He was indeed a prolific author (examples of which appear in the *Selected Bibliography*). His many successes as an advocate include the landmark House of Lords prisoners' rights ruling in *Raymond v Honey* ([1983] 1 AC 1). At his packed memorial event at Middle Temple Hall it was mentioned that, though courageous, he might often take an entrenched position which he would argue to the nth degree, occasionally causing him problems not least when defending (albeit successfully) a libel action against himself in Northern Ireland. His wife Joan was a justice of the peace and family members have inherited his reforming zeal.

The Jewish Contribution to English Law

Sir Louis Blom-Cooper was a correspondent of *The Observer*, *Guardian* and other newspapers, an academic at the London School of Economics, and one of the founders of Amnesty International. Appearing as a QC before the House of Lords he won the leading prisoners' rights case *Raymond v Honey*. Photo Waterside Press.

Into the Twentieth Century

Sir Clive Callman (1927–2019)

Born in Berlin, Germany into a Jewish professional family, when Clive Callman's father was taken to Sachsenhausen Concentration Camp plans were put into action for his release and, if successful, immediate departure to England in March 1939 on the *SS Bremen*. Virtually destitute, but with a place at school in Weybridge on offer, Clive Callman later attended Kingston (Surrey) Technical College, and the London School of Economics in 1947. He was called to the Bar 1951, building a practice in Probate and Family Law. He was appointed a circuit judge in 1973. Callman had a reputation for advancing the interests of children, and concerning education. He was Senator of London University, Governor at Birkbeck College, University of London, the London School of Economics and the Hebrew University of Jerusalem, and has acted as a mediator. He was knighted in 2012 for services to law, education and charity.

Sir Sydney Lipworth (1931–)

Sydney Lipworth merits mention here, although he held no judicial appointments at all. However, like Sydney Kentridge (above) he was born in South Africa, and educated there. He was co-founder with Sir Mark Weinberg and Lord Joel Joffe (*Chapter 12*) of Hambro Life Insurance, later called Allied Dunbar and now Zurich Insurance. He was chair of the Monopolies and Mergers Commission and Astra Zeneca, and deputy chair of the National Westminster Bank. Sydney Lipworth was knighted in 1991, called to the English Bar, and appointed Queen's Counsel in 1993.

Lord Peter Millet (1932–2021)

Educated at Harrow and Cambridge University, Peter Millet was awarded a double first. He was called to the Bar in 1955, then became a flying officer in the Royal Air Force. After a period in chambers at Lincoln's Inn he joined the Chancery Bar and was thereafter junior counsel to the Department of Trade and Industry, then a member of the Law Commission. In 1974 he was appointed

Queen's Counsel, and specialised, often on behalf of the then Inland Revenue, in Taxation and Insolvency, which led to the revision by Government of many tax avoidance schemes as well as the identification of outright evasion.

In 1986 Millet was appointed to the High Court and five years later made a Lord of Appeal in Ordinary in the House of Lords with a life peerage, from which active role he retired in 2004. From 2000, he was a non-permanent judge of the Hong Kong Court of Appeal.

Peter Millet gave the judgment in a leading House of Lords case *McFarlane v Tayside Health Board (Scotland)* ([2000] 2 AC 59), which concerned a claim for the cost of bringing up an 'unwanted' child following a vasectomy alleged to have been performed in a negligent manner. He said, 'The birth of a normal, healthy, baby is a blessing, not a detriment,' though he allowed a small amount of compensation to reflect that the parents 'had lost the freedom to limit the size of their family.' His other fields of expertise included Equity, Trusts, and Professional Negligence. He was active as a senior Freemason, and he served as President of West London Synagogue, Upper Berkeley Street.

Sir Harry Ognall (1934–2021)

Born in Salford into a middle-class originally Russian Jewish family, Harry Ognall's father Leo Horace Ognall (1908–1979), under names Hartley Howard and Harry Carmichael, was the prolific author of over 80 detective novels such as *The Last Appointment* and *The Death of Cecilia*. Harry Ognall his son later wrote *A Life of Crime: The Memoirs of a High Court Judge* (2017). Educated at Leeds Grammar School, Lincoln College, Oxford University and the University of Virginia, USA as a Fullbright Scholar, Ognall was called to the Bar in 1958, made Queen's Counsel in 1973 and was a Crown Court recorder (1972–1986). One of his most outstanding cases was his defence in 1983, in Harare, South Africa of six white Royal Air Force officers who had been charged with assisting South African saboteurs to blow up 13 war planes. He showed that confessions had been extracted by torture.

Appointed to the High Court in 1986 (at the time he was a good friend of mine in Leeds, where he practised initially), Ognall was a formidable advocate, who took over the prosecution in the trial of Peter Sutcliffe, the Yorkshire

Ripper, as he was more experienced in criminal matters than the then Attorney-General. By this time, he had transferred to the Church of England.

As a High Court judge he presided over the trial of Robert Napper for the high-profile 'Wimbledon Common' murder of Rachel Nickell;[14] the Lyme Bay kayaking manslaughter tragedy involving the proprietors of a small educational centre;[15] the trial of Nigel Cox;[16] and he conducted hearings in relation to former Chilean Head of State Augusto Pinochet.

Judge Michael Hyam (1938–2004)

It was unexpected when Michael Hyam, at the age of 66, and who did not appear to have a great number of connections with the capital was appointed Recorder of London in 1998. He sat in many high-profile and demanding cases and was described in his obituary in *The Guardian*[17] as 'firm, fair and courteous' if sometimes strict. Educated at Westminster School and Cambridge University he was called to the Bar in 1962. He spent much of his career as a prosecutor in Kent, and then moved to the Old Bailey, and became a recorder in 1983, the next year a circuit judge, later the resident judge at Norwich Crown Court, and thereafter the Old Bailey. He wrote *Advocacy Skills* which ran to several editions up until 1993.

Hyams route to the City was as a liveryman with the 'Fruiterers.' He was a member of Marylebone Cricket Club (the MCC) and became a deputy lord lieutenant. On the day of his death, he had ordered the retrial of members of the family of a suicide bomber, and he died at a dinner where he was due to speak. He was a fastidious after dinner speaker who prepared with great aplomb: this suited him perfectly for the demanding position of recorder. Although his health was not good, he always put work before anything else, making great sacrifices in this regard.

---

14. A cold case in which Napper had been convicted of the murder of Samantha Bisset and her daughter years earlier but where investigators ignored what with hindsight were obvious clues.
15. Britain's first and at the time of writing only successful corporate killing prosecution.
16. The first medical man to be tried in the UK for facilitating euthanasia.
17. 15 July 2004.

Sir Gavin Lightman (1939–2020)

Gavin Lightman graduated from University College London in 1961 and was called to the Bar1 in 1963. He rose to become Treasurer of Lincoln's Inn. He was appointed as a High Court judge in the Chancery Division in 1994, retiring in 2008. He was Vice-president of the Anglo-Jewish Association. His father, Harold Lightman, Queen's Counsel (1906–1998), was the son of a Lithuanian refugee who became a furniture manufacturer in Leeds, worked hard, and was rewarded by his father with the money to study accountancy, and at a young age wrote a book on company finance. Thereafter Harold studied for the Bar and was called in 1932. He overcame a reluctance by London solicitors to instruct the sons of immigrants, which gave him added determination, and his knowledge of accounts proved invaluable. He became a Queen's Counsel in 1955, a bencher and Head of Chambers. He was responsible for some important decisions in matrimonial finance, and his tenacity was again revealed when he had a stroke and had to learn to write with his left hand. His 90th birthday was celebrated with a highly attended dinner at Lincoln's Inn.

This talented family is currently represented at the Bar by Harold Lightman's grandson, Gavin's son, Daniel Lightman QC; an extremely well-thought of Chancery and Company Law specialist, especially by minority shareholders.

Judge Martin Stephens (1939–)

Martin Stephens was called to the Bar in 1963 and became Queen's Counsel in 1982. He was appointed as a recorder in 1979 and to be a circuit judge 1986. After sitting at Swansea Crown Court, he was then appointed as a permanent judge to the Old Bailey in 1999, where he dealt with a heavy caseload, including a considerable number of murder cases.

Judge John Samuels (1940–)

A circuit judge, deputy High Court judge, prison reformer and Queen's Counsel, John Samuels was born in Reigate, educated at Charterhouse, in Perugia and at Cambridge University. He was commissioned in the Queen's Royal Surrey Regiment. Samuels was called to the Bar in 1962, made Queen's Counsel in 1981, and was a deputy High Court judge, having become a circuit judge in 1997. He represented retired judges, liaised on their behalf with the Magistrates' Association and served on the Parole Board, and probation and drug treatment committees. He has also supported numerous prison reform bodies, for which he works tirelessly.

Sir Robert Raphael Hayim Jacob (1941–)

The son of Sir Jack Jacob (above), Robert Jacob read Physics at Cambridge and then Law at the London School of Economics and was called to the Bar in 1965, taking silk in 1981. His speciality was Patents and Intellectual Property and in 1983 he was appointed to the High Court as a designated patent judge, and then to the Court of Appeal in 2003. After eight years he retired, and in 2018 took a position with the Astana International Finance Centre in Kazakhstan, which was established that year to create a financial hub in Asia. It is the same organization to which Lord Woolf (*Chapter 11*), former Lord Chief Justice, gravitated.

Sir Jonathan Cohen (1941–)

Called to bar in 1974, Jonathan Cohen became Head of Chambers, having been appointed Queen's Counsel in 1997. He was engaged in Family Law then, unusually at his age, appointed to the High Court's then Divorce Division at the age of 66, meaning he would only have four years *in situ* before needing to retire!

Sir Richard Henriques (1943–)

Born in Lancashire, Richard Henry Quixano Henriques attended school in Lytham St Annes, Lancashire then went to Oxford University and was called to the Bar in 1967. Made Queen's Counsel in 1986, as an advocate he prosecuted

The Jewish Contribution to English Law

in some of the most serious cases in Lancashire and Eastern England. In 1993 he prosecuted the juveniles Robert Thompson and Jon Venables in the notorious James Bulger child murder case which was moved to Preston Crown Court due to strong local feeling. It involved an allegation of the murder of two-year-old Bulger by two ten-year-olds caught walking with their victim via CCTV footage. A central legal issue turned on the concept *doli incapax* ('lack of criminal capacity,' i.e. the question whether the two young defendants knew and understood what they were doing was wrong).

An equally notorious case of Henriques, was that of Dr Harold Shipman at Preston Crown Court in 1999, the serial killing general medical practitioner who possibly murdered well over 200 of his elderly patients under the guise of treating them.

Henriques was appointed to the High Court in 2000 and retired in 2013. His retirement did not last long, because he was asked by the Commissioner of the Metropolitan police to investigate the way in which the police had conducted investigations into allegations made against several political and public figures including Lord Leon Brittan (*Chapter 10*), as well as high-ranking armed services chiefs. The investigations revealed no evidence against these people, but this was not made known until after Brittan had died.

Henriques, although believed not to be a practising Jew, came from a very old established family descended from the Jews of Spain who had fled the inquisitions and moved to many parts of the world, including Portugal. It was there that in 1492, believing they could practice their religion in peace, they were forced to convert to Catholicism. They were thus known as *Conversationes*, Marranos or 'New Christians.' There is a clue to this in the name Quixano, for despite much assimilation and complete departure from their Jewish religion, they maintained that name as a subsidiary or 'middle' name. But, also, they adopted as a surname Henriques or Henry as a tribute to a man who had tried to save them centuries earlier. Henriques Dias Milao Cacares (1528–1609) was a wealthy Catholic businessman from Lisbon arrested by the Spanish — it is not known if his Catholicism was original or whether he was a Merrano, though that conversion was likely as he was charged with having dealings with Jews, and at least one of his servants practised Judaism. At 82-years-old he was put to death. His family witnessed this and took on the name Henriques in his memory. The family spread to many parts of the world, including India, Germany, Denmark and Sweden as well as England.

Judge David Pearl (1944–)

David Pearl is included in this list, for although a circuit judge his eventual status as President of the Immigration Appeals Tribunal in 1997 (and from which he retired in 2019) equates with high status. Educated at Birmingham University and Cambridge University he was called to the Bar in 1968. He lectured at Cambridge and then the University of East Anglia. Pearl was chief adjudicator on appeals prior to being President of that tribunal. He was Director of Studies at the Judicial Studies Board which was then responsible for judicial training. In 2006 he became a member of the Judicial Appointments Commission.

Sir Bernard Rix (1944–)

Educated at St Paul School and New College, Oxford University, Bernard Anthony Rix is the son of Otto Rix and Sadie Silverberg. He was elected a Kennedy Scholar and studied at Harvard Law School where he received an LLM to add to his Oxford University MA. Called to the Bar in 1970, he became a bencher and Queen's Counsel in 1981, and then a member of the Bar Senate, the Bar Council, and Treasurer of his inn of court, Inner Temple. After becoming a Crown Court recorder, he was appointed to the High Court in 1993, and was put in charge of the Commercial List, advancing to Lord Justice of Appeal in the Court of Appeal in 2000. He retired from the English bench in 2013.

Appointed a judge of the Singapore International Commercial Court in 2015, Rix was also Director of the London Philharmonic Orchestra and Vice-president of the Friends of Bar Ilan University, Ramat Gan, Tel Aviv, Israel. He also ran the Spiro Institute concerned with pioneering approaches to Jewish education.[18] His wife, Lady Karen Rix, is the daughter of Lord David Young and Lady Young (see *Chapter 14*).

---

18. See www.spiroark.org

Lord Anthony Grabiner (1945–)

Born to Jewish parents, Anthony Stephen Grabiner was educated at Central Foundation Boys' School, Islington, the London School of Economics (with first-class honours and an LLM with distinction) and called to the Bar in 1968. From 1976–1981 he was a junior Treasury Counsel. He was made Queen's Counsel in 1981, was a recorder and then deputy High Court judge. He is or was a non-executive director of various companies (Arcadia, Next) and advised News Corporation.

In 1999, he was awarded a life peerage and sat on the Labour benches as Baron Grabiner, but in 2015 he resigned the party whip (remaining a Labour party member) due I believe to his views concerning Labour leader Jeremy Corbyn (then being vilified by allegations of anti-Semitism). Grabiner has since sat on the cross-benches. He was or became a non-executive director of various companies, including Taveta Investments Ltd[19] and advised News Corporation.

Lady Hazel Cosgrove (1946–)

Born in Glasgow, Hazel Cosgrove attended Glasgow High School for Girls and the School of Law, University of Glasgow obtaining an LLB in 1966. She was admitted to Scotland's Faculty of Advocates in 1968 and was standing junior counsel to the Department of Trade 1977–79. Hazel Cosgrove was appointed Queen's Counsel in 1991. She was the first woman Sheriff of Glasgow (1979), and in 1996 the first woman Senator of the Court of Sessions, i.e. a judge of the Scottish Supreme Court. Awarded a CBE in 2004, she retired in 2006. She was deputy chairman of the Boundary Commission for Scotland.

---

19. Philip Green's holding company for his Acardia group that in 2016 attracted strong criticism in a Parliamentary report: See https://old.parliament.uk/business/committees/committees-a-z/commons-select/work-and-pensions-committee/news-parliament-2015/bhs-report-published-16-17/

Sir Michael Burton (1946–)

Educated at Eton and Oxford University, Michael Burton was called to the Bar and appointed Queen's Counsel. He worked at the Commercial Bar, and became Head of Lyttleton Chambers. He was appointed to the High Court in 1998, sitting to deal with Chancery matters, and served on the Employment Appeal Tribunal and in the Commercial Court. He retired from the bench in 2016. Burton was President of the Investigatory Powers Tribunal 2013–2018, dealing with important aspects of national security. At the time of writing, he acts as an arbitrator.

Sir Hugh Laddie (1946–2008)

Educated at Aldenham School, Elstree, Hertfordshire and St Catherine's College, Cambridge University, Hugh Ian Lang Laddie began by studying medicine, but changed his mind and entered law school. He was called to the Bar in 1969, and as an expert in Patents had an extremely busy practice. After 25 years, in 1995, he was elevated to the High Court where he worked in the Chancery Division and is credited with innovations including development of the so-called 'Anton Piller order,' which allows the search of premises and seizure of evidence without notice and to prevent it being destroyed.

Laddie caused something of a stir when after complaining that he found the job 'boring' and ten years in post he resigned.[20] It was all the more surprising because as an acknowledged expert in his field it was inevitable that he would have been elevated to the Court of Appeal, and having regard to his intellectual prowess, many observers thought, to the Supreme Court.

After several legal consultancy and similar roles, Laddie was appointed Professor of Intellectual Property Law at University College London in 2006, where he founded the Institute of Brand and Innovation Law and gave his name to the Sir Hugh Laddie Chair in Intellectual Property Law. However, illness struck, and sadly he died in 2008.

---

20. As with what appears to have been his only predecessor in this regard, Sir Henry Fisher, who resigned in 1970, he retained the knighthood usually given on appointment to the High Court. See also Sir Bernard Eder later in this chapter who I think was able to do much the same.

Judge Clement Goldstone (1949–)

Clement Goldstone was honorary Recorder of Liverpool, in which position he succeeded Sir Henry Globe (below), and previous to him Neville Laski (see earlier in this chapter). Born into a Jewish family in Liverpool, he was educated at Manchester Grammar School and Cambridge University. He was called to the Bar in 1971, made Queen's Counsel in 1993, and became a circuit judge in 2002. He was a formidable criminal advocate who retired in 2019.

Sir Henry Globe (1949–)

Henry Globe was educated at Liverpool College and then the University of Birmingham. He was called to the Bar in 1972 and made Queen's Counsel in 1994. In 2003, as a senior circuit judge, he became Recorder of Liverpool, and in 2011 was appointed to the High Court. From 2013 to 2016 he was a presiding judge on the Northern Circuit. He was elected an Honorary Fellow of Liverpool University for his contribution to the law over 40 years. He retired from the bench in 2017.

Sir Brian Leveson (1949–)

Born in Liverpool and educated at Liverpool College and Oxford University, Brian Leveson was called to the Bar in 1970, practised on the Northern Circuit, and became Queen's Counsel in 1986. Appointed to the High Court in 2000, he presided over the Northern Circuit, was appointed to the Court of Appeal in 2006, and in 2013 was made President of the Queen's Bench Division of the High Court.

He was involved in many notable cases. He prosecuted Ken Dodd the popular entertainer on tax evasion charges (Dodd was acquitted[21]), Rosemary West (serial killer wife of Frederick West who committed suicide in prison before he could be tried also), dealt with Barry George (wrongly convicted of the unsolved murder of TV Presenter Jill Dando and later released) and James Hanratty

---

21. The apocryphal tale is that no Liverpool jury would have convicted him. His statue stands there.

(hanged for murder in 1962). Also, the later posthumous appeal of Ruth Ellis (the last woman to hang in Britain in 1955). In 2011, he chaired the Leveson Inquiry, a major judicial public inquiry into the culture, practices and ethics of the press, involving in particular News International and phone hacking.

As President of the Queen's Bench Division, he was responsible for discipline amongst judges. One morning when I had been a judge for several years, he sent for me. Upon arriving at the Royal Courts of Justice in The Strand, in his room, he informed me he had received a complaint, I had given a talk to a charity organization, and in the course of it mentioned an exceptional, though lenient, course I had once taken which resulted in the defendant becoming successfully rehabilitated. Someone present complained of my 'favouritism,' and he needed to take me before the Lord Chief Justice, whom he said would see me straightaway. I asked the natural question, who 'snitched,' but he wouldn't tell me. Suffice it to say that after 20 mins with Lord Judge, then Lord Chief Justice, I walked out without a stain, or even the semblance of a stain, on my character.

Sir Brian Leveson became well-known beyond the courts and judiciary when he looked into phone hacking by the press. Photo Waterside Press.

Sir Michael Supperstone (1950–)

Michael Supperstone attended St Paul's School and Oxford University. He was called to the Bar in 1973, made Queen's Counsel in 1991 and a High Court judge in 2010. He presided over the Administrative Court and retired in 2020.

Sir Peter Roth (1952–)

Born into a Jewish family, Peter Roth was educated St Paul's School and Oxford University and became an associate professor of the University of Pennsylvania, USA (he was a Harmsworth Scholar). He was called to the Bar in 1977, made Queen's Counsel in 1997, appointed to the High Court in 2009, and was made President of the Competition Appeal Tribunal in 2013. He was the editor of *Bellamy and Child, Community Law of Competition* (current edition 2014).

Sir Kim Lewison (1952–)

Kim Lewison's mother was Jewish, and he was educated St Paul's School and Cambridge University. He was called to the Bar in 1975 and made Queen's Counsel in 1991, and a High Court judge in 2003. He was Chancery Supervising Judge, and a member of the Competition Appeal Tribunal. In 2011 he was made a Lord Justice of Appeal.

Sir Bernard Eder (1952–)

Born into a Jewish family, Bernard Elder was educated at Haberdashers' Aske's Boys' School and Downing College, Cambridge University. He was called to the Bar in 1975, made Queen's Counsel in 1991, and a High Court judge in 2011, from which he resigned in 2015 (compare Sir Hugh Laddie above). He was then appointed as a judge of the Singapore International Commercial Court; the following year an acting judge in the Eastern Caribbean Supreme Court; and was assigned to the Commercial Division in the British Virgin Islands.

He gives presentations and lectures and was a visiting professor at University College London from 1999–2003, giving talks on Shipping Law to masters degree students. A member of the Institute of Maritime Law at the University of Southampton, he is lead editor of *Scrutton on Charterparties and Bills of Lading* and an independent arbitrator.

Judge Nigel Peters (1952–)

Born in 1952 into to a Jewish family in Denmark Hill, Nigel Peters was educated at Hasmonean High School in Barnet (for pupils from orthodox Jewish families) and Leicester University. He was called to the Bar in 1976 and made Queen's Counsel in 1997, with a busy criminal practice. He became a circuit judge in 2012. He is a cricket enthusiast and chair of the Marylebone Cricket Club (MCC) Membership Committee, and also of London's Garrick Club.

Judge Richard Marks (1953–)

Born into a Jewish family, Richard Marks was educated at Clifton College, Bristol and the University of Manchester. He was called to the Bar in 1975. After practising on the Northern Circuit, of which he became leader, he held the office one rung down from Recorder of London, but of equal traditional eminence, Common Serjeant of London, to which he was appointed in 2015. His livery, and one would need one for appointment, is the Cooks Company.

Sir Clive Freedman (1955–)

Born into a Jewish family in Manchester, Clive Freedman attended Manchester Grammar School and Cambridge University. He speaks at least four languages, including Russian and Hebrew. A highly respected Commercial Law Queen's Counsel he is a forceful advocate. He was promoted to the High Court in 2018.

Dame Victoria Sharp (1956–)

Victoria Sharp is the daughter of Lord Sharp of Grimsdyke (1916–94), a principal at the Ministry of Power, a director of ICI Fibres, and chair of P & O Ferries. Her twin brother is Richard Sharp, sometime chair of the BBC. Educated at North London Collegiate School in Edgware, then Bristol University, she was called to the Bar in 1979. Although her first choice was to specialise in Labour Law the chambers she gained admission to did largely defamation work, and she also did Media Law. Made Queen's Counsel in 2001, Victoria Sharp acted for Associated Newspapers, and the *Sunday Times*. She was appointed a judge of the High Court in 2001, where she also presided over defamation cases. In 2013 she was promoted to the Court of Appeal and became President of the Queen's Bench Division in 2019, succeeding Lord Justice Leveson (above) in 2020, and becoming Deputy Head of Criminal Justice.

Sir Stephen Morris (1957–)

After attending Bradford Grammar School, Stephen Morris went to Cambridge University, was called to the Bar in 1981, then made Queen's Counsel. He became a leading Competition Law expert, and is also expert in European Law and Commercial Law, as well as the work of International Arbitration tribunals. He was appointed to the High Court in 2016

Sir David Waksman (1957–)

David Waksman attended school in Newcastle, went to Manchester University, and Oxford University and was called to the Bar in 1982. He was made Queen's Counsel in 2002. He had a Commercial Law practice, was appointed a circuit judge in 2007, placed in charge of the London Technical and Construction Court, and made a High Court judge in 2018.

Dame Ingrid Simler (1963–)

Educated at Henrietta Barnett School, Cambridge and the University of Amsterdam, Ingrid Simler was called to the Bar in 1987, becoming a Head of Chambers. She was chair of the Bar Equality and Diversity Committee, and was made Queen's Counsel in 2006, a High Court judge in 2013, then Court of Appeal judge in 2019. She was for a time President of the Employment Appeal Tribunal.

CHAPTER 11

Judicial Appointments High and Low

As can be seen from the pen portraits in the last two chapters, many Jews progressed to appointments in the High Court and Court of Appeal. Some went further, becoming Supreme Court justices and a number were ultimately appointed to the great legal roles of England, becoming President of the Supreme Court, Lord Chief Justice, Lord Chancellor or Master of the Rolls. As readers will see some progressed by holding several such roles. Two Jewish lawyers have already come to occupy senior international positions, with which this chapter opens. It closes with 'snapshots' of some further Jewish judges and barristers from the base of the 'judicial and legal pyramid.'

International Judicial Appointments

Sir Hersch Lauterpacht (1897–1960)
Born in 1897 in the Austro-Hungarian Empire, now the Ukraine, Hersch Lauterpacht moved to Galicia. He enrolled in the law school at the University of Lemberg but was unable to graduate due to being a Jew. He went to Vienna and subsequently London where he completed his doctorate at the London School of Economics, then practised law, wrote about and taught International Law, and became a member of Queen's Counsel. He was part of the prosecution team at the Nuremberg War Trials that dealt with the surviving Nazi leaders after World War II, led by English prosecutor Sir Hartley Shawcross QC.

A pioneer of human rights ahead of his time, Lauterpacht was a member of the International Law Commission (1952–1954) and a judge of the International

Court of Justice in the Hague (1955–1960). The Lauterpacht Centre for International Law in the Faculty of Law at Cambridge University is named after his son, Sir Elihu Lauterpacht QC CBE (1928–2017) its founder and first director.

Dame Rosalyn Higgins (1937–)

Born Rosalyn Cohen, Dame Rosalyn is married to Lord Higgins (1928–) (Sir Terrence Higgins the former MP and 1950s Olympic athlete). Having studied at Cambridge University, then Yale University, USA, she was called to the Bar, and made Queen's Counsel in 1986. She served on the United Nations Human Rights Committee for 14 years and was elected to the International Court of Justice in 1995, the first woman to be appointed to that court. She was made a dame in 1995, and then in 2006 President of that court. She was appointed adviser on International Law to the British Government during the Chilcot Inquiry of 2009–2016 (that under Sir John Chilcott, also known as the Iraq Inquiry into the UK's role in that war). Rosalyn Higgins holds a reported 13 honorary doctorates.

Supreme Court of the United Kingdom

The Jewish lawyers in this section were appointed to this country's highest court, the Supreme Court[1] that sits at Middlesex Guildhall across Parliament Square from the House of Commons. Supreme Court justices sit in judgement under the President of the court.

Lord Nicholas Phillips (1938–)

Nicholas Phillips' mother's *Sephardim* grandparents came to England from Alexandria, Egypt, making him *halachically* Jewish, though not so far as I know practising. He was educated at Bryanston School, Dorset and served as an officer in the Royal Navy, then went to Cambridge University, and was called to the

---

1. Formerly the House of Lords (more precisely its Judicial Committee), when Law Lords (also known as Lords of Appeal in ordinary) sat to hear appeals there. The Privy Council has an appellate function and comparable role dealing with cases from British territories abroad that still recognise it as their final court of appeal. The suffix PC (privy counsellor) applies to all members of the Sovereign's broader Privy Council, but its judicial functions are exercised via judges appointed for that purpose (often the same individuals as Supreme Court justices).

Bar in 1962 having been a Harmsworth Scholar of the Middle Temple. He was made Queen's Counsel in 1978, and in 1987 appointed to the High Court of Justice. He oversaw a large number of fraud trials, including in the early-1990s the Robert Maxwell pension scheme prosecution concerning the removal by the newspaper magnate of funds from his Mirror Group's coffers; and the trial involving Barlow Clowes International's fraudulent collapse in 1988.

Phillips was made a Lord of Appeal in 1999 and created a life peer as Baron Phillips of Worth Matravers. In 2000, he succeeded Lord Harry Woolf (see later in this chapter) as Master of Rolls, and then became Lord Chief Justice (2005–2008). In 2009 he was appointed as the first President of the newly formed Supreme Court until he retired in 2013. He has been President of the Qatar International Court, Hong Kong Court of Appeal, and of the English Maritime Law Association.

Lord Nicholas Phillips of Worth Matravers first Head of the UK Supreme Court in 2009 and a former Lord Chief Justice. As a judge he oversaw complex fraud trials, a specialism from his days at the Bar.

The Jewish Contribution to English Law

Lord Leonard Hoffman (1934–)
Leonard Hubert Hoffman (known as 'Lennie') was born in Cape Town, South Africa, the son of a leading solicitor there, and educated at Queen's College, Oxford University as a Rhodes Scholar, where he won a Vinerian Scholarship (for the student performing best in the Bachelor of Common Law examinations). He published a standard work on evidence as it affects his home country. He was called to the Bar in 1964, made Queen's Counsel in 1977, appointed to the High Court in 1985 (as a judge in the Chancery Division) and to the Court of Appeal in 1992, then made a Lord of Appeal in 1995 as Baron Hoffman of Chedworth. There among other things he gave key judgements on terrorism and national security. He retired from the English judiciary in 2009 when the House of Lords appellate jurisdiction transferred to the Supreme Court, taking-up an honorary chair in International Property Law at Queen Mary, University of London. He is an *ad hoc* judge at the Court of Final Appeal of Hong Kong.

Lord Simon Brown (1937–)
Educated at Stowe School, Buckinghamshire, then commissioned in the Royal Artillery, Simon Denis Brown went to Worcester College, Oxford University (where he is an honorary fellow). He was called to the Bar in 1961, became First Treasury Counsel, and was appointed to the High Court in 1984 sitting in the Queen's Bench Division. He was advanced to the Court of Appeal in 1992 and made a Lord of Appeal in 2004 with a life peerage as Baron Brown of Eaton-under-Heywood, sitting on the cross-benches. He transferred to the Supreme Court as a Supreme Court justice in 2009.

Lord David Neuberger (1948–)
Born in London, David Edmond Neuberger's father and all three brothers are academics holding chairs (in non-legal topics) in British Universities. His sister-in-law is Rabbi (now Baroness) Julia Neuberger (born 1950). Educated at The Hall School Hampstead, Westminster School, and Christ Church College Oxford University, he was called to the Bar in 1974 after working in banking for Rothschilds. He was made Queen's Counsel in 1987, appointed to the High Court in 1996, and to the Court of Appeal in 2004–2007. He was made a Lord of Appeal in 2007 and became Baron Neuberger of Abbotsbury, transferring to the Supreme Court in 2009 (becoming also Master of the Rolls) and in 2012

succeeded Lord Phillips (above) as its President. He now acts as a judge in the Hong Kong Court of Final Appeal on an *ad hoc* basis and chairs the Panel of Experts on Media Freedom.

Lord Lawrence Collins (1941–)

Born in London, Lawrence Collins was educated at City of London School and Cambridge University, obtaining a starred first in law, and an LLM at Columbia University, New York, USA. He was admitted a solicitor in 1968, becoming a partner in Herbert Smith (now Herbert Smith Freehills) in 1971. He was one of the first two solicitors appointed Queen's Counsel in 1997. He has appeared as a solicitor advocate in the UK appellate courts and the European Court of Justice and acted for Chile in the case of the extradition from the UK of the former dictator General Augusto Pinochet in 2000.

Collins was appointed to the High Court in 2000, being the first solicitor to achieve this status direct from private practice. In 2007 he was appointed to the Court of Appeal, and in 2009 made a Lord of Appeal, and created a life peer as Baron Collins of Mapesbury. In October 2009, he transferred to the Supreme Court.

The author or editor of respected and established legal works, and though retired from the bench, Lawrence Collins has since leaving the Supreme Court in 2011 been or acted among other things as Professor of Law at London University, an international arbitrator, a judge in the Hong Kong Court of Final Appeal sitting *ad hoc*, and a cross-bencher in the House of Lords. He has always been a practising Jew and is a regular attender at Saturday services in synagogue.

Dame Vivien Rose (1960–)

Born into a Jewish family in London, Vivien Judith Rose was educated at Kingsbury High School then Newnham College, Cambridge University, and for her post-graduate degree at Brazenove College, Oxford University. She was called to the Bar in 1984, and became standing counsel to the Director of Fair Trading in 2005, deputy counsel Office of the Speaker, and co-edited various legal textbooks. She was legal chair of the Competition Appeal Tribunal, and appointed to the High Court Chancery Division in 2013. She was made a Lady Justice of Appeal in 2019; and as Lady Rose of Colmworth was appointed a Supreme Court justice in 2021.

At her swearing-in, a list of her formidable qualifications in many spheres of the law was read out by the President of the Supreme Court, Lord Reed, amongst which it was indicated that she was the first former government lawyer to be so appointed.[2]

Lord Chief Justice

The Lord Chief Justice is the Head of the Judiciary and President of the courts of England and Wales. This dual role only began when the Lord Chancellor's judicial functions were transferred to the Lord Chief Justice under the Constitutional Reform Act 2005.[3] Apart from those individuals described below it should be noted that Lord Nicholas Phillips (above) held office as Lord Chief Justice from 2005–2008 *en route* to his presidency of the Supreme Court. Historically, the occupants of this role may sometimes have been famed for 'speaking truth to power' (a function that of course continues) as encapsulated by the title of Anthony Mockler's classic work, *Lions Under the Throne* (see *Selected Biogrfaphy*). So, what of some further 'Jewish lions.'

Lord Peter Taylor (1930–1997)

Peter Murray Taylor has already been mentioned in *Chapter 1* where I described his memorial service at St Paul's. His family originally came from Vilna in Lithuania, the home of a large Jewish community. They emigrated to England and lived in Leeds to begin with, where his father became a doctor. His mother's relatives, the Palterovitchs, are from the same family as Oscar-winning actress Gwyneth Paltrow. The family moved to Newcastle-upon-Tyne, where Peter Taylor was born.

Educated at the Royal Grammar School, Newcastle then Cambridge University, Taylor was an enthusiastic rugby player and represented his county. He was also a pianist, having a long friendship with Dame Fanny Waterman, eventually joining her in running of the Leeds International Piano Competition.

---

2. The swearing-in can be viewed at https://youtu.be/25637NgOXAg (Accessed 5 August 2021).
3. The official Courts and Tribunals Judiciary website sets out some 400 statutory responsibilities that fall under the remit of the Lord Chief Justice, that in routine administrative matters are discharged by civil servants in the Judicial Office: see www.judiciary.uk/about-the-judiciary/who-are-the-judiciary/judicial-roles/judges/lord-chief-justice/

Judicial Appointments High and Low

He gave concerts throughout his life at gatherings legal and otherwise; and was said to have been so competent that he might well have chosen to be a concert pianist. He was however called to the Bar in 1954 and practised out of Newcastle, also the formative area for a second Jewish Lord Chief Justice, Harry Woolf (below). He was appointed Queen's Counsel in 1967 at the age of 37.

Peter Taylor prosecuted the high-profile Pontefract corruption case of 1972, in which the architect and property developer John Poulson (said to be 'a man more sinned against that sinning') and local officials were jailed; that of Judith Ward (the M62 IRA coach bombing of 1974, later found to be a miscarriage of justice); and Stefan *Kiszko* (for the sexual murder of young Leslie Moleseed, later discovered to have been an impossibility as Kiszko could not produce semen as found on her clothing and concerning which another man was ultimately identified as the perpetrator by DNA many years later). There is nothing to say that Taylor did not act correctly throughout these cases on the then available evidence and standards at the time. He also prosecuted Jeremy Thorpe, leader of the Liberal Party (acquitted at the Old Bailey of conspiracy to murder), when Taylor was praised for his fairness of approach.

Peter Taylor was appointed to the High Court, and then the Court of Appeal in 1988, and shortly after this he was asked to conduct the Hillsborough Inquiry following the tragic deaths of 93 Liverpool Football Club supporters at the home of Sheffield Wednesday in 1989. His 'Taylor Report' led to the implementation of all seater stadiums for elite level sport across Britain.

He took over as Lord Chief Justice in 1992. Quite different from his predecessors he took part in BBC TV's 'Any Questions,' and BBC Radio's 'Desert Island Discs.' I would add a personal note here, in that as I was practising as a solicitor during his time at the Bar and I had the pleasure of instructing him on several occasions. He was very refreshing. Down to earth, and his clients were immediately at ease with him just as he was thorough in his approach to preparation. When I was sworn in by him at the Royal Courts of Justice as a recorder, he gave me a 'big wink.' I was at a tribute dinner at the Middle Temple in 1996 and as part of the evening's proceedings he played a magnificent sonata on the grand piano. It gained a standing ovation. As we drove home I switched on the news, and it was announced that he had decided to step down due to serious illness. Being the man he was, there had been no mention of this at the dinner, he clearly had not in any way wished to detract from the event. His memorial service, held at St Paul's Cathedral is described in *Chapter 1*. Taylor's daughter, Deborah, has followed him to the Bar and bench and is currently the well-liked resident judge at Southwark Crown Court.

Lord Harry Woolf (1933–)

Born in 1933 in Newcastle-upon-Tyne (as was Lord Peter Taylor (above)), Harry Kenneth Woolf spent his formative years in that city. His grandparents were of Russian Jewish and Polish origins. His father started out as a fine arts dealer, but progressed to the building trade, and Woolf was five years-of-age when the family moved to Glasgow. He attended Glasgow Academy and Fettes College, Edinburgh. Despite a stutter, he yearned for the Bar and overcame this disability through sheer force and determination. Although offered a place at Cambridge University he chose London University.

Once called to the Bar he began on the Oxford Circuit and was chosen as a junior counsel to the Treasury, and subsequently in 1974 appointed to the High Court bench; then in 1986 to the Court of Appeal. In 1990, he conducted the Woolf Inquiry and wrote (with Judge Stephen Tumim) a devastating report following the Strangeways (HM Prison Manchester) and other prison disturbances of 1990, in which he recommended major reforms concerning decency, justice and conditions less likely to cause resentment among inmates.

In 1992 he was granted a life peerage as Baron Woolf, upon becoming a Lord of Appeal, and four years later, in 1996, was appointed Master of the Rolls. Then in 2000 he was appointed Lord Chief Justice. In this capacity he was very much 'hands on,' and chose from time-to-time to see what was happening on the street. He would do something rarely done by his predecessors, he would go out of London 'on circuit' and not necessarily to the most highly populated Crown Court hubs, and not on a 'commanding officer's inspection' basis, but to sit in one of the courts, and do a normal day's judicial work. As an example, he indicated a wish to visit Harrow Crown Court at the time I was based there. Harrow was a well-constructed modern courthouse, built in 1990. The courtrooms, users and judges' facilities are excellent, and I was fortunate to have what had been described as 'the most pleasant judges' chambers in London.' They had a panoramic view stretching from Harrow-on-the-Hill (with the School Spire on the right) sweeping across London to the City and the NatWest Tower. I volunteered to vacate my room, having known Woolf through meetings at the school our sons both attended in Bristol. The following day I found that he had left a gracious note of thanks on my desk, agreeing with the reputation my chambers enjoyed.

Harry Woolf argued strongly for the creation of a Supreme Court; and retired in 2005. He was appointed a judge of the Court of Final Appeal in Hong Kong until 2012. His other responsibilities include or have included: Chancellor of the Open University of Israel; chair of the Institute of Advanced Legal Studies; chair of the Council of University College and Professor of Law. In 2018, he became Head of Justice at the Astana Financial Centre Court in Kazakhstan.

Lord Harry Woolf 'man of the people' who was a much-admired hands on Lord Chief Justice (and before that Master of the Rolls). His landmark report on the Strangeways Prison (Manchester) riots of 1990 transformed the treatment of prisoners concerning fairness, decency and human rights.

Lord Chancellor

The role of Lord Chancellor—that theoretically outranks that of Prime Minister—is nowadays combined with that of Justice Secretary. Until 2008, the occupant of this office also presided over the House of Lords, was Head of the Judiciary (see now Lord Chief Justice above) and presiding judge of the Chancery Division of the High Court. The title 'Lord Chancellor' has been retained for ceremonial and other purposes, but the role is inescapably a political one. So, I have dealt with it in the context of those chapters covering the achievements of Jewish lawyers who sought or progressed to it. See:

- Whether a Jew might become Lord Chancellor: *Chapter 5*.
- Farrer Herschell described as 'barely Jewish': *Chapter 9*.
- Sir Rufus Isaacs who received 'a Passover': *Chapter 9*.
- Lord Victor Mishcon, Shadow Lord Chancellor: *Chapter 14*.
- Dominic Raab who was appointed Lord Chancellor and Secretary of State for Justice as this book was going to press: *Chapter 1*.

Master of the Rolls

This ancient judicial office originated in the safe-keeping of public documents such as charters, patents and reports of court rulings, at one time using parchment rolls. The occupant is still chair of the Advisory Council on Public Records and of the Royal Commission on Historical Manuscripts.

The Master of the Rolls is automatically a judge of the Court of Appeal and the President of its Civil Division. He or she (so far all men) is responsible for the deployment and organization of the work of the judges of the division as well as presiding in court; and normally sits with two Lords Justices of Appeal and there is occasionally an additional member such as a retired Lord Justice.

The more complex civil cases traditionally come before the Master of the Rolls and leading judgements occur in this way, including from Jewish occupants of the office. It is possible—as with Lord David Neuberger and Lord Harry Woolf already mentioned above—that in addition to those listed below other Jewish lawyers may have been Master of the Rolls during their overall career path.

Lord John Dyson (1943–)

Born in 1943 and of Eastern European heritage, John Anthony Dyson's mother was Bulgarian and his father of Lithuanian origin. He was born in Leeds, educated at Leeds Grammar School, and like Peter Taylor (above) studied piano with Dame Fanny Waterman. He then went to Wadham College, Oxford University and was called to the Bar in 1968, becoming Queen's Counsel in 1982. He was Head of Chambers at 39 Essex Court. He was appointed to the High Court in 1993, and in 1998 President of the Technology and Construction Court.

In 2001, John Dyson was advanced to the Court of Appeal and in 2010 to the Supreme Court. When that court indicated that its members were entitled to the courtesy title 'Lord' he became Lord Dyson. He was then made Master of the Rolls from 2012 to 2016 when he was replaced by Terence Etherton (below). He is an honorary fellow of Wadham College and of the Hebrew University, Jerusalem, as well as a visiting Professor at Queen Mary University of London, and University College London, and works as an arbitrator. In 2021 he prepared a report in a commendably short space of time on the Princess Diana interview by Martin Bashir shown on BBC 1 in 1995.[4]

Lord Terence Etherton (1951–)

Terence Etherton was educated Holmwood House School and St Paul's School and studied Law at Corpus Christi College, Cambridge University. He was selected as a member of the British Fencing Team for the 1980 Olympics in Russia but boycotted these in protest at the Soviet invasion of Afghanistan. He was called to the Bar in 1974 and made Queen's Counsel in 1990, then advanced to the High Court in the Chancery Division in 2006. He was appointed to chair the Law Commission and promoted to the Court of Appeal, and in 2013 to be Chancellor of the High Court, before in 2016 being made Master of the Rolls. He was the first openly homosexual person so appointed. After entering a civil partnership in 2006, he later converted this to marriage at the West London Synagogue, where he held office as warden. He is visiting professor at various universities and received a life peerage as Baron Etherton in 2020.

---

4. See: 'Martin Bashir: Inquiry criticises BBC over "deceitful" Diana interview': www.bbc.co.uk/news/uk-57189371 —BBC News (Accessed 1 August 2021).

Sir Geoffrey Voss (1955–)

Educated at University College School Hampstead and Cambridge University, Geoffrey Voss was called to the Bar in 1977 and became Queen's Counsel in 1993, then was appointed a High Court judge in the Chancery Division in 2009. He was appointed to the Court of Appeal in 2013, and as Chancellor of the High Court in 2016. He was appointed Master of the Rolls in January 2021, having in the past also sat in the Courts of Appeal of Jersey and Guernsey, and the Cayman Islands.

Snapshots of Some Other Jewish Judges and Barristers

There have been many Jewish circuit judges and district judges. Together with Crown Court recorders (and at one time assistant recorders) they will have been called upon to take the oath and the original pre-1858–1868 constraints would have applied to them just as to those of higher status. In the short outlines below, some are described as 'resident judges.' This means the judge appointed at a local courts centre to be the regular supervisor, head administrator and ultimate arbiter on matters such as which judge tries a given case (called 'allocation'). But all judges are independent in matters judicial. Also listed in order of their year of birth are some notable Jewish barristers and their specialities.

Judge Myrella Cohen (1927–2002)

Born in Manchester into an orthodox Jewish family, Myrella Cohen was educated at Manchester Grammar School, Colwyn Bay Grammar School and Manchester University. She was called to the Bar and was the fifth woman to be appointed Queen's Counsel, and in 1971 one of youngest judges and women judges. She sat at the Old Bailey and was then appointed resident judge at the newly opened Harrow Crown Court. She married Lieutenant Colonel Mordaunt Cohen (a pure coincidence of names), a decorated Burma veteran. Myrella Cohen was active in the Jewish community and known especially for 'reversing'—in the English courts and through parliamentary campaigns leading to the Divorce (Religious Marriages) Act 2002—Jewish matrimonial laws which disadvantaged women.

Judicial Appointments High and Low

Judge Gerald Butler (1930–2010)

Born in Hackney, London into a Jewish family, Gerald Butler attended Ilford County High School, then the London School of Economics, and later Oxford University. Called to the Bar in 1955 (and a second lieutenant in the Royal Army Signals Corp) he was made Queen's Counsel in 1975, circuit judge in 1982, and resident judge at Southwark Crown Court in 1984. He was strict in his directives to the several judges and recorders, including myself, who sat at Southwark. One was that on no account whatsoever was a case to be adjourned on the application of a defendant: 'Too many cases are being delayed at their whim,' he decreed. I committed the unthinkable, and one day agreed to a case being adjourned. The following morning, Butler was standing at the door. It looked as though he was waiting for me to come in, for his window overlooked the judges' car park. I was greeted with,

'Barry, how did you come to adjourn Jimmy Robinson, despite my instructions?'

'I had to,' I said.

'What do you mean you had to … you knew my instructions?'

'Yes,' I replied, 'but word was that he had died the previous night and I had to put it off to get proof.'

Happily, he agreed that I had not blotted my judicial copy book!

Judge Brian Walsh (1935–2000)

Born in India, to Jewish parents, where his father, a solicitor, was working, Brian Walsh attended Leeds Grammar School, then Cambridge University. He completed his National Service in the Royal Air Force, was called to the Bar, and made Queen's Counsel in 1977. He had a largely criminal practice and was an accomplished after-dinner speaker. He was made Recorder of Leeds in 1996 and was chair of Yorkshire Cricket Club.

Judge Peter Fingret (1935–)

Born to Jewish parents in Leeds, Peter Fingret was educated at Leeds Modern School and Leeds University (where he was President of the Students Union). He qualified as a solicitor in 1960, was made a stipendiary magistrate (district judge) in 1982, circuit judge in 1992 and resident judge at Snaresbrook Crown Court.

Judge Dennis Levy (1936–2020)

Born into a Jewish family in London, Dennis Levy was educated at Clifton College, Bristol and Cambridge University. He was called to the Bar in 1960, and to those of Hong Kong, the Turks and Caicos Islands, and Granada. He was made Queen's Counsel in 1982, and a circuit judge in 1991.

Judge Valerie Pearlman (1936–)

Valerie Pearlman was born into a Jewish family, educated at Wycombe Abbey, High Wycombe and called to the Bar in 1958. She was appointed a circuit judge in 1985, and senior circuit judge in 2003 in the Principal Registry of the Family Division. She was awarded the CBE in 2008. She once received much praise for having started a lengthy, complex fraud trial when she then had an accident and was hospitalised, but with the aid of video links continued the trial from her hospital bed, saving considerable costs had the matter needed to be re-tried.

Eleanor Platt (1936–)

Born in Hove, Sussex into a Jewish family, Eleanor Platt was educated at Hove County School, University College London and called to the Bar in 1960, being made Queen's Counsel in 1982. She was at one time Head of specialist Family Law chambers and later a deputy High Court judge in the Family Division. She took part in the infamous 1988 Cleveland Inquiry into Child Abuse chaired by Baroness Butler-Sloss, advised on statutes relating to surrogacy, and was Vice-president of the Board of Deputies of British Jews. She has attended the New London Synagogue in Abbey Road, North-West London.

Judge Geoffrey Rivlin (1940–)

Born in Leeds into a Jewish family, Geoffrey Rivlin was educated at Bootham School in York (a Quaker school), Leeds University and called to the Bar in 1963, being made Queen's Council in 1979. He was quite young looking but this was deceptive for he was mature in his approach. Described as a brilliant advocate, and very painstaking on the particulars of fraud matters, he was made a circuit judge in 1989. He was appointed honorary Recorder of Westminster in 2008. After retirement from the bench, he was made an adviser to the Head of the Serious Fraud Office in 2012.

Judge Roger Sanders (1940–)

Born into a Jewish family, Roger Sanders attended Highgate School, and was called to the Bar in 1965. He was a Metropolitan stipendiary magistrate (district judge) from 1980–87, made a recorder in 1986, and a circuit judge in 1987. He became resident judge at Harrow Crown Court (1999–2005) (where I also sat). He was highly respected there, appreciated by his fellow judges and court staff alike. One day counsel, a Miss Dee Connelly, asked to see him in chambers (naturally with opposing counsel present as well). He granted her application. Some months later she granted his, and they have been married for over 20 years.

Michael Beloff (1942–)

The son of Lord Max Beloff (Baron Beloff (1913–1999)) the historian, Michael Beloff was educated at the Dragon School in Oxford, Eton College, and Oxford University where he was President of the Oxford Union. He was called to the Bar, made Queen's Counsel, and was President of Trinity College, Oxford University. He sat in the Jersey and Guernsey Courts of Appeal and the Court of Arbitration for Sport established in 1984 to settle sporting disputes via Arbitration rather than expensive litigation in the courts proper.

Judge Geoffrey Kamil (1942–)

Born to Jewish parents in Leeds, Geoffrey H Kamil was educated at Leeds Grammar School and Leeds University. He was admitted a solicitor, made stipendiary magistrate (district judge) in the West Midlands in 1987, then a circuit judge in 1993 on the North-Eastern circuit sitting in Bradford and elsewhere. A minorities liaison judge and concerned with diversity and the community, in 2007 he was described by *The Times* as 'leading the push by judges to forge links with their local communities—and encourage them to join the justice system—"This is a time of great change in the attitude of the ethnic minority population towards the legal system"' (26 June 2007). He was made a CBE in 2008 and sits on the Parole Board.

Judge Ronald Moss (1942–)

Ronald Moss was born into a Jewish family and educated at Hendon Grammar School and Nottingham University. He was admitted a solicitor in 1968, became a Metropolitan stipendiary magistrate (now district judge) in 1984, a circuit judge in 1993, resident judge at Luton Crown Court, then Harrow Crown Court. He has great affection for Watford Football Club, with a corresponding sign in his chambers, and he was said to wear a jersey with 'Watford' on it under his robes.

Judge Dawn Freeman (1942–)

Born in Westcliff-on-Sea into a Jewish family, Dawn Freeman was educated at Westcliff High School for Girls, University College London, and called to the Bar in 1966. She was made a Metropolitan stipendiary magistrate (district judge) in 1980, and became a circuit judge in 1991. Dawn Freeman was chair if the Jewish Marriage Council and (together with Judge Myrella Cohen above) advised on improvements to the law on Jewish divorce.

Baroness Ruth Deech (1943–)

Ruth Deech is chair of the Bar Standards Board. Born into to Jewish family, she was educated at Christ's Hospital School Hertford, then Oxford University. Called to the Bar in 1967, she was made an honorary Queen's Counsel in 2013. The Principal of St Anne's College, Oxford University, she was made a Dame of the British Empire (DBE) and elevated to the peerage as Baroness Deech in 2003.

Sir Alan Moses (1945–)

Born to Jewish parents, Alan Moses was educated at Bryanston School, Dorset, then Oxford University, and called to the Bar in 1968. He worked as junior counsel to the Crown and was made Queen's Counsel in 1990. He was raised to the High Court in 1996, then to be a Lord Justice of Appeal in the Court of Appeal in 2005. He is a member of the *Union Socialista La Sierra*.

David Goldberg (1947–)

Born in Plymouth (where his family had lived for several generations) into an orthodox Jewish family, David Goldberg was educated at Plymouth College, the London School of Economic, called to the Bar in 1971, and made Queen's Counsel in 1987. He became one of the great experts on Revenue Law; and has written or co-written several books on the subject, including his early works *Introduction to Company Law* (1971; 4th edition, 1987); and as co-author *The*

Law of Partnership Taxation (1976; 2nd edition 1979). He was extremely generous in that he hosted many religious services for colleagues and others.

Jonathan Goldberg (1947–)

The son of Rabbi P Selwyn Goldberg, Jonathan Goldberg attended Manchester Grammar School and Cambridge University. He was called to the Bar in 1971, became a member of the New York State Bar in 1985, and was made Queen's Counsel in 1989. He has appeared in over 100 murder trials, and one of his notable successes was the 'Marine A' appeal[5] which made him popular with the British Army. An online *Guardian* report[6] spoke of Goldberg being played by actor Al Pacino in a proposed feature film.

Goldberg is President of the International Association of Jewish Lawyers, has his own chambers and has represented many orthodox Jewish clients. Highly thought of by the *Charedi community* (in Jewish *Haredi*), characterised by a strict adherence to Jewish law and traditions as opposed to modern approaches to Judaism, he has been referred to as the 'Defender of the Faith.'

Hilary Heilbron (1949–)

Hilary Heilbron holds an MA from Oxford University and is the daughter of Dame Rose Heilbron (*Chapter 10*). She is a barrister at Brick Court Chambers, with extensive experience of International Arbitration and Commercial Litigation. Following in her mother's footsteps, she was called to the Bar in 1971, became a QC in 1987, and sat as a deputy High Court judge. She is now a mediator and international arbitrator whose trajectory includes her many published legal and historical articles, the book *Rose QC* (about her mother: see *Selected Bibliography*), chairing the City Disputes Panel (2006-07), and being a member of international task forces, the Bar of New South Wales, a bencher of Gray's Inn and being chosen by the Legal 500 (2020) which described her as belonging to the A-starred list of arbitrators.

---

5. In which the British marine was freed having served three-and-a-half years of a life sentence for 'murdering' a wounded Taliban fighter, replaced by manslaughter due to diminished responsibility.
6. 28 April 2017.

Philip Kremmen (1949–)

Called to the Bar in 1975, Philip Kremen became a specialist in Chancery Law, Property, Landlord and Tenant, Trusts and International Law. He did not take silk as his assistance was more readily available to solicitors and clients as a 'senior junior.' In this respect he followed a course of several other counsel in strong demand as juniors, such as Alter Hurwitz (see *Chapter 13*).

Henry Grunwald (1949–)

Born into a Jewish family in London, Henry Grunwald was educated at the City of London School, University College London, called to the Bar in 1972, and made Queen's Counsel in 1999, specialising in Criminal Law. He is a Fellow of University College London, President of the Board of Deputies of British Jews (2003–2009), President of World Jewish Relief, and chair of the National Holocaust Centre and Museum, *Beth Shalom* ('House of Peace) in Nottinghamshire which opened in 1995. A Crown Court recorder, he was awarded the OBE in 2009 for services to the Jewish community and inter-faith relations.

Judge William Bartfield (1949–)

Educated at Leeds Grammar School and Queen Mary College, William Bartfield was called to the Bar in 1971 and made a circuit judge in 1996.

Judge Joanna Greenberg (1950–)

Educated at Brondesbury and King's College London, Joanna Greenberg was called to the Bar in 1972 and made Queen's Counsel in 1994. Approved as an International Court counsel she was made chair of the Police Appeals Tribunal in 1999.

Judge Deborah Taylor[7]

Deborah Taylor is the daughter of Lord Chief Justice Peter Taylor (see earlier in this chapter). She became the resident judge at Southwark Crown Court, and is a deputy High Court judge, sitting in the Administrative Court, and was also a Judicial Appointments Commissioner.

---

7. In just a very few instances I have been unable to trace individuals' dates. Where I do give them I have relied on those in the public domain.

Jonathan Caplan (1951–)

Born into Jewish family London, Jonathan Caplan was educated at St Paul's School and then Cambridge University. He was called to the Bar in 1973, made Queen's Counsel in 1991. He sits as a Crown Court recorder.

Stuart Isaacs (1952–)

Born into Jewish family, Stuart Isaacs went to Haberdashers' Aske's Boys' School and Cambridge Universiy where he secured a double first, After his Master of European Law in Brussels he was called to the Bar in 1975 and made Queen's Counsel in 1991. He has been called to the Bar in New York, Singapore and several Caribbean jursidictions and became a deputy High Court judge in 2005.

Professor David Graham

Born of Jewish parents in Leeds and educated at Leeds Grammar School and Oxford University, David Graham was called to the Bar and became a Queen's Counsel. For many years an acknowledged expert on bankruptcy and Insolvency, some people considered him a little eccentric in that he would prefer to stand and walk around during a consultation. I knew him and was grateful to him for his assistance, and he was and is a brilliant lawyer.

Judge Martin Zeidman (1952–)

Born in Cardiff to Jewish parents, Martin Zeidman studied at the University of London, was called to the Bar in 1974, made Queen's Counsel in 1998, and a circuit judge in 2001, becoming resident judge at Snaresbrook Crown Court.

He is chair of the Jewish Marriage Council, and son-in-law of Judge Aaron Owen (see *Chapter 10*). He has written various publications on Land Law.

Judge Wendy Rose Joseph (1952–)

Educated at Cathays High School Cardiff, Wentbridge, California, and New Hall, Cambridge University, Wendy Joseph was called to the Bar in 1975, made Queen's Counsel in 1998, a circuit judge in 2007, and progressed to become resident judge at the Central Criminal Court (Old Bailey) in 2012.

Judge Alan Conrad (1953–)

Alan Conrad was born into a Jewish Family in Manchester and educated at Bury Grammar School, Greater Manchester and Oxford University. He was called to the Bar in 1976, made a QC in 1999, and a circuit judge in 2013. He was resident judge at Liverpool Crown Court, and then Manchester Crown Court.

Judge Jeremy Gold (1955–)

Jeremy Gold was educated at Brighton and Hove Grammar School and the University of Kent. He was called to the Bar in 1977, made Queen's Counsel in 2003, specialising chiefly in Criminal Law, and was appointed circuit judge in 2009.

Judge Alan Greenwood

Alan Eliezer Greenwood was a circuit judge assigned to the South Eastern Circuit. He was the resident judge at Harrow Crown Court.

Judge David Aaronberg (1958–)

David Aaronberg attended Merchant Taylors' School and the former Polytechnic of Central London before being called to the Bar in 1981. Made Queen's Counsel in 2010, he practised in Regulatory Law and Criminal Law.

Judge Lawrence Cohen (1958–)

Lawrence Cohen took his degree at Birmingham University before being called to the Bar in 1974. Made Queen's Counsel in 1993, he specialised in Chancery work and fraud, He was also called to the Bar of the Eastern Caribbean.

Judge Jonathan Rose (1958–)

Born into a Jewish family Leeds, Jonathan Rose was educated at Talbot Road School and Roundhay School in Leeds, Preston Polytechnic and Keeble College, Oxford University. He was called to the Bar in 1983 and made a circuit judge in 2008. He is the author of *Innocents: How Justice Failed Stefan Kiszko and Lesley Molseed* (1997) (with Steve Panter): see *Selected Bibliography*.

Judge Simon Monty (1959–)

Born into a Jewish family in Manchester, Simon Monty was educated at Alleyn's School, Dulwich, Manchester University and called to the Bar in 1982. He was made Queen's Counsel in 2003, is a professional negligence specialist, and was made a circuit judge in 2018. He also sits as a deputy High Court judge.

Jeremy Dein (1960–)

Jeremy Dein was born in Bow, raised in Redbridge, and graduated at Queen Mary College, University of London. He was called to the Bar in 1982 and made a QC 2003. A formidable Criminal Law silk, Joint Head of Chambers, and a former Director of Education for the Criminal Bar Association (who has represented high profile clients as well as those charged with the most serious offences), he is a Crown Court recorder. He also appears regularly on television including in the series 'Murder Mystery and My Family: Case Closed?' (BBC 1) (with Sasha Wass QC[8]) in which they re-examine and 'argue out' notable criminal cases.

Jonathan Arkush

Jonathan Arkush studied Jurisprudence at Mansfield College, Oxford University and was called to the Bar in 1977. He is a Deputy Chancery Master and a mediator. He was President of the Board of Deputies of British Jews (2015–2018). A bencher of Middle Temple, Jonathan Arkush is a member of the Chancery Bar Association, the Association of Contentious Trust and Probate Specialists (ACTAPS) and gives lectures and holds seminars for other professionals.

Simon Myerson (1962–)

The son of Judge Arthur Myerson (see Alter Hurwitz in *Chapter 13*) and Shirley Myerson an international raconteuse, Simon Myerson was educated Carmel College, Wallingford and Cambridge University. He was called to the Bar in 1986 and made a Queen's Counsel in 2001 and operates a considerable criminal and civil practice. A highly respected blogger, he sits as a Crown Court recorder.

---

8. Details of Sasha Wass' accomplishments and achievements can be viewed at www.6kbw.com/people/barristers/sasha-wass-qc

Dinah Rose (1965–)

Born in London into a Jewish family, Dinah Gwen Lison Rose was educated in the City of London School for Girls, at Oxford University, and City, London University. She was called to the Bar in 1989, made Queen's Counsel in 2006, and in 2020 President of Magdalen College, Oxford University. She has appeared in many high-profile cases including that of the Wikileaks founder and Ecuadorian Embassy asylum seeker from USA prosecutors Julian Assange, and been particularly involved in Human Rights cases, as well as acting for governments. In 2009 she was named 'Barrister of the Year' by *The Lawyer* newspaper. Rose investigated the BBC abuse scandal from 2012 following the Jimmy Savile disclosures when she and her team discovered numerous cases of alleged sexual harassment and bullying within that organization which had not been properly investigated by management. In 2016, Dinah Rose was appointed a deputy High Court judge.

Phillipe Sands (1960–)

Educated at University College London (where he is a Professor of Law), Cambridge University and Harvard University, USA, Phillipe Sands was called to the Bar in 1985 and made Queen's Council in 2003. He is a specialist in International Law and author of several books including the Baillie Gifford Prize-winning *East West Street*, *Lawless World: Making and Breaking Global Rules* and *The Ratline*: see Selected Bibliography.

Daniel Greenberg (1965–)

Educated at Trinity College, Cambridge, Daniel Greenberg became a Parliamentary Counsel, served in the former Lord Chancellor's Department (now Ministry of Justice), and as Speaker's Counsel. The editor of various books on English Law, he has been a teacher of Jewish Law. He was made a Companion of the Order of Bath (CB) in 2021.

Sam Grodzinski (1968–)

Sam Grodzinski attended University College School Hampstead, Oxford University and was admitted a solicitor in 1993 working at Freshfields, then was called to the Bar in 1996. He became Queen's Counsel in 2011 specialising in Public Law, Regulatory Law and Tax Law. A member of Blackstone Chambers he is regularly instructed by top City solicitors and accountants. He has appeared in all levels of court often in high profile cases in England and internationally. Named Legal 500 'Tax Silk of the Year' in 2020 (and shortlisted for comparable awards) he is also a Deputy High Court judge.

Ami Feder
Ami Feder was called to the English Bar in 1965 and to the Israeli Bar in 1985. She has chambers in both countries, and thus specialises not only in UK Criminal Law (amongst other things) but also in Israeli Law.

Judge Samantha Cohen (1970–)
Samantha Cohen was called to the Bar in 1995 before being made a circuit judge.

Dame Norma Ellenbogen (1970–)
Born in Liverpool to Jewish parents, Norma Ellenbogen's father was a medical consultant. Her uncle was Sir Harry Ognall (*Chapter 10*). She was educated at the King David High School, Oxford, called to the Bar in 1992, and specialises in employment, and professional negligence. She is co-author of *Butterworth's Employment Law* (Lexis Nexis-Butterworths, Edn.28, 2020) and was appointed as a High Court judge in 2021.

Robert Rinder (1978–)
Robert Michael Rinder was born into a Jewish family in Southgate, North London and educated at Queen Elizabeth's School, Barnet and Manchester University, where he gained a first-class degree. He was called to the Bar in 2001, practising at 2 Hare Court, mainly in Criminal Law (including bribery, corruption, fraud, money laundering and homicide). From the mid-2000s, having also been a student of the National Youth Theatre, he transitioned to working in media and entertainment, becoming a well-known television personality, journalist, writer and star of the reality series 'Judge Rinder' (an enhanced variant of the USA's 'Judge Judy' set in a courtroom). He has also appeared in and often written, e.g. 'The Rob Rinder Verdict,' 'Judge Rinder's Crime Stories,' 'Judge Rinder's Crown Court' and 'Raising the Bar' (the last on radio). His many other TV credits include 'Strictly Come Dancing' (as a contestant), 'Celebrity Gogglebox' and 'Who Do You Think You Are?' in which

he traced his Jewish roots including family tragedy and learning more about his grandfather, Morris Malenicky, who survived Schlieben and Bergen-Belsen concentration camps (visiting the remnants of the latter on camera). He was awarded an MBE in 2021 for services to Holocaust education and awareness. He is the author if *Rinder's Rules* (see *Selected Bibliography*).

As with the solicitors I write about in *Chapter 14*, I cannot hope to list every Jewish judge and barrister individually. Here is a short note of some further Queen's Counsel, each specialising in Criminal Law at the highest level, and achieving considerable success, who appeared before me as advocates when I sat on the bench. I was impressed by their professionally robust approach, courtesy, knowledge and endeavours for their clients. I recall Howard Godfrey (1946–) who attended the William Ellis School and the London School or Economics. Called to the Bar in 1970 he became a QC in 1991, and was also called to the Bar of the Turks and Caicos Islands, and later made a Crown Court recorder. David Nathan (1948–) went to City of London School and Manchester University, being called in 1971, and made a QC in 2002. Nigel Lambert (1949–) attended Cokethorpe School and the College of Law, was called in 1974, made a QC in 1999, and also appointed as a recorder. Joel Bennathan (1961–) went to Bristol Grammar, School and Queen Mary College, University of London, was called in 1985, made QC in 2006 and was again a recorder. Last but not least. Malcolm Wolkind was called in 1976 and became a QC in 1999. I remember them well.

CHAPTER 12

Jewish Lawyers in Politics

It was the determination of Jewish lawyers with political interests and would-be Jewish members of Parliament, lawyers or not, that brought about emancipation and the capacity for fully-fledged participation as politicians, lawyers and judges in England and Wales as described in earlier chapters. But who were these people?

Early Notable Lawyers in Politics

Lord Leslie Hore-Belisha (1893–1957)

Leslie Hore-Belisha was born in Hampstead into the Jewish family of an insurance company manager called Belisha who was the son of a *Sephardic* Moroccan. His father died when he was a baby and his mother remarried Sir Charles Hoare, a senior civil servant. He was educated at Clifton College Bristol in its Jewish Polack's House[1] then in Paris and Heidelberg. He served in World War I as a major then went up to Oxford and was later called to the Bar. He entered Parliament in 1923 and was appointed junior minister at the Board of Trade. He was described as energetic but still an 'outsider.' As Transport Minister he did an extremely visible job and gave part of his name to Belisha beacons. Then as Secretary of State for War he disagreed with the generals, and his attitude to Nazi Germany caused disaffection for him amongst appeasers of Adolf Hitler. He did much to enhance the Territorial Army, was moved from the War Office,

---

1. Pollack's House is described in *Chapter 10* under the heading Judge Neville Laski.

and offered the Board of Trade, but declined. There was much talk of anti-Semitism as the cause of his downfall. He was elevated to House of Lords in 1954.

Samuel Silkin (1918-1988)

Samuel ('Sam') Charles Silkin, later Baron Silkin of Dulwich, was a Labour party politician and county cricketer for Glamorgan and Cambridge University. The second son of Baron Lewis Silkin who was a noted solicitor (*Chapter 14*), he was a minister in Prime Minister Clement Attlee's Cabinet from 1945 to 1950 and served as Attorney-General. His younger brother, John (below), was also an MP and Cabinet minister. Sam Silkin was educated at Dulwich College and Trinity Hall, Cambridge. He was called to the Bar in 1941 and made Queen's Counsel in 1963. In March 1946, Silkin presided over (as a lieutenant colonel) the so-called 'Double Tenth War Crimes Trials' in Singapore when Japanese guards were accused of torturing internees, resulting in 15 deaths; eight defendants being sentenced to hang, others given long terms of imprisonment, and seven acquitted. A member of the Privy Council, he chaired the Society of Labour Lawyers and served on Camberwell Borough Council from 1953 until 1959.

John Ernest Silkin (1923-1987)

Third son of the solicitor Baron Lewis Silkin (*Chapter 14*) and a younger brother of Baron Samuel Silkin (above), John Silkin was educated at Dulwich College, the University of Wales and Trinity Hall, Cambridge University. He served in the Royal Naval Volunteer Reserve (1942–1946), in the East Indies, and with the Eastern Fleet and Pacific Fleet. He was admitted as a solicitor in 1950 and worked in his father's law practice in London. After several failed attempts, his persistence led to him becoming Member of Parliament for Deptford in 1963; and he occupied several (non-legal) Cabinet and shadow cabinet posts; in 1980 losing in the Labour party leadership election.

Lord Greville Janner (1928-2015)

Born in Cardiff of Jewish parents of Lithuanian extraction, Lord Barnett Janner (*Chapter 14*), Greville's father, was a notable solicitor (and Ruth, Lady Kenwood, his sister also became such) but this 'family tradition' was all part of Greville Janner becoming a lawyer of whatever kind. Evacuated initially to

Canada, then attending St Paul's School, London at age of 18 he served in the Army and after demobilisation went to Cambridge University. He was called to the Bar in 1954 and made Queen's Counsel in 1971. He succeeded his father in Parliament in the seat for Leicester, was President of the Board of Deputies of British Jews, and co-founded the Holocaust Education Trust.[2] After his House of Commons career, he was made the life peer Baron Janner of Braunstone in 1947. One daughter is Rabbi Layra Janner-Klausner, and his son, Daniel is a QC specialising in Criminal Law.

The onset of Alzheimers prevented him properly responding to certain historical allegations but a posthumous investigation by a High Court judge strongly criticised investigating bodies whose methods precluded a fair and proper determination of what were later shown to be false claims, for which an accuser was imprisoned for 18 years.[3] In 2019, Daniel Janner founded Falsely Accused Individuals For Reform (FAIR).

Lord Joel Joffe (1932-2017)

Joel Goodman Joffe, later to become the Labour peer Baron Joffe of Liddington CBE, was a South African-born solicitor from a Jewish family. 'Exiled' to England in 1965, as a UK businessman he co-founded Hambro Life Assurance (with Sir Mark Weinberg and Sir Sydney Lipworth (*Chapter 10*)), later Allied Dunbar and now Zurich Insurance. In his earlier incarnation as a Human Rights practitioner in the early-1960s Joffe instructed counsel for the leadership of the African National Congress (ANC) in South Africa's internationally observed 'Rivonia Sabotage/Treason Trial' (1963–1964) (as to which one correspondent said they 'ran rings round the prosecution' and the centrally accused Nelson Mandela in his book *The Long Road to Freedom* wrote that Joffe was 'the general behind the scenes'). In the House of Lords Joffe repeatedly sought to promote a private member's Bill on Assisted Dying for the Terminally Ill which after gaining considerable support was 'shelved' in 2006. His legacy also includes being a philanthropist, champion of the voluntary sector, author (see *Selected Bibliography*), patron of Humanist UK (he had become a 'Jewish

---

2. See www.het.org.uk
3. Another independent inquiry was due to report at the time of going to press.

aetheist'), chair of Oxfam (twice between 1980 and 2001) and founder of the Joffe Charitable Trust.[4]

Lord Leon Brittan (1939–2015)

Born in London, Leon Brittan's father was a doctor and his family from Lithuania. Educated at Haberdashers' Aske's Boys School and Cambridge University, he was President of the Cambridge Union, before attending Yale University, USA. Malcolm Rifkind (see below) was a cousin. Brittan was first elected to Parliament 1974 and became a Queen's Counsel in 1978. In 1981 he became Minister of State at the Home Office, then Chief Secretary to the Treasury (as the youngest member of the Cabinet); was appointed Home Secretary in 1983; and Secretary of State for Trade and Industry in 1985, from which he resigned in 1986 over the 'Westland Affair' being at odds with Michael Heseltine, the prime mover in the leaking of a letter. Some allegations of anti-Semitism are also believed to have brought about this resignation.

In 1989 Leon Brittan was made European Commissioner, but he left that role in 1999. He was given a life peerage in 2000. In 2010 he was appointed Trade Adviser to the Government. He died in 2015 after a long illness. His final years were darkened by a number of bizarre accusations comparable to those against Lord Greville Janner above, that after Brittan's death were found to be false and unsubstantiated.

Lord Michael Howard (1941–)

Born in Swansea, Michael Howard's Jewish father was Rumanian. His mother originally from Europe was also Jewish. He took the eleven plus examination obtaining a place at Llanelli Grammar School, Wales then a scholarship to Cambridge University where he became President of the Cambridge Union. He was called to the Bar in 1964 undertaking Employment Law and Planning Law. He was made Queen's Counsel in 1982.

Howard entered Parliament in 1983 becoming Secretary of State for Trade in 1985, seeing in the technology 'Big Bang.' He then became variously Minister of State for Local Government, Housing, Employment, and the Environment, and in 1993 was appointed Home Secretary. There he became known for his

---

4. See https://joffetrust.org/joel-joffe/

attack on crime and 'prison works' mantra, clashing with penal reformers. He was criticised by the Master of Rolls for increasing the sentences of juveniles Robert Thompson and Jon Venables in the James Bulger Liverpool child murder case. Howard had many problems over prisons, and notoriously in 1997 the BBC TV's Jeremy Paxman asked him the same question 12 times on the 'Newsnight' programme without a direct response. The question concerned whether Howard had threatened to overrule the then Director-General of the Prison Service concerning whether a prison governor was to be removed from his post following the escape of three high security prisoners.

He attempted the Conservative Party leadership (at one stage with William Hague on what was described as a joint 'Golden Ticket'). He became Shadow Chancellor of the Exchequer, and in 2004 leader of the Opposition. But he failed in the 2005 general election so resigned (when David Cameron took over). In 2010 he became a life peer as Baron Howard of Lympne CH, PC. He is a practising Jew, and although a member of the Upper Berkeley Street Reform Synagogue (West London Synagogue), he has attended Western Marble Arch Synagogue in Great Cumberland Place to say memorial prayers, and has actually taken the service there more than once.

Sir Malcolm Rifkind (1946–)

Of a Jewish family, Malcolm Leslie Rifkind was born in Edinburgh, his grandparents having emigrated there from Lithuania. He is a first cousin of Leon Brittan (see above). He was educated at George Watson's College and Edinburgh University. Then he worked in Rhodesia from 1967–68 as a university lecturer. In 1970 he was called to the Scottish Bar, where he practised as an advocate and was appointed Queen's Counsel in 1985. He entered Parliament in 1974 and was soon appointed spokesman for Scottish Affairs, but he resigned in a tactical protest. He served for 18 continuous years (the longest since Viscount Palmerston (1784–1865)) under Margaret Thatcher, Prime Minister and her successor John Major. He was variously at Home Affairs, Europe, the Foreign Office, the Scottish Office, Transport and Defence, becoming Foreign Secretary in 1995, then losing but regaining his parliamentary seat in 1997 and 2001, respectively. He has been the chair of the Parliamentary Standards and Privileges Committee, the Intelligence and Security Committee and a Minister for International Trade. Hugo Rifkind, *The Times* columnist is his son.

Sir Ivan Lawrence (1936–)

Born into Jewish family of Russian Rumanian descent, Ivan Lawrence was educated at Brighton Grammar School and Oxford University, doing his National Service in the Royal Air Force. He was called to the Bar in 1962 and had a heavy criminal practice, being made Queen's Counsel in 1981, then a recorder of the Crown Court.

As a lawyer Lawrence defended in countless serious case including those of the Kray twins (gangland murders), serial killer Dennis Nilsen, the 'Babes in the Wood' murders by Russell Bishop and the Brink's-Mat gold bullion case. He was Conservative Member of Parliament for Burton-upon-Trent (1974–1997).

It was expected that Lawrence would become either Attorney-General or Solicitor-General in 1992, but instead he was appointed chair of the Home Affairs Select Committee (and awarded the knighthood which would have followed either of those legal appointments) serving in that role until 1997.

Lord Anthony Lester (1939–2020)

Born into a Jewish family Lester was educated at City of London School then Trinity College, Cambridge University and Harvard Law School, USA, being called to the Bar in 1963, and made Queen's Counsel in 1975. He was appointed a Crown Court recorder in 1987. A member of various Labour legal organizations, he was chair of the Runnymede Trust,[5] a charity which describes itself as the United Kingdom's foremost independent race equality think tank seeking to 'generate intelligence to challenge race inequality in Britain through research, network building, leading debate, and policy.' Lester was special adviser to Home Secretary Roy Jenkins and later to the Justice Secretary. He was raised to the peerage in 1993 as Baron Lester of Herne Hill.

Following historic allegations of sexual impropriety, a recommendation was made that he be suspended from the House of Lords but this was rejected following intervention by Lord David Pannick (see below) saying this was unfair. However, he resigned from the Lords in 2018, claiming he hadn't the strength or health to continue. He wrote several books including *Five Ideas to Fight For* (2016).

---

5. See www.runnymedetrust.org

Lord Alex Carlile (1948–)

Brought up in North Wales the son of Polish Jewish immigrants, Alex Carlile was educated at Epsom College and King's College London before being called to the Bar in 1970 and made Queen's Counsel in 1984. He entered Parliament as a Liberal Democrat in 1982 and received a life peerage in 1999. Carlile sat as a deputy High Court judge (2001–2011) and was an Independent Reviewer of Terrorism Legislation. He has fervently supported the provision of legal aid to those arrested and was President of the Howard League for Penal Reform.

Lord Peter Goldsmith (1950–)

Of Jewish descent, Goldsmith was born in Liverpool where he attended Quarry Bank School, then Cambridge University and University College London. He was called to the Bar in 1972 and made Queen's Counsel in 1987. Raised to the peerage by Labour in 1999, he became Attorney-General in 2001. He was the founder of the Bar's *Pro Bono* Unit (2003). The nature of his legal advice to Government on the invasion of Iraq and its legality saw him at the eye of the political storm and was a matter of controversy. The words of Lord Chief Justice Lord Bingham indicate the nature of certain feelings, when he said this advice contained 'No hard evidence that Iraq had defied UN resolutions in a manner justifying resort to force, and that the invasion [by the USA and UK] was a serious violation of the rule of law and International Law.' Upon leaving office, Goldsmith qualified as a solicitor and joined Debevoiuse and Plimpton as a full equity partner.

Lord David Pannick (1956–)

Although now a cross-bench peer, David Philip Pannick's place in the list of those involved in politics is merited I think by the sheer number of issues upon which his advice and assistance have been sought. He has been described as one of the finest brains in the law, of his time, and even prior to that.

Born in Islington, into a Jewish family, David Pannick attended Bancroft's School, Woodford Green, Hertford College, Oxford University and is a fellow of All Souls, Oxford University. Called to the Bar in 1979 he was junior counsel to the Crown, and made Queen's Counsel in 1992, later a Crown Court recorder and deputy High Court judge. He has appeared in many famous cases in this country and abroad including challenging Governments and authority and in a reputed 100 appeals in the House of Lords/Supreme Court, as well as writing books (including *Advocates* (1982); and *Judges* (1987): see *Selected Bibliography*) and is a regular contributor to *The Times*. He is an expert in Human Rights, Judicial Review and Sex Discrimination among other topics and, so far as his career is concerned, he can surely decide to do what he wants, when he wants. He was made a life peer in 2008 as Baron Pannick of Radlett: announced by the journalist Joshua Rosenberg with the memorable line: 'Popular Pannick picked as people's peer.'

Members of the Government at the Time of Writing

Attorney-General

The Rt Hon. Michael Ellis (1967–)
Michael Tyrone Ellis was born into a Jewish family in Northampton, and educated at Wellingborough School and Buckingham University where he became student editor of its *Denning Law Journal*. Ellis was called to the Bar in 1993 and practised in Criminal Law. Elected to Parliament in 2010 as MP for Northampton, his progress included being Minister for Transport, Parliamentary Under-Secretary for Digital Culture, Media and Sport, and Leader of the House of Commons. He was appointed Solicitor-General in 2019 and made Queen's Counsel in accordance with that office. In 2021, when Suella Braverman (whose husband is Jewish), the then Attorney-General, was designated 'Minister on Leave' (i.e. maternity leave), Ellis served as Attorney-General during her absence (becoming Paymaster-General in 2021 in a Government reshuffle that coincided with her return).

Solicitor-General

The Rt Hon. Lucy Frazer (1972–)
Born into a Jewish family in Leeds, Lucy Frazer's father is a solicitor, and her paternal grandmother one of first women barristers in Leicester. Her grandfather, Jewish immigrant Dr Hyman Frazer CBE was the Headmaster of Leicester's Gateway Grammar School. Educated at Leeds Girls' High School

and Newnham College, Cambridge University where she was President of the Cambridge Union, she was called to the Bar, and has a busy Commercial Law practice. She was made Queen's Counsel in 2012, entered Parliament as MP for South Cambridgeshire in 2015, was appointed Minister for Prisons and Parliamentary under Secretary for Justice in 2018, Solicitor-General in 2021 then Financial Secretary to the Treasury in a Government reshuffle later that same year.

Under Secretary of State for Justice

Lord David Wolfson (1968–)

Born into a Jewish family in Liverpool and educated at King David High School, Yeshiva Hakotel, Jerusalem, then Selwyn College, Cambridge University, Lord David Wolfson of Tredegar was called to the Bar 1992, becoming a leading commercial lawyer and Queen's Counsel in 2009. He has been described as a 'legal heavyweight,' and 'one of finest legal minds in the country.' A Commercial Law practitioner and a bencher of the Inner Temple, he was 'parachuted' into the Government as a minister in 2020 at the Ministry of Justice. Unpaid I understand though I am sure that does not reflect his true worth to the department nor his acumen and experience having been declared 'Commercial Litigation Silk of the Year 2020' by the Legal 500 and 'Commercial Litigation Silk of the Year' in the Chambers UK Bar Awards of the same year.

In addition to those noted above, I have already mentioned in *Chapter 1* the progress of Dominic Raab, who became Lord Chancellor and Secretary of State for Justice as this book went to press.

CHAPTER 13

The Doors Were Open to All

The effect of the 1858 Act and its amended versions was not only of benefit to the Jews, but it opened the way for people of other faiths. Its effects soon began to show in terms of the presence of Jews in public life and their ambitions became more visible to society. They had of course been around for many centuries apart from the period of exclusion or covertly. So had people of other minority faiths.

Although there is a reference to Muslim scholars in Geoffrey Chaucer's *Canterbury Tales*, the first record of an Englishman converting to Judaism was in the 16th century. There followed a few more during the next century and some Jewish sailors who worked for the East India Company settled around port areas. It seems they just abandoned ship and took up residence. Quite a few Muslims came from the Yemen, as many ships had called at Aden before coming here. The greater immigration was from the 1950s. Hindus mainly settled here after Indian independence in 1947, then there was encouragement to doctors once the National Health Service was born, and later in the 1970s people came from East Africa, after being expelled from Uganda. It was this influx that provided a more literate group, keen on further education and advancement.

It is hardly surprising that advancement in the law and on the bench came for this group from more recent immigrant backgrounds. They did not have to struggle on the question of taking an oath as Jews did, the matter had already been resolved and put quite simply a Muslim could take an oath on the *Koran*, and a Hindu by swearing to *Gita*, or the holy water of the River Ganges. It was purely prejudice which slowed their progress.

Judge Sir Mota Singh (1930–2016)

Mota Singh was educated in Nairobi, called to the Bar in London in 1955, returned to practice at the Bar in Nairobi, re-joined the English Bar in 1967, and was the first person from any minority ethnic group to be appointed to the bench in 1982. He held high office in his Sikh community and was the first judge to sit on the bench wearing a turban. Knighted in 2010 for services to charity and the judiciary, I had the pleasure of sitting with him for a period when I was a Crown Court recorder at Southwark. He was a most popular judge, especially at lunch time, when his religion prescribed fruit as the safest dish. Every day he would bring in a large bowl of the most exotic fruits, it was placed on the centre of the table in the dining-room and everyone was invited to partake, which we did to our blissful satisfaction.

Judge Usha Karu (1958–)

Usha Karu (short for Karunairetnam) was called to the Bar by Middle Temple in 1984 and practised on the South-Eastern Circuit specialising in Criminal Law. One of the first female Asians to be made a Crown Court recorder (2000) then circuit judge (2005), she sits at Inner London Crown Court where she is now resident judge, a Diversity and Community Relations judge, Co-ordinator of Judicial Mentors for Recorders in the London area, and New Recorder Training Judge. Judge Karu who is (so I believe) a Hindu also sits at the Old Bailey and was made Honorary Recorder of Southwark in 2017. Additionally a member of the Mental Health Review Tribunal, Circuit Judge Commissioner at the Judicial Appointments Commission, and a bencher of her Inn of Court, in 2018 she was awarded an honorary doctorate by London South Bank University School of Law and Social Sciences in recognition of her 'outstanding contributions to the law and the judiciary.' She has been quoted as saying: 'Throughout my career I've never had a day when I wake-up and don't want to come to work.'

Judge Avik Mukharjee

Educated at Nottingham Polytechnic where he obtained his LLB (Bachelor of Laws) degree in 1989, Avik Mukharjee, a Hindu, was called to the Bar in 1991, becoming a circuit judge in 2015. He was Honorary Professor, Nottingham Trent University and the Diversity and Community Relations Judge.

Judge Kaly Kaul (1960–)

Kaly Kaul was educated Heathfield School Harrow, then the London School of Economics. A Hindu, she was called to the Bar in 1983, made Queen's Counsel in 2011, and was chair of Association of Women Barristers, and Diversity Officer for the South-Eastern Circuit. At the time of writing, she sits at Snaresbrook Crown Court. There are currently several Hindu members of Queen's Counsel and it is expected that more judicial appointments are inevitable.

Alter Hurwitz

When I qualified as a solicitor in Leeds in 1956, my preparatory period of articles meant contact with the chambers of Alter Hurwitz, up three sets of staircases to a lofty group of rooms bang opposite Leeds Town Hall, where the 12 magistrates' courts a day, and three jury courts used for Assizes and Quarter Sessions were located.[1] Alter Hurwitz was an orthodox Jew, the son of a rabbi, and with a fine academic record. He had done a pupillage[2] in Leeds but was unable to obtain a tenancy (a 'seat' in a set of barristers' chambers). I believe he was the only Jewish barrister in Leeds at that time. And so Hurwitz set up his own chambers above a bank in Park Square, an oasis in Leeds city centre, a green space, surrounded by Georgian houses that had become the city's legal hub.

Hurwitz, being Orthodox, put his religious knowledge into practice believing the tract (gospel), including the need to show love for an alien: 'For you were aliens in the land of Egypt.' His chambers were open to all barristers, provided they had a qualification. And so it was that the only non-white barrister around, a man reputed to be a prince of the Indian Raj called Peter Das came to join him. The chambers grew and had to move to the spot previously described, opposite the law courts, which became Park Square Chambers.

---

1. Both now parts of the Crown Court.
2. A barrister's practical training, a bit like being articled to a practising solicitor, but attached to an experienced member of the Bar.

They were joined by Vivian Hurwitz, who was Alter's Cambridge-educated son, by Arthur Myerson QC, Geoffrey Rivlin QC, and Paul Hoffman, each of whom became a circuit judge, together with William Barfield, Paul Hoffbrand and Bryan Bush, and also Harry Ognall QC (*Chapter 10*), who went on to become a High Court judge. There were also Lionel Scott and Stephen Brodie QC (though I cannot recall if they served on the bench) as well as Louise Godfrey who also became a silk, but sadly died young. Arthur Myerson became resident judge at York, as did Paul Hoffbrand, who also became the first honorary recorder of that city.

Alter Hurwitz remained a junior barrister throughout his busy practising life[3] and retained his orthodoxy to the extent that he would not work on the Sabbath.[4] However, if as sometimes happened in autumn or winter and if the case was slow-moving so that he might need to be there on a Friday afternoon when the Sabbath came in, he would continue the case but put down his pen, memorise his work, and walk the four miles home.

Hurwitz was number 250 on a list compiled by the Nazis of those who should be arrested on Germany invading Britain. Unusual for a junior, he was appointed Recorder of Halifax, and at the time it was within the remit of recorder to appoint his assistant recorder if the list of cases was heavy. Hurwitz and Myerson both enjoyed their 'practice,' and not to be left out Peter Das also took up the mantle, and so took the oath on the *Koran*.

Lord Justice Rabinder Singh (1964–)

Born in Delhi to a Sikh family, educated at Bristol Grammar School and Cambridge University where he achieved a double first, Rabinder Singh then studied at the University of California. He was called to the Bar in 1989 and became junior counsel to the Crown and then the Inland Revenue. His fields of Public Law, Administrative Law, Employment Law, Human Rights and European Community Law made him a prime candidate for Matrix Chambers.

---

3. Many talented barristers remain juniors if earning good fees and they are cautious about how promotion might impact on this; others the 'legal hacks' whose talents are less fitted to being a QC may have little choice — as cleverly portrayed by John Mortimer with his fictional Horace Rumpole.
4. From a few minutes before sunset on Friday evening until the appearance of three stars in the sky on Saturday night.

He was said to be one of the most successful high earners at the junior Bar, and this translated easily to him being made Queen's Counsel. At the age of 39 he was appointed a deputy High Court judge, one of youngest, then in 2011 to a permanent position in the High Court, and in 2017 to the Court of Appeal, the first black and minority ethnic (BAME) candidate to gain such an appointment. A quite sterling career.

Three more Muslim Judges

There are now so far as I can tell two further Muslim circuit judges and at least one Muslim deputy district judge who I should mention.

Judge Anuja Ravindra Dhir (1968–)
Raised in Dundee, Anuja Ravindra Dhir was born of parents there who emigrated to Scotland from Pakistan. She was educated at Harris Academy Dundee and Dundee University, called to the Bar in 1989, and made a circuit judge in 2012. She was the first 'non-white' woman judge to sit at the Old Bailey. She is also properly called Lady Lavender, as her husband is Sir Nicholas Lavender, a High Court judge.

Judge Khatun Sapnara (1967–)
Educated at Chadwell Heath School and the London School of Economics, Khatun Sapnara is a Bangledeshi born judge (the daughter of a liberationist, i.e. from Pakistan) and practising Muslim. She was called to the Bar in 1990, specialising mainly in Family Law. She was made a Crown Court recorder in 2006 and a circuit judge in 2014, believed to be the first such person to be so appointed.[5] She became chair of Ashiana Network (2003–2014) (a women's refuge and support group) and Rights of Women and has written and made many other contributions to related issues particularly around forced marriage.

---

5. Certainly, in January 2015, she was declared 'Person of the Year' in the British Bangladeshi Power and Inspiration 100 rankings and this was stated to be for her 'outstanding achievements as the first person of British Bangladeshi origin to acquire a senior judicial position.'

The Jewish Contribution to English Law

Raffia Arshad

Raffia Arshad hails from Burton-upon-Trent. She was called to the Bar in 2002 and practices out of St Mary's Chambers, Nottingham, including in the civil and family aspects of finance, child law, forced marriage (of wives or husbands) and female genital mutilation. Her expertise also extends to Islamic Family Law, Trust Law and she has acted for and against applicants seeking to intervene in cases involving Third Party Rights. BBC News (27 May 2020) described her as a 'trailblazer' after she became the first hijab-wearing member of the judiciary in England and Wales when appointed to sit as a deputy district judge on the Midland Circuit.

Errata: Please note that on page 190 line 3 the words 'not the' should appear before test cricketer.

CHAPTER 14

Some Notable Jewish Solicitors

I have already touched on several Jewish solicitors when this seemed to fit into earlier chapters, e.g. because they were (maybe still are) members of the higher judiciary or served in political office. I will now describe a number who may be harder to categorise but who certainly deserve special mention for their individual contributions to public life and legal affairs.

Sir George Henry Lewis (1833–1911)

History does not record the first Jewish solicitor, but by 1880 there were about 50 across England. George Henry Lewis was perhaps the first to achieve fame.

He came from a family of *Sephardim* Jews who arrived from The Netherlands and settled here in the 18th century. Their name was Loew, changed to Lewis. George's father, James Graham Lewis, became a solicitor in 1829 and set up a practice in Ely Place just north of High Holborn close to the heart of 'legal London,' the Law Courts and the four inns of court. As was the custom with some Jewish people he lived 'over the shop,' and the practice remained at that address for over 100 years.

George Lewis was born in 1833 and had a governess called Miss Parry, who later became the Headmistress of Queen's College in Harley Street. Because at that time he would not have been able to go to Oxbridge (see *Chapter 1*) as since the time of Charles II, like all Jews, Catholics, Methodists or Congregationalists, or anyone not Church of England, those universities were barred to him. In 1847 he went to University College London, a pioneer in freedom from sectarian prejudices, so much so that UCL became known as 'The Godless Tower of Gower Street.' He attended UCL for three years and was then articled to his father.

Once qualified, the firm became Lewis & Lewis, and they specialised in Criminal Law. James, the father, was known as 'the poor man's lawyer,' a name given to a form of legal aid before the real version developed some 70 years later. It was James, it was said, that inspired Mr Jaggers in Charles Dickens' *Great Expectations* where Jaggers, a lawyer, was central character Pip's guardian, Miss Haversham's attorney and trial lawyer for Magwitsch (the ex-convict who it eventually transpires bestowed on Pip his 'expectations'). Dickens described Jaggers as:

> '…a burly man of an exceedingly dark complexion, with an exceedingly large head, and a corresponding large hand. He took my chin in his large hand and turned up my face to have a look at me by the light of the candle. He was prematurely bald on the top of his head, and had bushy black eyebrows that wouldn't lie down but stood up bristling. His eyes were set very deep in his head, and were disagreeably sharp and suspicious. He had a large watch-chain, and strong black dots where his beard and whiskers would have been if he had let them.'

Jaggers it seems also had unique standing amongst the criminal classes, saying, 'I never lock the doors at night' thereby extending an open invitation to all burglars by saying, 'Why don't you try it on?' Nobody responded to this challenge, as no burglar could afford to make an enemy of Mr Jaggers.

So, how did the real-life James Lewis come to prosper? John Juxon, in his book *Lewis and Lewis: The Life and Times of a Victorian Solicitor* (1983) (see *Selected Bibliography*) gives a graphic description of criminal activities in what is now largely known as Soho, and where the success of a criminal solicitor followed from the fact that in the mid-19th century this and other areas of London were enclaves of crime.

According to Luxon (paraphrased), the capital was a mixture of squalor and elegance, the windows of the rich overlooked terrible alleyways and courtyards rife with crime. Slums were no-go areas, and such was an area known as 'The Holy Land' between Great Russell Street and St Giles High Street. A labyrinth of tortuous alleys and foul intercommunicating cellars provided a valuable sanctuary for villains operating in the West End. There were different kinds of street thieves, from wretched children to 'the swell mob' who were superior pickpockets, well-dressed, targeting victims also well-dressed, and of course, well-off. There were women who specialised in stealing from shops who wore ankle length skirts which facilitated concealment; and 'dragsmen' who stole from coaches. A coach would leave the railway station, amidst traffic congestion nowhere near as orderly as today, just a jumble of vehicles, criss-crossing the highways and it was easy to follow the coach in a light cart driven by one person whilst another jumped from the cart onto the coach and dislodged pieces of luggage from the roof and drove quickly away. There were the 'rampsmen' who would use an attractive woman to decoy a man away from his companions and rob him.

In 1861 there was an epidemic of 'garroting' whereby a team would attack people by approaching them from behind with a piece of rope or a tightly furled scarf, throwing it over their head and choking them, in the course of which they would be robbed. A Member of Parliament was thus killed in Pall Mall, then a jeweller, and vigilante groups were formed, carrying swordsticks. An act to deter this *modus operandi*, the Garroting Act 1862 was quickly taken through Parliament, the penalty a public flogging, and the epidemic was virtually eliminated.

There always will be the professional criminal, then as now, the cracksmen, the fences, the coiners (those who scraped valuable metal off coins of the realm), and of course prostitutes and those who maintain them and supervise their trade. It was through one of many royal mistresses that George Lewis had been introduced to King Edward VII, and become part of his set. He acted for Edward when he was embroiled in the 1869 Mordaunt adultery case[1] and, on the introduction of Edward, for the defendant in the famous Royal Baccarat Scandal.[2] He also instructed leading barrister Sir Edward Carson who acted

---

1. As a result of which Lady Harriett Mordaunt the co-respondent wife of baronet, MP and barrister, Sir Charles Mordaunt ended-up being committed to an institution.
2. Also known as the 'Tranby Croft Affair' (after its Yorkshire setting) when the future king played cards with Sir William Gordon-Cumming of the Scots Guards who was accused of cheating.

The Jewish Contribution to English Law

for George Archer-Shee in the High Court in 1910 in 'The Winslow Boy' case.³ George's wife, Elizabeth, ran a salon in Portland Place to whence they moved.

Lewis was knighted in 1893 and a baronetcy followed. I will deal with other solicitors who helped Government leaders later, and who were awarded peerages for such service, and ironically one of whom who also moved to live in Portland Place.

Spy cartoon of Sir George Henry Lewis whose solicitor father James is said to have been the inspiration for Charles Dicken's fictional Mr Jaggers in *Great Expectations*. After joining his father in what became the solicitors' firm Lewis & Lewis, George went from representing the criminal classes of Soho to advising the Prince of Wales. Picture Alamy.

---

3. A father's fight to clear his son's name after the latter was expelled from Osborne Royal Naval College, Isle of Wight, for allegedly stealing a five-shilling postal order, later in 1948 a play of the same name by Terence Rattigan and a 1999 film.

Some Notable Jewish Solicitors

Lord Lewis Silkin (1889-1972)

Born of Jewish parents, Lewis Silkin became a solicitor and in 1925 a member of the former London County Council. He entered Parliament as Labour MP for Peckham in 1936. He was Minister for Town and Country Planning under Prime Minister Clement Attlee from 1945 to 1950, responsible for some of the most important planning legislation of the age, giving his name to the 'Silkin Test' planning mechanism designed to preserve areas if natural beauty. Having earlier turned-down a knighthood, he was granted a life peerage as first Baron Silkin of Dulwich in 1950; and made a Companion of Honour in 1965. His son, Sam Silkin, became Attorney-General and was also granted a life peerage; another son John was also a lawyer and politician (see *Chapter 12* for both).

Lord Barnett Janner (1892-1982)

Born in Lithuania, at the age of nine Barnett Janner moved to Barry in Wales. Educated at a local school and then University College (South) Wales, he graduated with a BA. In World War I he served in the Royal Garrison Artillery. He had started his legal studies before the war and qualified as a solicitor in 1919 then began practising in Cardiff.

Janner stood several times for Parliament as a Liberal, then, having moved to London, stood twice, lost each time, but won the third time around, only to lose his seat at a subsequent election. He later joined the Labour party and sat as an MP for various seats in Leicestershire from 1945 until 1970, when he was given a life peerage. He was succeeded as MP by his son Greville (see *Chapter 12*). From 1955-1964 Janner was the much-respected President of the Board of Deputies of British Jews.

Sydney Silverman (1895-1968)

A tenacious reformer and politician, Sydney Silverman is someone whose name will forever be associated with the struggle to end capital punishment in Britain. Leaving poverty behind in Jassy, Romania his parents arrived in the UK as Jewish immigrants escaping tyranny, after which Silverman was born. He was educated at his local Liverpool Institute and Liverpool University where he studied English Literature, having obtained scholarships (he in fact turned down one to Oxford University on the ground of expense).

Silverman became a solicitor in 1927. As a socialist and someone who had witnessed atrocities in Europe, he conscientiously objected to World War I; which led to him serving three prison terms after refusing to obey orders in barracks. He then became a Labour Member of Parliament when he won the seat for Nelson and Colne, Lancashire in the 1935 general election. Silverman founded the National Campaign for the Abolition of Capital Punishment, and he wrote widely about miscarriages of justice including the case of Timothy Evans (wrongfully hanged in 1952 for the murder of his baby daughter, who it transpired was almost certainly a victim of the serial killer John Reginald Christie). Having only partly succeeded with a private member's Bill for abolition in the House of Commons in 1956 that failed in the House of Lords, he was instrumental in arranging for the Bill that led to the Murder (Abolition of Death Penalty) Act 1965.

Silverman's other involvements in key moments in history are that the so-called 'Riegner Telegram,' was addressed to him in London. It was sent by Gerhart Riegner, Secretary of the World Jewish Congress based in Geneva, in August 1942, and was the first convincing evidence of the Final Solution and the Holocaust (as a result of which Silverman renounced his pacifism). He was also one of the leading opponents of Sir Oswald Moseley and the British Union of Fascists in the 1930s; and a founder of the Campaign for Nuclear Disarmament (CND) in 1961.

Some Notable Jewish Solicitors

Without Sydney Silverman's persistence capital punishment in the UK might not have been abolished in 1965. As a socialist who witnessed atrocities in Europe, he was a conscientious objector leading to three prison terms. In 1942 he was the recipient of the 'Reigner telegram' from the World Jewish Congress that verified suspicions about the Holocaust. Photo Alamy.

Leonard Sainer (1909–1991)

Educated at the Central Foundation Boys' School in Islington, then University College London, Leonard Sainer qualified as a solicitor in 1933 but was also a retailer. He founded the law firm Titmus, Sainer & Webb in 1938 which became one of London's largest, and was particularly active in post-World War II property transactions. He succeeded one of his clients, Charles Clore, as President of Sears Holdings[4] the British-based international conglomerate listed on the London Stock Exchange and once part of the Footsie 100, which Sainer had helped Clore to establish.

Sainer created the Leonard Sainer Legal Education Foundation, Sainer Dementia Centre and, via his estate, Leonard Sainer Trust which sponsors charitable activities such as the Leonard Sainer Centre, Ilford, for children with special needs.

Lord Victor Mishcon (1915–2006)

Born in Brixton, the son of a rabbi who had arrived in England from Poland, Victor Mishcon was educated in the City of London, became a solicitor, and founded Victor Mishcon & Co in 1937. Active in the Labour party, he was a councillor (1945), and chair of the old London County Council (1954). He stood without success in three general elections but in 1978 was created a life peer as Baron Mishcon, and was shadow Home Affairs Minister, then Shadow Lord Chancellor.

A solicitor in many notable cases, including the divorce of Ruth Ellis (the last woman to hang in Britain) and acting as instructing solicitor for MP and novelist Jeffrey Archer (later Lord Archer) in the libel trial that many years later led to Archer being jailed for perjury), he became an honorary Queen's Counsel, was a board member of the National Theatre, President of the Board of Deputies of British Jews, and Vice-president of the Council of Christians and Jews. He acted as a confidential intermediary between King Hussein of Jordan and Shimon Peres in Middle-East peace attempts.

---

4. Sears was acquired by entrepreneur Philip Green in 1999.

Some Notable Jewish Solicitors

On a personal note, when I was about to leave the Army, in 1958, I was interviewed by him and offered a position, which I accepted, but later declined due to family reasons, needing to return to Leeds.

Sir David Napley (1915–1994)

Born in London into a Jewish family, David Napley qualified as a solicitor in 1937 and set-up his own practice which rapidly grew, attracting many notable private clients, some of whom were household names. Jeremy Thorpe, leader of the Liberal party, was possibly the person involved in Napley's most high profile case (see further below). In World War II, he served in the Queen's Royal Regiment as a captain.

Napley chaired the Law Society Standing Committee on Criminal Law, before becoming President of the Law Society (the solicitors governing body), for which he was knighted as was then customary. He worked extensively with leading criminal defence barrister George Carman QC of the Northern Circuit.

Before Jeremy Thorpe was acquitted at the Old Bailey on a conspiracy to murder charge in 1978, the old-style (or 'steam') committal in which the prosecution evidence was rehearsed was held at Minehead Magistrates' Court where Napley represented Thorpe.[5] There was an atmospheric 'fuzz,' the gold Rolls-Royce, the assistant bearing piles of law books, etc. Some years later, at the Helen Smith hearing in Leeds (below), with similar accessories, Brian Walsh QC was heard to whisper stage left, 'Ah, Minehead revisited.'

I met Napley frequently through the British Academy of Forensic Sciences, and when he came to Leeds in connection with the long-delayed 1982 inquest into Helen Smith, who had died in mysterious circumstances after apparently falling from a balcony in Jeddah, Saudi Arabia in 1979, he came to dinner at my home in Harrogate when the other guest that day was my old friend Gilbert Gray QC. It was quite a memorable evening. The West Yorkshire coroner had refused an inquest on a deceased who died outside the jurisdiction, a decision reversed on appeal that changed the law on inquests into deaths of UK citizens abroad.

---

5. In modern times serious cases are 'whisked-off' to the Crown Court almost straightaway so that Minehead now seems somewhat quaint.

Napley was a prolific author of articles and books, many of which ran to subsequent editions, including: *The Technique of Persuasion* on courtroom tactics and *Not Without Prejudice* his memoirs as President of the Law Society. These and some of his other works are listed in the *Selected Bibliography*. He was a regular presence at literary gatherings at the Garrick Club and other venues where publishers and writers gather.

Solicitor Sir David Napley represented many high profile clients including Liberal party leader Jeremy Thorpe when accused of conspiracy to murder. A dapper President of the Law Society and a frequent author of books on crime, evidence and lawyerly skills, he drove a gold-coloured Rolls-Royce and was one of the UK's better-known solicitor advocates. Photo Alamy.

Leo Abse (1917–2008)

Leopold ('Leo') Abse was born Cardiff. The son of Jewish solicitor Rudolf Abse (who was also the local Cinema owner), his grandparents had emigrated to England from Poland. He attended Howards Garden High School Cardiff then studied law at the London School of Economics. He joined the Labour party and visited Spain during its Civil War. In World War II he served in the Royal Air Force.

Abse was admitted as a solicitor, practised in Cardiff, and established the law firm Leo Abse & Cohen in 1951. In the same year he was elected chair of Cardiff Labour party, then two years later to Cardiff City Council, becoming Labour Member of Parliament for Pontypool in 1958 in a by-election. In the House of Commons, Abse introduced private Bills to decriminalise homosexuality and liberalise divorce law, matrimonial causes and abortion, concerning the last of which he chaired a Parliamentary Select Committee (1975–1978). According to Geoffrey Goodman writing in *The Guardian* (20 August 2008), Abse introduced more private Bills in the 20th century than any other MP. He was appointed to the Advisory Council of the Penal System in 1968.

A sometimes flamboyant-dresser and rarely deflected by controversy, he became the main sponsor for the Bill to enact the recommendations of the 1957 Wolfenden Report (Report of the Departmental Committee on Homosexual Offences and Prostitution chaired by Sir John Wolfenden) which eventually, with the support of the Government, became the Sexual Offences Act 1967 that finally legalised homosexuality in England and Wales.

An opponent of Welsh devolution, opposed to nuclear weapons, British troops being stationed in Northern Ireland, and a supporter of the European Community, Abse was elected for the re-aligned Torfaen, Wales, constituency in 1983 but retired as a career politician four years later after 30 years on the back benches. His nomination for the House of Lords was vetoed by Prime Minister Margaret Thatcher.

Abse's many writings include *Margaret, Daughter of Beatrice: A Politician's Psycho-biography of Margaret Thatcher* about Thatcher not acknowledging her mother's influence and *The Man Behind the Smile: Tony Blair and the Politics of Perversion*. These with others are listed in the *Select Biography*.

The Jewish Contribution to English Law

Leo Abse, a Welsh solicitor turned Labour Member of Parliament who was 'the House of Commons' most flamboyant dresser.' Abse introduced more private Bills in the 20th century than any other MP, including that for the Sexual Offences Act 1968 which legalised homosexuality in the UK. After 30 years on the back benches his expectation of a peerage was blocked by Prime Minister Margaret Thatcher. Photo Alamy.

Stanley Berwin (1926–1988)

Another old friend of mine, born in Leeds, Stanley Berwin's Jewish family had established a well-known tailoring firm, Berwins. Educated at Roundhay School, Leeds he then went into the Royal Navy, and afterwards Cambridge University, and then Leeds University (where we met, and where I assisted him when as a law student he tried to enter Parliament for Wakefield as a Liberal candidate: he came a 'long' third as he did at Shipley, also in West Yorkshire, a year later).

Berwin did his articles with Booth & Co, a refined and established firm of solicitors in Leeds. The nexus was presumably the Liberal Party and Sir Donald Wade, the member for Huddersfield, one of their partners. He then transferred to the London firm of Oppenheimer, Nathan & Vandyk where he remained after qualifying.

He started Berwin & Co in the 1960s specialising in mergers and corporate finance, which drew him to the bankers Rothschild, of which he became a director, British Land and Wickes. In 1970, Berwin & Co merged with Leightons, to become Berwin, Leighton — then they added Paisners — and still later in 2018 the firm became Bryan Cave Leighton Paisner LLP.[6] His commercial interests occupied him to the extent that he withdrew from the 1970s incarnation, however after a period he returned to the law as S J Berwin in 1982.

The name Stanley Berwin is known throughout the legal profession and is particularly referred to amongst commercial practitioners. He endowed the S J Berwin Chair of Corporate Law in his name at Cambridge University.

Benedict Birnberg (1930–)

Born of Jewish parents, both teachers, in Stepney, Benedict Birnberg was educated at Cambridge University and admitted as a solicitor 1957. He set-up Birnberg & Co specialising in radical causes and miscarriages of justice. In 1993

---

6. As with many other firms or groupings mentioned in this book the line of progression can also be traced through other partnerships, entities or amalgamations.

he secured a post-humous pardon for Derek Bentley who was hanged for murder in 1953 and in 1998 the quashing of his conviction in the Court of Appeal.[7]

Birnberg practised with Imram Khan (test cricketer and later Prime Minister of Pakistan) and Gareth Pierce (the highly-respected Human Rights lawyer who acted for the wrongly convicted Guildford Four and was played in the 1993 feature film 'In the Name of the Father' by the actress Emma Thompson). The firm is now Birnberg Pierce. He has acted for many people ranging from the 'eccentric to the eclectic,' including those wronged by the police or State. A truly reforming character, he has fought for gay rights and those prejudiced by the colour of their skin. He became a trustee of and adviser to the Koestler Trust; the prisoner-related arts charity.[8]

Ronald Teeman (1930–)

Born into a Jewish family in Leeds, Ronald Teeman attended Roundhay School and Leeds University where he obtained an LLM and became a lecturer. Admitted as a solicitor in 1952, he was a specialist in sports cases and crime. He was President of British Rugby League. Retired at 82 years-of-age he remains a larger than life character.

Professor Michael Zander (1932–)

Michael Zander was born in Berlin to parents of Jewish background, who when he was aged four left Berlin for London at a time of increasing Nazi oppression towards the Jews. A legal scholar of note, Professor Emeritus of Law at the London School of Economics and an honorary Queen's Counsel (1997), he was a member of the Royal Commission on Criminal Justice (aka the Runciman

---

7. This *cause célèbre* of the shooting of a police officer by Bentley's juvenile accomplice Christopher Craig (born 1936 and believed to have since died) who was death penalty exempt, under the much criticised law of joint enterprise, and notoriously whilst Bentley was already under secure arrest, was one that helped to drive the abolition of capital punishment in the United Kingdom.
8. The Koestler Trust is highly regarded across prison interest groups. Named after Arthur Koestler (1905–1983) a refugee, activist and sometime political prisoner from Budapest, of Jewish parentage, not a lawyer but the author of *Darkness at Noon* (1940) that has been described as one of the most highly influential anti-Soviet tracts.

Commission) which began work in 1991, and later a member of the Police and Criminal Evidence Act (1984) (PACE) strategy board. He is perhaps one of the earliest legal commentators to have emerged on radio and television.

Educated at the Royal Grammar School High Wycombe, then Cambridge University, he obtained a double first in law. He then attended Harvard University, USA, qualifying as a solicitor with Ashurst, Crisp in London. His chair in Law at the LSE dates from 1977. He holds several honorary degrees and lifetime achievement awards.

Michael Simmons (1933–)

Born in London and educated St Paul's School and Emmanuel College, Cambridge University, Michael Simmons gained a first-class degree and was then commissioned in the RAF. He became a specialist in law firm amalgamations and International Law. He is the author of *The Lawyer Who Couldn't Sit Still* (see *Selected Bibliography*). He remains a non-practising legal consultant. As a lawyer, legal journalist and writer he has delivered lectures worldwide.

Jeffrey Gordon (1933–)

Jeffrey Gordon was admitted as a solicitor in 1956. A Criminal Law advocate for many years, he has taken part in 40 London Marathons. He stood as a conservative Parliamentary candidate repeatedly, but even more famously gave birth to the concept of the McKenzie Friend: the principle that, with the court's permission, another individual (a 'friend') can assist a litigant in person even though not legally trained or qualified—i.e. by 'giving quiet assistance.' This iconic ruling occurred when in 1970 one of Gordon's clients, Levine McKenzie, had his legal aid withdrawn. Gordon offered to represent him *pro bono* (gratis) then asked Australian barrister Ian Hanger, who was not qualified to practise in the UK, to stand in for him at court. Ordered from the courtroom by the judge, Hangar left McKenzie to fend for himself. He lost his case – but the Court of Appeal granted a retrial on the basis that he had been denied representation.[9]

---

9. See *McKenzie v McKenzie* [1970] 3 All ER 1034 CA.

Sir Geoffrey Bindman (1933–)

Geoffrey Lionel Bindman was born in Newcastle-upon-Tyne where his father was a general medical practitioner, the family being descended from Jewish immigrants. He was educated at the Royal Grammar School, Newcastle, then Oriel College, Oxford University. He became a solicitor in 1959, was knighted in 2007, and appointed an honorary Queen's Counsel in 2011.

Bindman was legal adviser to the Race Relations Board (1966–1983), Amnesty International, and the International Commission of Jurists sent to South Africa to investigate apartheid (institutional and political racial segregation), and has represented satirical magazine *Private Eye*. In 1947, he established the solicitors Bindmans LLP (nowadays award-winning on several chiefly Human Rights related and prisoners' rights fronts), based in central London. Geoffrey Bindman has dealt with many high-profile cases. In 2001 he was brought before the Solicitor's Disciplinary Tribunal for taking a case with a 'conflict of interest' (and breach of confidentiality) and fined £12,000 by the Solicitors Disciplinary Tribunal; a finding subsequently strongly criticised by other legal authorities, including an independent review by a member of Queen's Counsel, Anthony Hopper, who stressed the quality and high standards of Bindman's legal work and suggested that, in short, his strong views and legal challenges may have made him a target. Among other criticisms of authority, he has expressed support for the opinion that Tony Blair should be prosecuted for starting the Iraq War (2003–2017: allowing for its 'domino effect' and resurgences) with President George Bush Jnr of the USA.

Jeffrey Greenwood (1935–)

Born in London into a Jewish family, Jeffrey Greenwood was educated at Cambridge University and became senior partner at Nabarro Nathanson. He was chair of the Jewish Welfare Board, later known as Jewish Care.

Ruth Morris, Lady Morris of Kenwood (1937–)

Daughter of Lord Barnett Janner (above) and Elsie Janner, Ruth Morris was admitted as a solicitor and became senior partner of Janners; and then a consultant at Berwin Paisner, Manuel Swaden. A tribunal chair and trustee of several charitable rusts she was awarded the CBE. Her father in law was Harry Morris (1894–1954), Labour MP for Sheffield who was enobled in 1950 as the first Baron Morris of Kenwood.

Sir Victor Blank (1942–)

Maurice Victor Blank was born into a Jewish family in Stockport, Greater Manchester, and was educated at Stockport Grammar School, then St Catherine's College, Oxford University. He qualified as a solicitor, and at age 26 was made the youngest ever partner in Clifford Chance (then Clifford Turner). He specialised in Corporate Law and co-wrote *Weinberg & Blank on Take-overs and Mergers*, which became the leading work on the topic, current editions of which are still produced by publishers Sweet & Maxwell.

In 1981, he was appointed Head of Corporate Finance at Charterhouse Bank; he dealt with a buyout of Woolworths; and was then chair of Charterhouse and also a director of the Royal Bank of Scotland. In 1999, he became chair of Mirror Group Newspapers, which became the largest newspaper publisher in Britain. He was chair of Great Universal Stores (GUS) (1993–2006). He was made chair of Lloyds Trustee Savings Bank in 2006. Following a sharp contraction in the world economy and certain policy problems, relations within the company were somewhat strained. He decided to retire in 2009, though stayed on until an appropriate successor was found. He was knighted in 1999.

Blank took over Halifax Bank of Scotland and was chair of the Industrial Development Advisory Board. He was appointed as a business ambassador by Prime Minister David Cameron. He is reported to have donated £150,000 to the Labour party and has made several generous donations to research into women's health in particular, and he also raises a considerable amount each year at a private cricket match at his country home. The list of his charitable donations and interests is formidable.

Martin Paisner (1943–)

Born into a Jewish family, Martin Paisner was educated St Paul's School, The Sorbonne, Oxford University and Michigan University. He qualified as a solicitor in 1970, set-up Paisner & Co, then, in 2001, Berwin Leighton, Paisner & Co, dealing with Charity Law and acting as a trustee of many family trusts. These include the Wolfson[10] and Wohl[11] trusts. Awarded the CBE he is Vice-president of Jewish Care, and the American Jewish Joint Distribution Committee (known as 'the JDC') a Jewish relief body based in New York.

Michael Caplan (1953–)

Educated at Henry Thornton School and King's College London, Michael Caplan qualified as a solicitor in 1977. He was appointed as one of first solicitor members of Queen's Counsel in 2002, with rights of audience in the higher courts. He became a partner in Kingsley Napley, chair of the Police Appeals Tribunal, and a member of the Sentencing Council.[12] He represented former Argentinian President Augusto Pinochet.

Anthony Julius (1956–)

Educated in the City of London and Cambridge University (where he obtained a first-class honours degree), Anthony Julius joined solicitors Mishcon de Reya (now LLP) in 1979, where he became Deputy Chairman. He specialises in Defamation Law. He acted for Diana Princess of Wales; and defended Deborah Lipstadt and her publisher in the famous, long-running case of *David Irving v Penguin Books and Deborah Lipstadt* that began in 1996 and in which Irving unsuccessfully claimed that Lipstadt libelled him in her 1993 book *Denying the Holocaust* (see *Selected Bibliography*). Anthony Julius holds a chair at the University of London and is active in fighting anti-Semitism.[13]

---

10. See www.wfct.org
11. See www.wohl.org.uk
12. See www.sentencingcouncil.org.uk
13. For the final appeal ruling see *Irving v Penguin Books Ltd and Another* (2001) EWCA Civ 1197.

David Price (1963–)

Educated at Haberdashers' Aske's Boys' School, Harvard High School and Manchester University, David Price was admitted as a solicitor in 1990, called to the Bar in 1991, then re-admitted as a solicitor, becoming a member of Queen's Counsel in 2011. His well-established practice includes defamation as a specialism.

John Fenner

Born in Kent into a Jewish family, John Fenner was educated at Tonbridge School and University College London. He qualified as a solicitor, winning the Grotius Prize[14] in 1960. He became senior partner at Berwin Leighton in 1990, specialising in town centre schemes and urban regeneration. A lecturer on property tax and VAT, he was awarded the OBE and recognised for his work for the Helsinki Accords Conference in 1996 (named after agreements signed at a meeting of the multi-national Conference on Security and Co-operation in Europe held in Finland in 1975). He is a past master of the Fletchers Company.

'Divorce Tigers'

I hesitate to describe women lawyers as Divorce or Family Law experts as the criticism is that they were so categorised by their male counterparts, or pigeon-holed if you like, perhaps to keep them from more lucrative or what for many years historically was described as 'difficult' or 'complex' work, a self-serving way of male lawyers inhibiting women's legal careers or advancement to and within the judiciary. With this strong caveat and an assurance that I fully-acknowledge equality, I have to record that three of the top Family Law solicitors in this country are Jewish, or of Jewish origin, and they are women.

---

14. Named after the Dutch humanist, diplomat, lawyer, theologian, jurist, poet and playwright Hugo Grotius (1583–1645).

Baroness Fiona Shackleton of Belgravia (1956–)

Born in London, Fiona Shackleton's mother was of the Salmon family, her grandparents being Barnet and Molly Salmon of the J Lyons Salmon and Gluckstein 'dynasty' (see Sir Cyril Lyon in *Chapter 10*). Though her mother was Jewish it is understood neither her father nor husband are. Educated at Benendon School, Kent, then Exeter University for her degree in law, unusually she trained as a chef, catering for boardrooms, then qualified as a solicitor in 1980. She joined Farrar & Co LLP, the 'royal solicitors' becoming a partner later. She then joined Payne Hicks Beach as a partner in 2001. She has frequently acted for royal and other high profile clients.

Lady Helen Ward (1956–)

Born to Jewish parents in Golders Green, Helen Ward was educated at King Alfred School in Golders Green, then Birmingham University. She qualified as a solicitor in 1978 and has worked at Ward Bowie, Manches, and since 2010 Stewarts where she is a partner. She has many high-flying clients, and she specialises in the financial aspects of marital strife. She is a Crown Court recorder, and a deputy judge in the Family Division of the High Court. Her title refers to her marriage to Sir Alan Ward, a judge in the Court of Appeal, who is not Jewish. Her credentials as a solicitor who has successfully taken in many legal challenges, including international success, are amply documented at Stewarts' website[15] where she is described as 'the ultimate tactician,' with a 'tremendous work ethic.' It is also noted there that: 'The Legal 500 2021 named Helen in the Hall of Fame saying "Helen Ward is the standout family lawyer of her generation. In any contested family situation, she must be on your client's side."' Also that she has been described as, 'the first choice for the rich and famous.' She featured in *Tatler's* top 50 divorce lawyers.

Marylyn Stowe (1957–)

Bright, innovative and enterprising, Marylyn Stowe was born in Leeds into a Jewish family. She was educated at Leeds University and founded her own firm in 1982. Starting as a legal aid lawyer she rapidly progressed to private and notable clients and opened several offices in the Yorkshire area and then in

---

15. www.stewartslaw.com

London. She has worked with the Law Commission and has advanced the work of family mediation. Marylyn Stowe is a philanthropist, aiding several needy organizations in Yorkshire. She sold her group of firms for what is believed to be a substantial sum. Her husband is also a solicitor and part-time tribunal judge.

And many others...

Finally, there are a great number of solicitors whose specialist skills may keep them out of the limelight, but their contribution to the law is nevertheless invaluable. Clive Boxer, now retired, in the field of Insurance and Pension Law, Charles Corman of what is now Dechert LLP (Charity Law), Colin Jaques (whose paper on computers assisted Lord Harry Woolf's Civil Law Review), and Mark Prinsley, Head of Intellectual Property and Technology at Mayer Brown are just two examples. I must also mention Jonathan Black of BSB Solicitors in London, who has served two separate terms as President of the London Criminal Courts Solicitors Association not the least of his challenges being those he has made to Government about legal aid cuts. Posterity will record him as the last solicitor to practice at Bow Street Magistrates' Court before it closed in 2006. Less usually, he was in practice at the Bar later 'crossing-over.' With full rights of audience he has appeared in the Crown Court, High Court and the Court of Appeal. 'Legal Aid Lawyer of the Year in 2015,' he has represented many of those facing serious, violent, high profile and complex criminal allegations. And I must mention an absolute gentleman whom I knew well over many years, and who encapsulated all that is good in the law, Martin Compton, a magistrates' court solicitor of the old school, for whom no effort was too much, and who was always willing to help his clients, often without payment... they adored him.

Solicitors Who Answered the Call of Government

When I examined the way in which the leaders of political parties were presented with difficult decisions, or needed immediate help, it was clear that their first choice frequently appeared to be the type of lawyers described in this section: shrewd, lucid, proven, and as it happens Jewish. Fortunately, each of them is someone whom I have had the pleasure of knowing personally. The Conservative party produced David Young and David Gold, and James Levi CBE, QC of Gibraltar, not himself a politician, was called upon by politicians amongst others. Their similarity will become self-evident. Their degree of religious observation differed widely, but their loyalty, and acknowledgment of their faith and ancestral history, were ever present. I begin with another, the 'politically adaptable' Arnold Goodman.

Lord Arnold Goodman (1913–1995)

Arnold Goodman was referred to frequently and rather cruelly by the satirical magazine *Private Eye* as 'Two Dinners.' This emanated from an occasion when he arrived late at the home of Max Aitken (Baron Beaverbrook the newspaper magnate). It was a chance remark, made in jest, that he had already dined and that it was his practice to have no fewer than two dinners, probably several more. A perhaps unwise comment given his not inconsiderable bulk. He was a jovial, pleasant man, apart from his brilliance, and this might have been one of the factors making him so much in demand. He had an enviable memory as demonstrated by the detailed conversations described in his autobiography *Tell Them I'm On My Way: Memoirs* (1993). That title is thoroughly descriptive of his being the popular choice for individuals, companies, and even governments who were 'in a pickle' and needed immediate help, or probably more frequently having been surrounded by well-wishers, moaners, or doomsday prophets, were seeking an independent view, fresh ideas for the solution of an otherwise seemingly insurmountable dilemma.

It was the Conservative Edward ('Ted') Heath (who was to become Prime Minister) who provided Goodman's first contact with the political elite, but it was the Labour party that issued the call and was responsible for his subsequent ennoblement. Goodman was born in 1913, his parents having travelled to England in 1850 from Lithuania. It is amazing how often Lithuania and Poland have figured in Jewish immigration to England, and one wonders, if they had been able to stay and been allowed to contribute their brain power and energy to those then cold barren lands, what Utopian states they might have become.

Although Arnold's father was not over-wealthy, 'a shipbroker without any ships,' perhaps more correctly described as an export agent, his family were certainly more comfortable than the majority of immigrants. Everything is comparative, and their comparison was that they lived in the less salubrious part of Hampstead, though eventually they crossed the barrier of the Finchley Road and enjoyed at least sight of a few more blades of grass. They were passionate Jews but not religious, though his mother spoke Hebrew fluently, and later taught it to 1950s Labour leader Hugh Gaitskell's wife, Anna, who was Jewish.

Goodman went to University College London and then Cambridge University, where he remained after obtaining a degree for two years as a lecturer, during which time he was friendly with Harold Abrahams the Olympic athlete whose 100 metre sprint was depicted in the movie 'Chariots of Fire' (Jewish and again the son of Polish Lithuanian immigrants). Then as a fledgling solicitor, Goodman did his articles of clerkship, as they were then called, they consisted of a document signed by the solicitor, who promised to instruct, the pupil who promised not only to learn and follow all dutiful commands, but also not to 'nick the stamps or rifle the petty cash box.' Another party to the agreement, a parent, often agreed to pay the solicitor a sum calculated in guineas. The firm of solicitors known to Goodman's mother was Rubinstein Nash, one with the musically talented amongst their many interesting clients.

After qualification, Goodman worked for a time with Roy Kisch, another solicitor who had a room above Rubinstein's. Kisch, from an Anglo-Jewish family had been a major in the Army and held the Military Cross. To his credit, together with two or three contemporaries, they devoted several hours a week to working on a *pro bono* (i.e. free and charitable) basis in the East End of London. Kisch was fond of growing roses, a pleasure he shared with Goodman and when visiting Kisch's country garden the discussion turned to the building of a garden shed. A local carpenter called William Heath agreed to do this and he had a son called Edward to whom Goodman was introduced in the course of that work.

Possibly influenced by Kisch's military bearing and gravitas, Goodman joined the Territorial Army as war was clearly due to break out and conscription seemed inevitable. He became an officer, had an uneventful war but retained both his dignity and commission till the end. Upon demobilisation Goodman went back to Kisch as a salaried partner, earning £600 a year. He supplemented his income by reverting to his appointment as lecturer in Cambridge, travelling there on an early morning train, performing before students who had been urged to awaken at an hour, to which many of them were totally unaccustomed, but necessary so that Goodman could return to London in time for a late-morning's legal work. His energy paid off and the firm did well, so much so that they became an attractive enough proposition for Rubinsteins to make an offer of amalgamation. The result was an opening into the literary world, with clients such as J B Priestley, Graham Green and Evelyn Waugh.

He would brief D N Pritt a left-wing barrister, whom he described as 'the fiestiest and most tenacious advocate to grace the English Bar.' It is not known precisely why Goodman left that practice in 1954, but the ways and wiles of English law partnerships are varied. Lawyers are often effervescent and self-regarding, and it takes little to upset them, many have chopped and changed their allegiances. And so, the firm Goodman Derrick was formed.

Even before considering the political nature of Goodman's work, it is worth noting that he was involved in cases of public interest involving people in the public eye. He acted for Jack Hylton (1892–1965), pianist, composer, band leader, leading impresario, and beacon in the world of entertainment, at a time when commercial television channels and films were emerging, particularly Granada, and many of its actors and actresses. Although he would later become known for his connections with the Labour party, one of his earlier friends in politics was, as already noted, Edward Heath, the carpenter's son.

One man in particular prior to Heath of note here was Leslie Hore-Belisha mentioned in *Chapter 12* of this book. Prior to coming into contact with Goodman, Hore-Belisha was a Conservative politician, known to the public largely as the Minister of Transport who created 'Belisha beacons,' and less happily for his period as Minister of War and disagreement with the generals over what turned out to be his correct analysis of the uselessness of the Maginot Line.[16]

Goodman's connections with Hore-Belisha on legal matters were, sadly, trivial and involved the sort of problems retirees tend to conjure up in their minds. Even more sad was the story Goodman recounts of making arrangements for Hore-Belisha's funeral. It involved a problem arising from his origins as a *Sephardi* Jew, and his wish to be buried in an *Ashkenazi* cemetery at Willesden, North-West London, but Goodman swiftly re-arranged for the Golders Green Jewish Cemetery in Hoop Lane. A greater problem than calculating how many

---

16. The 'row' of concrete fortifications and other obstacles between France and Germany in World War II that the latter appear to have simply circumvented.

angels could dance on a pin head: getting a *minyan*.¹⁷ On the appointed day Goodman stood at the bottom of Middle Temple Lane and approached anyone passing who 'looked Jewish.' He succeeded.

It is perhaps little known that Edward Heath was one of those who, to my personal satisfaction, believed that solicitors were as capable of serving on the bench just like barristers are, but who for many years had held a monopoly. Heath pressed for a compromise when this was discussed, as it frequently was, namely that solicitors should be eligible for appointment as recorders, that is part-time judges, and that after five years in that office should be able to be selected for appointment to the Crown Court as a circuit judge. As we shall later see, it was also by the persuasion of Heath that Goodman was encouraged, despite initial reluctance, to use his abilities as a mediator in the lengthy transition to independence of Rhodesia. It was a year after Harold Wilson won the election with a small majority in October 1964 that he was elevated to the House of Lords; however this was not at the behest of Wilson but resulted from his friendship with Lieutenant Colonel George Wigg in his Army days.

Goodman could not really be described as politically active. As a student his sympathies were with the Republicans in Spain and the anti-Facists in Italy, and he did admire Prime Minister Margaret Thatcher. He had in fact been offered the chance to stand in a Conservative constituency as a Labour candidate, but declined. In the event, that seat did fall to Labour at the next election. Over the years he held great respect for and became increasingly friendly with several then current Labour stalwarts: Anuerin ('Nye') Bevan (pioneer of the welfare state), Hugh Gaitskell (already mentioned) and George Brown (deputy leader of the Labour party and Foreign Secretary), despite Brown's inability as someone who struggled with alcoholism to comprehend Goodman's abstemious disposition. Goodman gave advice on the Vassall Tribunal in 1963.¹⁸ There were also problems upon which he was invited to intervene concerning a leak of Labour Party minutes to *The Guardian*; and he gave constructive advice to the Government on land law, including the laws on eviction, although Property Law had not been one of his specialisms.

---

17. Hebrew for the quorum of ten male Jews who need to be present for the reciting of one of the holier prayers, the *Kaddish*.
18. When William John Vassall an ex-senior civil servant at the Admiralty was exposed as a Soviet spy.

There were criticisms of the influence which he had on senior ministers and Governments, one particular example being that when a minister was confronted with a problem the minister had not followed the established legal channels in his department but had dispatched three secretaries with a list of questions on troublesome matters to Goodman's flat in Upper Portland Place on a Saturday afternoon to obtain his immediate advice. He was deeply involved in the day-to-day (and sometimes night-time) happenings of the Profumo affair[19] and was on one occasion confronted by a minister on his doorstep at six o clock in the morning, one presumes to give advice rather than to simply wonder why the ministers was still in his pyjamas. Of all the politicians by whom Goodman was called, Harold Wilson (whether in office as Prime Minister or in opposition) was the most frequent.

Hugh Gaitskell died in 1963 (I often pass his grave when I walk from my home into Hampstead Village, it abuts the pavement in Church Row opposite St John Church, quite close to that of Anton Walbook whose film 'Dangerous Moonlight' and its haunting Warsaw Concerto cause me to hum a few bars as I amble into Hampstead, wondering why Walbrook, an Austrian refugee from the Nazis because of his mother's Jewishness, making him halachically Jewish, lies in a churchyard. That churchyard is just a few moments' walk to what was the home of the Gaitskells, just around the Corner in Frognal Gardens).

Goodman describes being summoned by Wilson to their first meeting. Wilson of course, was in opposition at that time, and he took the view that he viewed him with suspicion because he knew of the close relationship he had enjoyed with the Gaitskells in the 1950s. Goodman had found Gaitskell easy to deal with, their relationship having been described by the latter as being far more of a client-lawyer relationship than one influenced and sometimes therefore marred by close friendship. The way Goodman put it is that Gaitskell was a 'joy' to work with. He went on to explain that what he meant by that adjective is that 'He didn't argue, he didn't dissent, he agreed or disagreed.'

And then came Harold Wilson. It was clear from the start that Marcia Williams, Wilson's personal secretary, for one reason or the other had an enormous amount of influence over Wilson, but more and more did Wilson call upon

---

19. Events of the 1960s involving society osteopath Stephen Ward, showgirl-cum-hostess Christine Keeler, John Profumo MP, who was Minister for War at the time, and Russian naval attaché Yevgeny Ivanov, that rocked the British Establishment and precipitated the demise of the Conservative Government of Prime Minister Harold MacMillan,

Goodman for advice, not only legal but increasingly political, for after all these were the days when politicians did not rely on advice from 'advisers' barely out of their teens. One subject about which they talked was housing. Goodman was later flattered to realise that his thoughts on this were transposed into Labour policy. And at this time Goodman, as previously described, was not even a member of the Labour party. Harold Wilson became Prime Minster in 1964, although his majority was tiny, only five Members of Parliament. Following Goodman's elevation to the House of Lords in June 1965 where he sat as a cross-bencher, during Wilson's first and second terms in office, they would meet every few days, sometimes once a week. Goodman described those visits as akin to playing in a fives court with the ball banging at him continuously, only the ball being the various thoughts of Wilson. Realising what was happening a growing number of Labour politicians would use the existence of this conduit as a river into which their own tributaries could pour.

Goodman had long had an interest in and was a patron of the Arts, so it was natural that when matters relating to the Arts Council, theatres and the film industry came to the fore his aid would be sought, not only in the promotion of this, but also concerning any swelling of disturbances or strife in the employment fields which bordered upon any of them, such as a strike by television technicians and camera crews which threatened to bring programmes to a standstill.

It was his work between 1967 and 1972 in connection with the Unilateral Declaration of Independence (UDI) of November 1965 by Rhodesia which caused him to be granted the accolade Companion of Honour (CH). Originally a British colony, Rhodesia had governed itself since 1923, but in 1965 regarded itself as an independent sovereign state, as opposed to acknowledging the considerable powers Britain nevertheless still held there since 1923. Although pronounced with the intention of strengthening black power, when one examined the fine print, it was otherwise. Due to voting qualifications which had been imposed, Parliament was controlled by a white minority of five per cent of the population. There had been an impasse since the mid-1960s between Ian Smith (1919–2007) the Rhodesian Prime Minister and UK Prime Minister Sir Alec Douglas Hume. Ian Smith once said that from the very first secret meeting with him 1968, Arnold Goodman was the only person from England whom he really trusted.

In 1968 Harold Wilson asked Goodman if he knew anyone who could be sent to Salisbury, Rhodesia to engage in 'talk, talk.' Without actually indicating 'nudge, nudge, wink, wink.' Goodman realised he was the suggested nominee. He dodged the invitation by suggesting Max Aitken (1879–1964), who had been in the Royal Air Force with Smith. Aitken agreed on condition Goodman went with him. This was the first of about half-a-dozen trips. Goodman was always anxious that it should not be deemed that he was going out at the behest of a particular politician, even less that it be for the benefit of a political party, but that if he went it would be on behalf of the Government. And so it was, when the Conservatives came back into power, and on the fifth trip, in the company again of Douglas-Hume. Goodman was little impressed by the Foreign Office representatives and felt they were obstructing progress. When progress was made, the so-called 'Lancaster Talks' were held, with Margaret Thatcher at the helm in 1979, but his opinion of the Foreign Office had not improved.

It was in 1972 that Edward Heath said the Government would like to put Goodman forward for the award of Companion of Honour for the part he had played, with which suggestion Queen Elizabeth II graciously agreed. He also played an important part in the dispute within the National Health Service concerning the inclusion of daybeds in NHS hospitals, the Dockland Committee regarding the redevelopment of the Wapping area of London, and in the Arts with both the Royal Opera House and English National Orchestra, and all the while, because of his independence, and the ability to steer his practice along a progressive and profitable course. Lord Hailsham (some time Lord Chancellor) once said, 'If one wished to attain eminence in the law, one went to the Bar, but if one wished to become rich, one became a member of Goodman Derrick.' Goodman also spent many-years as President of the Observer Trust, and the Newspaper Publishers Guild. He was instrumental in the creation of the Open University and became Master of University College Oxford.

As happens with many Jewish people towards the end of their life, although always sympathetic, there is an increase in the strength of their support for Zionism. What can perhaps be summarised as one of the most important and far-reaching mediations which Arnold Goodman performed was in 1978. An impasse on one of the details had arisen in the course of the Camp David Accords. Goodman was called to Paris, and with the agreement of the Israeli Government met with President Anwar Sadat of Egypt. Suffice it to say agreement was reached.

Some Notable Jewish Solicitors

'Tell them I'm on my way...' Lord Arnold Goodman, jovial, pleasant, brilliant and said by *Private Eye* never to turn down an invitation to supper—it labelled him 'Two Dinners.' Founder of solicitors Goodman Derrick and the 'go to' lawyer of wealthy media clients, this caused a Lord Chancellor to say, 'If you wish for success at the law go to the Bar, but if you want to make money join Goodman Derrick.' Photo Alamy.

Lord David Young (1932–)

In his autobiography, *The Enterprise Years: A Businessman in the Cabinet* (1990) David Ivor Young devotes barely a line, in fact eleven words, to his having been a solicitor. This in no way reflects on his admiration for the profession. Young merits mention in this book for many reasons, one of which is that he confirms my belief that to qualify as a lawyer is a fine a foundation for a career in other fields.

At present there are open, or part-open book exams, which means you can take a book or notes into the examination room which may assist you in developing an answer to questions. When Lord Young took his Solicitors Final Examination it involved about ten papers on a wide expanse of legal subjects, much of which you were expected to have learned by heart. No lawyer, in chambers, the office, or court is expected to know everything by heart, what is far more important is to know where to look for legal answers that fit the questions, a skill in itself. David Young held a greater number of posts than most, illustrating an ability of knowing where to look for the answers. One other quality comes out which is a familiar theme in those stalwarts who at one time had lived in Lithuania. It is the combination of sheer hard work, but that time is also found for study. Although he died before Young reached his eighth year, his grandfather and family lived in a two-roomed wooden building in Minsk, and the former perhaps spent a greater portion of his life studying than filling the bottles in his shop. They preceded him to London, living in the East End and had a shop with a bakery. The family worked from four am to two am the following day, but the Sabbath was sacrosanct. Time to breath, time to recharge. The long hours paid off, the bakery grew, then they became flour factors, and the name 'Yankelovitch' became Young, the East End moved to Stamford Hill, membership of a golf club was secured, and, undreamt of in Minsk, they owned a motor car.

David Young was educated at Christ's College, Finchley and University College London. He was admitted as a solicitor in 1956, having been persuaded by his father to accept an offer of articles with an uncle who was a successful solicitor. The real attraction of this for Young was that a spell at university would enable him to obtain colours at golf. Although able to walk a golf course, the Royal Air Force would not have him due to 'flat feet' (fallen arches), his not theirs. Young protested, 'What's that to do with flying?' But the RAF was rigid, and the Army even more so, in those days flat feet was a no-no.

Young married Lita the same year that he qualified, but his time as a solicitor did not last long, for although he had been offered a legal post at his wedding reception he was introduced to the Head of Great Universal Stores (GUS), and rather than stay a solicitor in practice became assistant to the chairman of GUS, Sir Isaac Wolfson (1897–1991). He describes this as five years of amazing training, from a man with a magnetic personality, who charmed people into allowing him to follow the roads he wanted to travel along, the challenging roads of commercial life. There was one intriguing problem to solve after another and the days flew by.

GUS used as their solicitors a firm (no longer in existence) called Oppenheimer, Nathan & Vandyk. Described as 'one of the leading solicitors', Openheimer's Stanley Berwin (noted earlier in this chapter) and Young became friendly and suffice it to say over time various proposals and plans developed which resulted in Young, and others, entering a property development company. This was on condition that he leave GUS and devote his full-time to this group, however after some time he decided he would prefer to be his own master and tempted by the prospect of making his own decisions did just that, hitting particularly upon one great idea. It was the time of the building of the motorways, and they were the key to commercial viability. It followed that the areas to which goods needed transportation, and often storage, would be alongside them, or even better at their junctions.

A common factor amongst successful Jewish entrepreneurs has been an urge, having achieved success, to reflect this by way of thanks and put something back into the community. It might differ whether this 'something' should be by way of philanthropy, and there were always many hungry mouths to feed in this direction, or by practical service on a *pro bono* basis, that would be either by using their commercial acumen to assist a project, or participating, as in politics. Young had, in common with many of his contemporaries supported the more equitable ideas of Labour, and it would have been natural for his predecessors or ancestors to have come to this country without wealth and in the main, if assistance had been offered, for it to have been by their co-religionists. So, the principle of helping one another, and particularly the less fortunate, was in-built. Young had never participated in politics, and it was only when he came across a speech of Edward Heath at a shadow cabinet gathering in Selsdon Park that he 'perked up.' This gathering produced a radical free market agenda, one which in later times would be adopted by Margaret Thatcher, who played an important part in Young's career, as did her successor John Major. As this was happening, he believed that it was restricting his potential to continue handling the day-to-day problems of his company and that he would have more chance to look for more interesting pursuits if he became a non-executive director. He had been offered the opportunity of becoming chair of the British Rail Property Board and was about to accept when certain scandals were revealed via the Sunday newspapers, so he reversed out. Once again fate had played a master hand by brokering an introduction to Jeffrey Sterling, who had followed Young as assistant to Isaac Woolfson at GUS. Sterling suggested a joint property venture involving town and city centres and the upcoming demand for conference centres.

Young was to become engaged with many charitable organizations, but one in particular immediately struck a chord with him, and he has remained active in it for many years. It is called the Organization for Rehabilitation through Training (ORT);[20] international in scope it was created in Russia at the time of the gathering of Jews particularly into the Pale of the Settlement, an area stretching from Lithuania down to the Ukraine, and which at the time of oppressive czars and their pogroms caused many young people to wish to leave and secure employment in the West, or for that matter anywhere. With the war in Europe, the organization became instrumental in helping displaced persons start a new life in either Israel or the USA. One of its main functions today, and I am proud that my daughter Anna plays a prominent part, is in the mentoring of young people, providing them with training for new jobs. The attraction of ORT to Young may well have been his own firm belief that it was as important to provide training in industry and commerce straight after school as it was education in the arts, and that the economic success of any civilised country depends upon the work force available, the enterprise shown, and the direction indicated by the State. Young has firmly taken on board the success of America which has stemmed from the Declaration of Independence to the Age of Enterprise.

---

20. See www.ort.org/en/

It was in this light that Young read speeches made by Margaret Thatcher and Keith Joseph. He was the holder of a baronetcy granted initially to his father as Lord Mayor of London, but also a great creator of understandable policies. He served as a Cabinet minister under four prime ministers. This group had examined a number of sites, and large buildings, designed to employ many hundreds if not thousands, but the requirement for such space was not so great as the demand by many smaller businesses which, given the opportunity, would eventually grow. This needed smaller facilities to start with. The idea developed into thoughts of sub-dividing the large spaces to give smaller businessmen the chance to prove themselves.

I had a personal admiration for Keith Joseph, at that time I lived in North Leeds and Joseph was the parliamentary candidate for Leeds North-East. I was chair of a small youth group, a kind of debating society, with ideas well above its station, built on the style of a 'lodge' of masons. It had its origins in America, with secret hand signals and that kind of paraphernalia. As election day drew near, I wrote to invite Sir Keith to come and address us, which he accepted for three nights before the election. He must have been rather disappointed to turn-up and find about 25 schoolboys, none over the age of 16, and therefore way short of voting material. He never batted an eyelid, came in, gave us the talk, answered questions, and left. I wondered what sort of trouble he got into with his election agent. Nevertheless, it was a safe seat, and he was returned to Parliament.

Young was appointed a special adviser to Joseph, and he had a great talent and insight for dealing with companies engaged in information technology. He writes of flying back from the USA in 1977 and seeing an advert for something called an 'Apple' computer. After landing, he contacted Apple in California and claims to be the second owner of one of their computers in UK. Seeing the potential, he got in touch with Kenneth Baker (later Baron Baker of Dorking, CH, PC but then Education Secretary), and Cambridge-based inventor and entrepreneur Clive Sinclair,[21] and computers entered school life thereafter. When Joseph was moved to the Department of Education, Young was asked to remain as adviser to his successor Patrick Jenkins, but still advised Joseph on a part-time basis.

---

21. (1940–2021). Creator of micro-electronics, portable computers and the C5 electric runabout.

In 1982 Young was appointed chair of the Manpower Services Commission created by Edward Heath in 1973. He was instructed to coordinate employment and training services in the UK. The commission oversaw the ultimately ill-fated Youth Training Scheme (YTS).[22] To many people, Whitehall is a wide avenue, in the centre of which is a memorial around which the Sovereign, Government and armed services assemble once a year, near one particular street in which the Prime Minister lives and pops in-and-out of in his or her car (sometimes at a speed which the normal person would not dream of doing on the M1 at two o'clock in the morning). No.10 Downing Street is, of course, more than that, it is a village of thousands of rooms of varying sizes the use of which is allocated in relation to their importance to the person on a given rung of the governmental ladder. The place where someone can be readily found in an emergency, or can quietly beaver away at specific and allotted tasks. There are phones, there are messengers, but there is nothing like being able to bang on the door, it's far more reliable. Once David Young got the Manpower Services Commission moving in a progressive manner it included nearly 20 sub-offices and employed 24,000 people. Unemployment is a frightening word in politics, and where youths are involved particularly so. With great energy he achieved much, along with the people responsible for implementing his programmes throughout the country. He worked with Norman Tebbit (later Baron Tebbit CH, PC) who at various times was Secretary of State for Employment, and for Education, then with Keith Joseph. It was essential that new schools be planned which worked in tandem with YTS schemes. He may have had an office in Whitehall but would spend several days each week travelling the length and breadth of the country.

Young's policy was not always popular for there were those who believed the world of schools and that of work should be kept separate, but this was also the time when technical innovations were being introduced into schools, and this was clearly something to attract the interest of pupils One wonders how remarkable it was that at that time he could have envisaged the situation today where virtually every child believes technical knowledge is a vital part of his or her life. His aim was to achieve 40,000 places on YTS schemes, and he

---

22. YTS had its critics and it was replaced by other schemes in 1987.

succeeded, even though the scheme ran into allegations of discrimination and exploitation before its demise.

In October 1984, David Young was given a life peerage by Margaret Thatcher and became Baron Young of Grafham CH, OPC DL; a month later he was appointed to the Cabinet, as Minister Without Portfolio. He knew this would happen, this had been why he was ennobled, and he knew what the portfolio would be that he would be without. The non-sequitur continues because although his responsibility related to unemployment, he became Secretary of State for Employment. There was one more aspect of the job, he would not receive any salary because the statutory number of Cabinet members had been reached. There was however a problem about the first Cabinet meeting, it was on *Rosh Hashanah*, the Jewish New Year, and Young like the majority of Jews in England, despite all other indiscretions, at that time observe three holy days, the two for New Year, and ten days later *Yom Kippur*, the Day of Atonement. When 'Sir Humphrey' was told he could not attend, the response was to the effect, 'But you must.' However a quick phone call to Margaret Thatcher resolved that, and Lord and Lady Young duly went to synagogue together.

It was just a week later that the Conservative Party Conference was due to be held in Brighton. Young was heavily engaged in assisting writing the leader's speech. There was much to include, and excitement about the Channel Tunnel project. It was late at night, and rather than stay at the hotel he preferred to sleep in his home about an hour's drive away. He chose well. It was the night an IRA Bomb tore apart the Grand Hotel causing five deaths and injuring 31, including Norman Tebbit and, more severely, his wife.

A few days later, David Young was sworn in as Baron Young when he wrote: 'Preparing for the oath I caught sight of my father. What would he have said if told this would happen to his grandson when he arrived at the Port of London nearly 80 years before?' There followed two highly charged years in Cabinet, involving reviews of social security and overseas trips particularly to China. He tells of one particularly interesting gathering at the home of Foreign Secretary, Sir Geoffrey Howe and Lady Howe, with Leon Britain and Soviet Leader Mikhael Gorbachov. Lady Howe commented that everyone present was a lawyer, and Gorbachov asked Young, 'Why are there so many lawyers in the United Kingdom?' To which Young replied, 'Well you see we are a society founded upon individual rights.' The poignancy of this comment was that at that time

211

emigration from the Soviet Union was almost impossible. Gorbachov laughed and raided his glass to Young.

Young's remit at Employment included supervising a scheme for City Action Teams (CATS) to encourage regeneration of provincial areas. He was later to take over the Department of Employment with small firms and tourism 'on the side,' as they say in America. And still without salary! Presumably, the classic phrase can be stretched, if they are sufficiently motivated then sometimes when you pay peanuts you get giants. The following years were a combination success and failure. In short, the normal run of politics. Throughout the period it was clear that Thatcher knew which of those surrounding her she could trust, and those whom she should beware. Young was clearly in the first group, time-and-time-again she would seek his mature advice. It was at this time that she coined the oft-quoted phrase, 'Everyone brings me problems, but David always brings me the Answers.'

There was a wobbly time in politics before the 1987 election, but after a successful result Young was promoted to Trade and Industry, where he presided over the privatisation of several State industries. Having originally entered politics for two years, after ten he returned to private business as chair of Cable and Wireless, and of University College Council, and as President of Jewish Care, Chai Cancer Care, and Chichester Festival Theatre.

Uniquely perhaps when approaching the age of 80, Young was invited back and given an office at No 10 Downing Street, where he advised on Enterprise, Business Start-up, and Career Development, all of which were matters which had also engaged him at ORT (above), and three years later was appointed Companion of Honour. Thatcher's choice of Jewish Ministers and advisers is well chronicled: David Wolfson and Stephen Sherbourne (both later enobled) in her office; and in her team: Leon Brittan (*Chapter 10*), Malcolm Rifkind, Keith Joseph, Nigel Lawson, Michael Howard (*Chapter 12*), Irwin Bellwin, and Geoffrey Finsberg but I would wager none higher in her regard than David Young.

Some Notable Jewish Solicitors

Lord David Young who 'knew where to look for legal answers' was so valued by No 10 Downing Street that Cabinet meetings were re-scheduled to accommodate *Rosh Hashanah* and *Yom Kippur*. A key aid to Margaret Thatcher he excused himself overnight from the Tory party conference in Brighton in 1984 narrowly missing becoming a casualty of the IRA bombing of the Grand Hotel. Photo Alamy.

Lord David Gold (1951–)

Born into a Jewish family David Gold attended Westcliff HIgh School for Boys, Westcliff-on-Sea, Essex and the London School of Economics. He was admitted as a solicitor 1975, becoming Head of Litigation at Herbert Smith, an International Law firm, with which he had commenced his career (now Herbert Smith Freehills). His client list varied from the most well-known Russian oligarchs to major PLCs, being also consulted by those in the media, politicians, and professional firms. He progressed to become senior partner (2005–2010), after which in 2010 he was created a life peer. He was appointed by the US Department of Justice from 2010 to 2013 to monitor BAE Systems, then in 2013 to review Rolls Royce's global anti-corruption compliance policies following bribery allegations in the Far East. There followed requests by other international commercial bodies, including Serco PLC (providers to among others the Ministry of Justice and other Government departments) to provide a similar form of ethical monitoring, and matters of compliance which continues to take him all over the world.

Probably one of the most significant indications of Gold' being invited to accept a peerage is that he also assumed the chairmanship of the Conservative Party Disciplinary Committee. He is a governor of the London School of Economics, head of a company providing high level strategic litigation advisers, a role which appeals to individuals and companies who already are embroiled in litigation, have their own legal team but require, with their knowledge, consent, and often, encouragement outside lawyers to seek a 'second opinion' on the route they are following.

Gold, as is immediately apparent to even the most practised interviewer, is the mildest of men, someone of charm despite the reputation which many arch-litigators have of Rottweiler-like behaviour. He has always said that the talent of a litigator is to keep his client out of litigation, except as a last resort, then go to law only if inevitable, and with the utmost care, devotion to detail and necessary tenacity: one of the 'hold back for a moment and just think about it' school.

For many years Gold was President of the Westcliff Hebrew Congregation, where he maintained a peaceful reign. He presently attends his synagogue in London each week, surrounded by his family, and when called upon delivers an impressive rendering of the weekly portion of the *Torah*.

Some Notable Jewish Solicitors

'The mildest of men, someone of charm,' solicitor Lord David Gold advised Government, gave second opinions, and said, 'The talent of a litigator is to keep his client out of litigation, except as a last resort, then go to law only if inevitable, and with the utmost care, devotion to detail and necessary tenacity.'

James ('Chaim') Levy

The names Hassans Solicitors and James (Haim) Levy are known throughout Gibraltar, and probably a large portion of surrounding Spain, in fact, in legal circles throughout the world. James was born in Gibraltar and obtained a law degree at Manchester University before being called to the Bar in 1972, and he was made Queen's Counsel in 2002. His mother was the sister of Sir Joshua Hassan, the Chief Minister of Gibraltar for many years, and the founder of Hassans Solicitors in 1939. The firm, of which James Levy is senior partner, now houses 90 Lawyers and a staff of around 250 and is without doubt Gibraltar's most highly reputed Law firm. It deals with Commercial Law, Taxation, Trusts, Property and Shipping Law, virtually every aspect of the law is covered, but this book is mostly concerned with the extent to which the Government of the territory relies upon its assistance, and the answer is in one word, 'considerably.' Levy advises public companies on mergers, advises on the family disputes of the wealthy, and above all has the great gift of common sense and is a qualified mediator.

His knowledge of Taxation Law enables him to contribute to *Tolley's Tax Planning Manual*, the bible of those who practice in that realm. His CBE was awarded 2013 for services to the economy and community of Gibraltar and he did much to establish Gibraltar's place as a financial centre, dealing with laws to prevent Money Laundering as well as Banking and Trust legislation.

Levy began working with his uncle, Sir Joshua in two rooms, with a clerk and a part-time secretary. Quite a contrast to the towering building which now hits the eye and to which his practice moved in 2019. Although started by two members of the same family, they made up their minds that others could join on merit, and not through blood, or even religious kinship. A strange example of this is that the present First Minister of Gibraltar was a partner, as was and at the same time as taking part in politics, the leader of the Opposition. Some little time ago a former Minister of Justice, who had also been a partner, returned to his desk at the firm after completing his stint in Government. Hassans has acted for construction companies, particularly those engaged in Gibraltar, banks, and many private clients.

The relationship between England and Europe over recent decades provided problems so far as implementation of EU directives were concerned. It became necessary that Levy gather a team together, at the behest of the Gibraltar

Government, including an eminent former British parliamentary draftsman, to consider directives on companies, insurance and mutual assistance, nationalisation of coal and steel, the use of rivers, and matters of tax jurisdiction. Moreover, Gibraltar was the first British offshore territory to adopt legislation against money laundering, and in this it became a world leader. Because of its strategic position in Europe special requirements and constraints were necessary in dealing with banking, and the ever-popular gaming industry, always a honeypot for the less scrupulous.

Gibraltar has been an English protectorate since the Treaty of Utrecht of 1704, and although many people think of it as an island, it is in fact a promontory at the most southerly point of the Iberian Peninsular, just a half-hour crossing by ferry to Morocco. It retains red post and telephone boxes, British-style police officers, a Gibraltar regiment which looks proud and smartens any parade ground, and its law is based on that of England and Wales. The main difference, however, is in the legal profession, for which English qualification is needed, and in which the judges wear red robes, long wigs on special occasions, otherwise short bench wigs, and tabs, and counsel wear short wigs, as do Queen's Counsel, but again on special occasions also wear long wigs and black gowns. Also they have a fusion of the professions of solicitor and barrister, thus James Levy, senior partner of a firm of solicitors, is also a member of Queen's Counsel, and most firms of solicitors there have at least one partner who is also a QC.

James, or as he is known 'Chaim' in the Jewish community, of which he is also the local President, is a strongly observant *Sephardi* Jew, attending synagogue each day, careful in his eating habits, often murmuring a prayer as he moves around Gibraltar, known and acknowledged by one and all, and above everything not only eager to study the *Torah* and other works, but anxious each day to find time in his busy life to sit down and teach his sons, and pass on his great knowledge in all matters relating to his faith and its history

In the same way that Arnold Goodman (see earlier in this section) came to the help of Harold Wilson, James Levy, with his trademark black fedora, is often seen dashing down Main Street from his offices to the those of the Governor, or more likely Chief Minister, no doubt uttering the same words as Arnold Goodman … 'Tell them I'm on my way.'

The Jewish Contribution to English Law

Epilogue

At the time of writing this book there have been reports that anti-Semitism is once again on the increase. Anti-Semitism, however, is a word with which I struggle.

The description of a Semite is far more wide-reaching than a Jew, it also includes members of any of various ancient and modern peoples originating in South-Western Asia, and therefore amongst others, Canaanites, Phoenicians, and Arabs. Ideally, rather than using that term one should be more specific as to whether an attack is anti-Jewish or perhaps as seems more common these days, anti-Zionist. Or even more precisely by distinguishing between the cause of Zionism itself, or against the actions of a particular Government in office. The latter is currently more prevalent, and there are those who believe such feelings to be fuelled by selective reporting within the media. Whilst I believe that it is possible to be anti-Israel without being anti-Jewish, sadly in the minds of many people the two are deeply interlinked, meaning that prejudice against one is readily loaded against the other.

During the mid-nineteenth century—the central time sphere of this book—there was not much known about Israel, in fact it did not exist as a State, nor was at that time such a happening visualised in the minds of Jews or others in this country. It was a dream being discussed in the coffee shops of Central Europe. Any anti-Jewish feeling was therefore directed against the foreigner in our midst, and it did exist. It has always existed, and probably always will, and can be more frighteningly exemplified by a closer examination of some of the speeches reported in *Hansard* in 1833, as to which see *Chapter 5*.

Ironically, any sentiments expressed which were anti-Israel as a State were from the Establishment, the aristocracy—the Cousinhood—of the Jewish community, at that time a small group who'd settled well, were established, and whose success manifested itself in a comfortable way of life. They did not want it to be endangered by the arrival of 'Johnny Foreigner,' even though they themselves had filled that self-same role not so much earlier. This was an attitude which later manifested itself in concerted opposition to the Balfour Declaration (*Chapter 10*).

Despite all this, and no matter how settled they felt, it would have been rare to find any Jewish person who had never been at the receiving end of some taunt. I have accepted that prejudice will always exist, you cannot remove it entirely, but you can mitigate its effect by education, though such education can be more practically levelled today at those who may be anti-Israel rather than simply anti-Jewish. In the case of the former you can point out the extent to which Arabs receive education and medical help in Israel itself and protection, and thus attempt to destabilise any untoward treatment considered to have been meted out to them. In the case of the latter, alas there's no easy treatment, it is a state of mind and its elimination is problematic.

The selection of the judiciary in this country is a fair and democratic process, depending largely upon ability exhibited over many years as a legal practitioner. To be a successful practitioner one needs the confidence of one's clients, including defendants and litigants. Clients can hardly have been prejudiced as to the background or religion of those in whose hands they chose to put their lives.

Thus do I conclude that any anti-Jewish feeling must have been put aside in the choices made by those who have had cause to go to law, and to be properly represented in the courts of this country—and I believe that the Jewish lawyers, as advisers, advocates, and eventually judges have accepted and appreciated the value of such confidence.

Let me end by one recall of Gibraltar, where I concluded my own legal career. Much of Gibraltar is today built on reclaimed land below the famous Rock. This small area was originally occupied by the Moors in the year 711, then came a Muslim presence led by a Berber called Tariq. The Spanish for Rock is *Gebal*, to which was added the first three letters of his name, so it became 'Gebaltar,' later Gibraltar.

By 1356 the population included a few Jews. The seas around were plagued by Barbary pirates who raided the mainland and on one incursion took hostage a rather fiery, black-haired 'Jewish beauty' who screamed, struggled and shouted, but they bound her and took her. The community were distraught and crowd-funded a sum to redeem her. Sure enough the pirates came back and shouted from their boat, 'Five pieces of silver.'

The Jews replied, 'We haven't got that much.'

'No,' yelled the pirate chief, 'That's how much we'll give you to take her back home with you!'

Selected Bibliography

Abse, Leo (1989), *Margaret, Daughter of Beatrice: A Politician's Psycho-biography of Margaret Thatcher*, Jonathan Cape.

(1998), *Wotan, My Enemy*, Robson Books.

(1996), *The Man Behind the Smile: Tony Blair and the Politics of Perversion*, Robson Books (revised as *Tony Blair: The Man Who Lost His Smile* (2003) for the USA);

(2000), *Fellatio, Masochism, Politics and Love*, Robson Books.

Bermant, Chaim (1971), *The Cousinhood*, The Book Service Ltd.

Blom-Cooper, Louis (1963), *The A6 Murder, Regina v James Hanratty: The Semblance of Truth*, Penguin.

(2015), *Power of Persuasion: Essays of a Very Public Lawyer*, Hart Publishing.

Blom-Cooper, Louis and Drewry, Gavin (1972), *Final Appeal: A Study of the House of Lords in its Judicial Capacity*, Oxford University Press.

Blom-Cooper, Louis and Morris, Terence (2011) (Foreword Lord Judge, Lord Chief Justice), *Fine Lines and Distinctions: Murder, Manslaughter and the Unlawful Taking of Human Life*, Waterside Press.

Bourne, Judith (2016), *Helena Normanton and the Opening of the Bar to Women*, Waterside Press.

Gilbert, Sir Martin (1990), *Jewish History Atlas*, William Morrow.

Goldberg, Jonathan and Panter, Steve (1997), *Innocents: How Justice Failed Stefan Kiszko and Lesley Molseed*, Sage Publications.

Goodman, Lord (1993), *Tell Them I'm On Way*, Chapmans.

Heilbron, Hilary (2019), *Rose QC: The Remarkable Story of Rose Heilbron, Trailblazer and Legal Icon*, Hart Publishing. Re-issued in paperback November 2019.

Henriques, Henry Straus Quixano (2010), *The Return of the Jews to England: A Chapter in the History of British Law*, Kessinger Legacy Reprints.

Hyam, Michael (1993), *Advocacy Skills* (Edn 4), Blackstone Press.

Joffe, Joel (1995), *The Rivonia Story*, Mayibuye Books, Cape Town.

(2007), *The State Versus Nelson Mandela: The Trial That Changed South Africa*, Oneworld Publications.

Lester, Anthony (2016), *Five Ideas to Fight For: How Our Freedom is Under Threat and Why it Matters,* Oneworld Publications.

Lipstad, Deborah (2006), *Denying the Holocaust: The Growing Assault On Truth And Memory*, Penguin.

Luxon, John (1983), *Lewis and Lewis: The Life and Times of a Victorian Solicitor,* Collins.

Mockler, Anthony (1983), *Lions Under the Throne,* Frederick Muller.

Montagu, Ewen (1953), *The Man Who Never Was,* Evans Brothers.

Morton, Frederick (1964), *The Rothschilds: A Family Portrait,* Penguin.

Napley, David (1971), *The Technique of Persuasion,* Sweet & Maxwell.

   (1988), *Murder at the Villa Madeira: The Rattenbury Case,* Weidenfeld & Nicolson.

   (1982), *Not Without Prejudice: The Memoirs of Sir David Napley, President of the Law Society 1976–77,* George G Harrap & Co.

   (1987), *The Camden Town Murder,* Weidenfeld & Nicolson (Great Murders of the Twentieth Century series).

Ognall, Harry (2017), *A Life of Crime: The Memoirs of a High Court Judge,* William Collins.

Pannick, David (1982), *Advocates,* Oxford University Press.

   (1987), *Judges,* Oxford University Press.

Rinder, Robert (2015), *Rinder's Rules: Make the Law Work For You,* Century.

Roth, Cecil (1964), *A History of the Jews in England,* Clarendon Press.

Sands, Phillipe (2016), *Lawless World: Making and Breaking Global Rules,* Penguin.

   (2017), *East West Street,* W & N.

   (2021), *The Ratline: Love, Lies and Justice on the Trail of a Nazi Fugitive,* W&N.

Schama, Simon CBE (2014), *Belonging: The Story of the Jews: Finding the Words (1000 BCE–1492),* Vintage.

Shapiro, James (1997), *Shakespeare and the Jews,* Columbia University Press.

Simmons, Michael (2011), *The Lawyer Who Couldn't Sit Still,* The Book Guild.

Skelly, George (2019), *The Cameo Conspiracy: A Shocking True Story of Murder and Injustice* (revised), Waterside Press.

Tovey, D'Blossiers and Pearl, Elizabeth (Translator) (1990), *Anglia Judaica: A History of the Jews in England,* Weidenfeld & Nicolson.

Young, Lord (1990), *The Enterprise Years: A Businessman in the Cabinet,* Headline.

Index

A

Aaronberg, David *156*
Aaron of York *38*
Abraham *29*
Abse, Leo *187*
Abse, Rudolf *187*
academic lawyers *129, 141, 145, 155, 165, 193, 194*
Advisory Council on the Penal System *187*
affirmation *27*
Alba Radios *118*
Albert, Prince *85*
Alexander III *32*
aliens *49*
American Jewish Joint Distribution Committee *194*
Amnesty International *192*
Anglo-Jewry *103*
   Anglo-Jewish Association *75, 103, 124*
anti-Semitism *14, 32, 47, 82, 162–163, 194, 219–221*
Anton Piller order *129*
apartheid *108, 192*
arbitration *129, 133, 134, 141, 147, 151*
Archer, Jeffrey *184*
Arkush, Jonathan *157*
arsenic *95*

Arshad, Raffia *176*
Ashiana Network *175*
Ashkenazi 36, 101, 200
Assizes *38, 74*
Association of Women Barristers *173*
Astana Financial Centre Court, Kazakhstan *145*
Attorney-General *162, 167, 168*

B

Babylon *29, 35*
badge *43*
Balcombe, Alfred *118*
Balcombe, John *118*
Balfour, Arthur *85*
Balkans *31*
Bar Council *86, 127*
Barfield, William *174*
Bar Ilan University *127*
Barlow Clowes International *139*
Barrow, Eliza *95*
Bartfield, William *154*
Belisha beacons *161*
Beloff, Michael *151*
Ben Israel, Rabbi Menasseh *62, 69*
Benjamin, Judah *77*
Bennathan, Joel *160*
Bentley, Derek *190*

Berlin *87, 117, 121, 190*
Bermant, Chaim *14*
Bernard, Dr Simon *75*
Berwin, Stanley *189*
Beth Din *39*
Beth Hamidrash Hagadol Synagogue *116*
Bevan, Aneurin *116*
Biko, Steve *118*
Bindman, Geoffrey *192*
Birnberg, Benedict *189*
Birnberg & Co *189*
Bishop, Russell *166*
Black Death *32*
Black, Diana *39*
Black, Jonathan *197*
Blair, Tony *192*
Blank, Victor *193*
Blom-Cooper, Louis *119*
Bloom, Louis *114*
Board of Deputies of British Jews *87, 103, 117, 163, 181, 184*
Boleslav (King Boleslav) *32*
Booth & Co *189*
Boundary Commission for Scotland *128*
Bow Street Magistrates' Court *197*
Boxer, Clive *197*
Brampton, Edward *59*
Brighton Grammar School *166*
Brink's-Mat gold bullion case *166*
British Academy of Forensic Sciences *185*
Brittan, Leon *164*
Brixton *184*
Broadmoor Special Hospital *89*

Brodie, Stephen *174*
Brondesbury *154*
Brown, Simon *140*
Bryan Cave Leighton Paisner *189*
Bryanston School *138*
Bucknill, Thomas *97*
Buddhism *49*
Bulgaria *147*
Bulger case *126, 165*
Burton, Michael *129*
Bush, Bryan *174*
Butler, Gerald *149*
Byzantine Law *26*

C

Cacares, Henriques *126*
Calcutta *92*
Callman, Clive *121*
Camberwell Borough Council *162*
Cambridge Union *164, 168*
Cambridge University Act 1856 *56, 85*
Campaign for Nuclear Disarmament *182*
capital punishment *181, 190*
Caplan, Jonathan *155*
Caplan, Michael *194*
Cardiff *116, 162, 181, 187*
Carlile, Alex *167*
Carlill v Carbolic Smoke Ball Company *100*
Carman, George *185*
Carson, Edward *98, 179*
Catholics *51, 63, 177*
Cayman Islands *148*
Cecil Peace Prize *111*

Chancery 71, 88, 102, 121, 141
Charterhouse Bank 193
Chaucer, Geoffrey 171
Chesterton, Cecil 97
Chesterton, Gilbert Keith 97
Cinq Ports 87
Clifford Chance 193
Clifford's Tower 38
Clifton College, Bristol 103
Clore, Charles 184
Cohen, Arthur 85
Cohen, Benjamin 85
Cohen, Jonathan 125
Cohen, Lawrence 156
Cohen, Levi Barent 85
Cohen, Lionel 101
Cohen, Myrella 14, 148
Cohen, Samantha 159
Collins, Lawrence 141
commerce 39
Common Serjeant 133
Competition Appeal Tribunal 132, 141
Compton, Martin 197
conflict of interest 192
Conrad, Alan 156
conscience 27
Constitutional Reform Act 2005 142
conversion 12, 25, 44, 59, 171
   forcible conversion 37
   House of Converts, 60
Corman, Charles 197
corruption 98
Cosgrove, Hazel 128
Council of Christians and Jews 184
courts

Court of Sessions 128
   International Court of Justice 138
   Jewish courts 26
Cousinhood 14, 55, 102, 105
criminal capacity 126
Cromwell, Oliver 46, 62, 70
Crusades 35, 36

D

Dando, Jill 130
David (King David) 30
Deech, Ruth 152
Dein, Jeremy 157
De Medina, Solomon 64
Deuteronomy 19, 65
Dhir, Anuja 175
Dickens, Charles 178
Disraeli, Benjamin 49, 63
diversity 173
Dodd, Ken 130
Dodwell, Henry 89
Dulwich College 162
Dyson, John 147

E

Eastern Caribbean Supreme Court 132
eccentricity 108
Eder, Bernard 132
Edict of Expulsion 1290 45
Edict of the Badge 43
Edinburgh 165
Edward I 39
Edward IV 59
Edward VII 179
Egypt 19, 35

Elizabeth I *19, 41*
Ellenbogen, Norma *159*
Ellis, Michael *168*
Ellis, Ruth *109, 131, 184*
emancipation *47, 54, 64, 67, 85, 161*
Employment Appeal Tribunal *135*
envy *38*
Epsom College *167*
Etherton, Terence *147*
Eton College *20, 100, 102, 129, 151*
Europe *141*
    European Commissioner *164*
Evans, Timothy *182*
expulsion *39*

F

Faculty of Advocates *128*
Falsely Accused Individuals For Reform *163*
Family Law *175*
fascism *182*
favour *66*
Feder, Ami *159*
Fenner, John *195*
Fetes College *144*
Final Solution *182*
finance *44, 63*
Finer, Morris *116*
Finestein, Israel *117*
Fingret, Peter *149*
food *11*
Foreign Secretary *165*
France *31*
fraud *94, 139, 150*
Frazer, Hyman *168*

Frazer, Lucy *168*
Freedman, Clive *133*
Freeman, Dawn *152*
Freemasonry *97, 122*
friars *39, 48, 74*
Fullbright Scholar *122*

G

Gardiner, Lord *109*
garroting *179*
Gay News *108*
gay rights *190*
George, Barry *130*
George Watson's College *165*
Germany *85, 105, 107, 117, 190*
ghetto *37*
Gibraltar *20, 216, 220–221*
gifts *65*
Gillis, Bernard *109*
Glasgow *144*
Globe, Henry *130*
Godfrey, Howard *160*
Godfrey, Louis *174*
Godless Tower of Gower Street *178*
Goldberg, David *152*
Goldberg, Jonathan *153*
Gold, David *214*
Gold, Jeremy *156*
Goldsmid, Asher *110*
Goldsmid, Francis Henry *71*
Goldsmid, Isaac *64, 71*
Goldsmith, Peter *167*
Goldstone, Clement *130*
Goodman, Arnold *198*
Gordon, Jeffrey *191*

Grabiner, Anthony *128*
Graham, David *155*
Grant, Robert *48*
Gray, Gilbert *185*
Gray's Inn *111*
Greenberg, Daniel *158*
Greenberg, Joanna *154*
Greenwood, Alan *156*
Greenwood, Jeffrey *192*
Grodzinski, Sam *158*
Grunwald, Henry *154*
Guernsey *60, 118, 148*
Guildford Four *190*

H

Haberdashers' Aske's Boys' School *108, 132, 155, 164*
Hain, Peter *108*
Hanratty, James *130*
Harrogate *185*
Harrow Crown Court *144*
Harvard University *105, 166, 191*
Hassans *216*
hatred *32*
Hebrew *16, 29, 72, 78, 133*
  Hebrew University *121*
Heilbron, Hilary *153*
Heilbron, Rose *113*
Heilpern, Godfrey *112*
Helsinki Accords *195*
Henriques, Richard *125*
Henry VIII *40*
Herod (King Herod) *31*
Herschell, Farrer *57, 87*
Higgins, Rosalyn *138*

hijab *176*
Hillsborough Inquiry *143*
Hindley, Myra *112*
Hoare, Charles *161*
Hoffman, Leonard *140*
Hoffman, Paul *39, 174*
Holland *33, 42, 55, 62*
Holocaust *13, 182*
  Holocaust denial *194*
  Holocaust Education Trust *163*
  National Holocaust Centre *154*
Holy Land *36*
Home Affairs *165, 166, 184*
Home Secretary *164*
Hong Kong *122, 139, 141, 145*
Hopper, Anthony *192*
Hore-Belisha, Leslie *161*
House of Commons *47*
Howard League for Penal Reform *167*
Howard, Michael *164*
human rights *168, 174, 190, 192*
Hurwitz, Alter *173*
Hurwitz, Vivian *174*
Hussein of Jordan (King Hussain) *184*
Hyam, Michael *123*

I

idolatry *49, 67*
immigration *171, 198*
  Immigration Appeals Tribunal *127*
India *30, 92*
  East India Company *48, 110, 171*
  Viceroy of India *98*
Inglis, Robert *49*
Inner Temple *86, 127, 169*

intellectual property *125*
International Commission of Jurists *192*
Investigatory Powers Tribunal *129*
Iraq *33*
Isaacs, Godfrey *97*
Isaacs, Rufus *57, 91*
Isaacs, Sarah *93*
Isaacs, Stuart *155*
Isiah *30*
Islington *167, 184*
Israel *11, 12, 13, 219–220*
    ancient Israel *27*
    anti-Israel *219*
    Israelites *29*
Italy *31, 62*

J

Jacob, Jack *111*
Jacob, Robert *125*
Janner, Barnet *181*
Janner, Daniel *163*
Janner, Greville *162*
Janner-Klausner, Rabbi Laura *163*
Jaques, Colin *197*
Jersey *118, 119, 148*
Jerusalem *30, 36, 147, 169*
Jessel, George *57, 88*
Jessel, Toby *90*
Jewish/Jews
    chattels of the king *39*
    degrees of Jewishness *12*
    first Jewish lawyers *69*
    Jew Bill 1753 *46*
    Jewish Care *192, 194*
    Jewish Historical Society *117*

Jewish law *65*
Jewish Municipal Relief Act 1847 *51*
Jewish Relief Act 1858 *52*
Jewish Welfare Board *192*
Jews College *87, 110*
'stiff-necked' people *19*
Joffe, Joel *163*
Johns, Adrian *20*
Jones, Janie *108*
Joseph, Wendy *155*
Judah the Maccabean *31*
Judea *30, 35*
judge advocate *107*
    Judge Advocate of the Fleet *105*
judiciary *56*
    Judicial Appointments Commission *127*
    Judicial Studies Board *127*
Julius, Anthony *194*
justice
    'justices of the Jews' *44*
Justice Secretary. See *Lord Chancellor*

K

Kaddish *16*
Kamil, Geoffrey *151*
Karminski, Seymour *107*
Karu, Usha *172*
Kaul, Kauly *173*
Kentridge, Sydney *117*
Kerr, Michael *117*
Kerr, Timothy *117*
Kew *88*
Khan, Imran *190*
King-Hamilton, Alan *108*
King's College London *154, 167*

King's/Queen's Counsel 74
kippah 16
Kiszko, Stefan 143, 156
Koestler Trust 190
Kol Nidre 20
Kray twins 166
Kremmen, Philip 154

L

Laddie, Hugh 129
Lambert, Nigel 160
Laski, Harold 104
Laski, Marghanita 103
Laski, Neville 103
Lauterpacht Centre 138
Lauterpacht, Elihu 138
Lauterpacht, Hersch 137
Law Commission 121, 147
Law of Return 59
Lawrence, Ivan 166
Law Society 185
Leader of the House of Commons 168
learning 19
Leeds 142, 147, 155, 168, 173, 185–186
legislation 43–58
Leonard Sainer Foundation 184
Lester, Anthony 166
Leveson, Brian 130
Leveson Inquiry 131
Levin-Smith, Archibald 99
Levy, Dennis 150
Levy, James 216
Lewis, George 177
Lewis & Lewis 178
Lewison, Kim 132

Lightman, Daniel 124
Lightman, Gavin 124
Lightman, Harold 124
Lincoln's Inn 66, 71, 79, 121
Lipworth, Sydney 121
Lithuania 142, 147, 162, 165, 181
Liverpool 113, 167, 182
Lombards 46
London County Council 181, 184
London School of Economics 116, 137, 173, 187, 190
Lopez, Roderigo 19, 40
Lord Chancellor 146
  Shadow Lord Chancellor 184
Lord Chief Justice 57, 98, 131, 137, 142
Lyon's corner houses 107
Lyons, Rudolph 112

M

Macaulay, Thomas 50
Maccabeans 51, 118
Maccabias, Judas 119
Maimonides 19
Mandela, Nelson 118, 163
Marconi scandal 97
Maritime Law Association 139
Marks, Richard 133
Marranos 39, 62, 126
massacres 63
Master of the Rolls 140, 144, 146
Maxwell, Robert 139
McKenzie Friend 191
Mediccis 69
Melford Stevenson, Aubrey 109
Mendes, Diogo 40

Index

Mendoza, Daniel *47, 91*
Mental Health Commission *119*
Mental Health Tribunal *117*
Mesopotamia *29*
Middle-Ages *19*
Middle Temple *119, 139, 143*
Millet, Peter *121*
Minehead Magistrates' Court *185*
Mirror Group Newspapers *193*
miscarriage of justice *114, 143, 182, 189*
Mishcon, Victor *184*
Mishnaic period *26*
Mocatta, Alan *110*
Mocatta, David *110*
Mocatta, Moses *110*
money lending *37*
Montagu, Ewen *104*
Montagu, Samuel *104*
Montefiore, Joseph *69*
Montefiore, Moses *64*
Monty, Simon *157*
Moors Murder Trial *112*
Mordaunt adultery case *179*
Morocco *62*
Morris, Ruth *193*
Morris, Stephen *134*
Moses, Alan *152*
Moss, Ronald *151*
Mukharjee, Avik *172*
Murder (Abolition of Death Penalty) Act 1965 *182*
Muslims *35, 36, 37, 175*
Myerson, Arthur *39, 174*
Myerson, Simon *157*

N

Nabarro Nathanson *192*
Nairobi *172*
Napley, David *185*
Napper, Robert *123*
Nathan, David *160*
National Campaign for the Abolition of Capital Punishment *182*
National Theatre *184*
Nazis *11, 12, 174, 190, 202*
Netherlands *177*
Neuberger, David *140*
Neumegens School for Jews *88*
Newcastle-upon-Tyne *142, 192*
New Orleans *78*
New World *33*
Nilsen, Dennis *166*
Nottingham Polytechnic *172*
Notting Hill Riots *107*
Nugee, Christopher *13*
Nugee, Richard *13*
Nuremberg War Trials *137*

O

oath *23–26*
  Jew's oath *37*
  judicial oath *20*
  Oaths Act 1978 *27–28*
  witness oath *27*
Ognall, Harry *122, 174*
Ognall, Leo *122*
Old Bailey *94, 107, 108, 109, 114, 175*
Open University of Israel *145*
Operation Mincemeat *105*
Oppenheimer, Nathan & Vandyk *189*

Orthodox Judaism 12
Owen, Aaron 116
Oxbridge 56, 85
Oxford University Act 1854 56

P

pacifism 182
Paisner, Martin 194
Pale 32
Palestine 13, 85, 104
    High Commissioner of Palestine 104
Pannick, David 166, 167
paranoia 40
patents 125
patriotism 85
Pearl, David 127
Pearlman, Valerie 150
Peres, Shimon 184
persecution 37
Persia/Persians 30, 33
Peters, Nigel 133
Phillips, Nicholas 57, 138
phylacteries 14
Pierce, Gareth 190
Pinochet, Augusto 141, 194
plague 32
Platt, Eleanor 150
pogroms 33, 109
Polack's House 103
Poland 32, 109, 167, 184, 187
Portland Place 178, 202
Portugal 40
Poulson, John 143
poverty 32
prejudice 32, 40, 178, 190

Price, David 195
Prinsley, Mark 197
prison reform 125
Private Eye 192
public life 171

Q

Qatar International Court 139
Queen Mary College 154
Queen's Remembrancer 112

R

Raab, Dominic 13
rabbi 24, 36, 184
    Chief Rabbi 38
    rabbinical court 39
    Rabbinic period 26
race 166
    Race Relations Board 192
radical causes 189
reform
    legal reform 181
    Reform Judaism 12, 75
'respectable occupations' 45
Restrictive Practices Court 110
return 59
    Law of Return 12
Richard I 38
Richard III 59
Riegner, Gerhart 182
'Riegner Telegram' 182
Rifkind, Hugo 165
Rifkind, Malcolm 165
Rights of Women 175
Rinder, Robert 159

Index

Rivlin, Geoffrey *150*, *174*
Rix, Bernard *127*
Romania *181*
Roman Law *12*
Romans *31*
Rose, Dinah *158*
Rose, Jonathan *156*
Rose, Vivien *141*
Rosh Hashanah *25*
Roth, Peter *132*
Rothschild, Baron Lionel *52*
Rothschild dynasty *48*, *64*, *101*, *189*
Rothschild, Nathan *85*
Rothschild, Nathaniel *54*
Royal Commission *108*, *190*
Rumania *164*
Runnymede Trust *166*
Russell, Earl *52*
Russia *31*, *32*, *202*, *208*, *214*

S

Sabot, Elias *40*
Sainer, Leonard *184*
Salmon, Cyril *107*
Salomons, David *51*
Samuel, Herbert *97*, *104*
Samuels, John *124*
Sanders, Roger *151*
Sands, Phillipe *158*
Sapnara, Khatun *175*
Savundra, Emil *108*
scholars *19*
Scotland *175*
Scott, Lionel *174*
Seddon, Frederick *95*

Sentencing Council *194*
Sephardim *33*, *36*
serjeant-at-law *74*
servants *43*
settlement *38*
Sexual Offences Act 1967 *187*
Shackleton, Fiona *196*
Shakespeare *40*
Sharp, Victoria *134*
Shaw, Sebag *109*
sheriff *45*
   Sheriff's Declaration Act 1835 *51*
shtetl *32*
Shipman, Harold *126*
Sicily *31*, *105*
Silkin, John *162*
Silkin, Lewis *181*
Silkin, Samuel *162*
'Silkin Test' *181*
Silverman, Sydney *181*
Simler, Ingrid *135*
Simmons, Michael *191*
Simon, John *74*
Simon, Oswald *75*
Singapore International Commercial
   Court *127*, *132*
Singh, Mota *172*
Singh, Rabinder *174*
S J Berwin Chair of Corporate Law *189*
Smith, Frederick ('F E' Smith) *98*
Smith, Helen *185*
Snaresbrook Crown Court *173*
Society of Labour Lawyers *162*
Solicitor-General *86*, *90*, *166*, *168*
Solomon *30*

South Africa *33, 117, 140, 163*
Southwark Crown Court *172*
Spain *31*
  Spanish Inquisition *35*
Spilsbury, Bernard *96*
Spiro Institute *127*
sponsorship *38*
Statute of Jewry 1253 *44*
Statute of Jewry 1275 *45*
St Bartholomew's Hospital *41*
Stephens, Martin *124*
Stepney *189*
Stockport *193*
Stowe, Marylyn *196*
Stowe School *140*
Suez Canal *54*
Supperstone, Michael *132*
Supreme Court *138–141*
Sutcliffe, Peter *122*
Swansea *164*
synagogue *11, 43*
  Bevis Marks Synagogue *62, 101*
  Federation of Synagogues *104*
  Montefiore Synagogue, Ramsgate *110*
  Reform Synagogue *107, 118*
  Spanish and Portuguese Synagogue *110*
  Western Marble Arch Synagogue *165*
  West London Synagogue *72, 108, 122, 147, 165*
Syria *19*

T

taxation *45*
Taylor, Deborah *144, 154*
Taylor, Peter *16, 57, 142*

Technology and Construction Court *147*
Teeman, Ronald *190*
terrorism *140, 167*
Thatcher, Margaret *187*
Thorpe, Jeremy *143, 185*
Torah *19*
trade *62, 63*
Treasurer *124*
tribes *30*
turban *172*
Turkey *31, 62*
tyranny *182*

U

Ukraine *137*
University College London *177, 184*
university degrees *56*
urban regeneration *195*
USA *20, 77, 164, 166, 192*

V

Victoria (Queen Victoria) *54, 64*
Victor Mishcon & Co *184*
Voss, Geoffrey *148*
vow *23–26*

W

Wade, Donald *189*
Wakefield *189*
Waksman, David *134*
Walsh, Brian *149*
Warbeck, Perkin *59*
Ward, Helen *196*
Ward, Judith *143*

Waterman, Fanny *142*, *147*
Welfare Board *107*
West, Rosemary *130*
wet-nurses *43*
White Book *111*
William III *64*
William the Conqueror *34*, *36*
Winchester College *118*
Wolfenden Report *187*
Wolfson, David *169*
Wolkind, Malcolm *160*
women *12*, *24*, *44*, *113*
  'chained women' *116*
  first 'non-white' woman judge *175*
Woolf, Harry *16*, *57*, *144*
Woolf Inquiry *144*
Woolworths *193*
World Congress of Faiths *108*
World Jewish Congress *182*
Wright, Whittaker *94*

Y

Yale University *164*
yarmulke *16*
Yiddish *31*
Yom Kippur *25*
York *38*
Young, David *206*

Z

Zander, Michael *190*
Zebrugge *118*
Zeidman, Martin *155*
Zionism *59*, *104–105*, *219–220*
  anti-Zionists *104*, *219*

Both Sides of the Bench
Barrington Black

'Interesting and entertaining… His story is told with skill and tact.'
The Law Society Gazette.

'Filled with anecdotes and observations from a lifetime in court that will be of interest to any practising or student lawyer. There is much to learn from Mr Justice Black's anecdotes, which are often laced with dark humour and dry wit… [and] lined with nuggets of practical advice.'
Gibraltar Chronicle.

'An excellent set of views and opinions from a leading well-known and controversial lawyer of our time.'
Phillip Taylor MBE and Elizabeth Taylor of Richmond Green Chambers.

Paperback | ISBN 978-1-909976-31-3 | 2015 | 224 pages

www.WatersidePress.co.uk